Fear at the Edge

Sponsored by the Joint Committee on Latin American Studies of the Social Science Research Council and the American Council of Learned Societies, with funds from the Andrew W. Mellon Foundation.

Fear at the Edge

*State Terror and Resistance
in Latin America*

Edited by Juan E. Corradi,
Patricia Weiss Fagen, and
Manuel Antonio Garretón

UNIVERSITY OF CALIFORNIA PRESS
Berkeley · Los Angeles · Oxford

University of California Press
Berkeley and Los Angeles, California

University of California Press, Ltd.
Oxford, England

© 1992 by
The Regents of the University of California

Library of Congress Cataloging-in-Publication Data

Fear at the edge : state terror and resistance in Latin America /
    edited by Juan E. Corradi, Patricia Weiss Fagen, and Manuel Antonio
    Garretón.
        p.   cm.
    Includes bibliographical references and index.
    ISBN 0-520-07704-0 (cloth: alk. paper) — ISBN 0-520-07705-9 (paper: alk. paper)
    1. Political persecution—Southern Cone of South America.
    2. Terrorism—Southern Cone of South America. 3. Fear—Southern
    Cone of South America. I. Corradi, Juan E., 1943–   . II. Fagen,
    Patricia Weiss, 1940–   . III. Garretón Merino, Manuel A. (Manuel
    Antonio)
    JC599.S57F43   1992
    303.6'25—dc20   91-30628
                                                                              CIP

9 8 7 6 5 4 3 2 1

Contents

Introduction

Fear: A Cultural and Political Construct

Juan E. Corradi, Patricia Weiss Fagen, and
Manuel Antonio Garretón

Efforts to understand the foundations and internal processes of public life, culture, and discourse are gaining importance in several disciplines. They inform democratic theory in political science, discussions in comparative literature and other cultural-critical disciplines, new approaches in ethics and jurisprudence, debates in philosophy, and empirical studies in sociology, anthropology, history, and communications. This book toils in the same vineyard: it examines civil society and political life, but "through a glass darkly," by focusing on what we may call the culture of fear that developed in a number of South American nations in the 1970s.

The culture of fear has not yet been systematically analyzed for those nations, nor even for places like Guatemala and El Salvador, despite the fact that it is central to the most vital matters of our day, those of life and death. The importance of the issue and the gap in the literature have led the various contributors to this book to delve into the social, psychological, and ideological underpinnings of the terror-laden regimes that spread in South America in the seventies and eighties. This book seeks to be a genuinely interdisciplinary work, with contributions from specialists in sociology, political science, psychology, literary studies, education, communications, and human rights. We were not daunted by the sheer catholicity of the enterprise. We believed instead that the time was ripe for a coordinated intellectual approach to an important issue.

In the United States and in other advanced industrial democracies,

1

there is a marked reluctance to consider fear as something other than a personal emotion and, hence, a phenomenon within the exclusive purview of one discipline: psychology. This reluctance, however, is itself a product of deep-seated social habits and political traditions. The decentralization of power, the exercise of self-governance in local communities, the existence of myriad voluntary associations, the separation of state and religion, the plurality of sects and creeds within religions, the possibility of rapid social and geographical mobility, and, above all, the functioning of representative institutions are among the factors (masterfully analyzed by Tocqueville a century and a half ago) that have relegated fear to being either an intimate or a transcendent experience. Free societies do suffer the occasional occurrence of collective frights or panics, but they do not know fear as the permanent and muffled undertone of public life.

This, unfortunately, is not the experience in large areas of the world where, since the end of World War II, dictatorships of all stripes, ranging from the unstable but recurrent military regimes of the Third World to the more thorough and longer-lived totalitarianisms of the now defunct Eastern bloc, have dominated. For decades, the populations of many countries have been subject to generalized or centralized violence; they have experienced the erosion of public values, of legal and even primary social bonds. Uncertainty, self-doubt, insecurity have been the staples of public life. In such contexts, fear is a paramount feature of social action; it is characterized by the inability of social actors to predict the consequences of their behavior because public authority is arbitrarily and brutally exercised.

This book is a contribution to the sociological and political understanding of fear; it is based on the collective experiences of one particular area of the world—the Southern Cone of Latin America—in the 1970s, when the four countries of the area (Argentina, Brazil, Chile, and Uruguay) were ruled by military regimes of a special kind.

Between the 1960s and the 1980s, successive military regimes in these countries transformed the social fabric. By means of systematic state terror that penetrated more deeply into society than ever before—even in previous regimes dominated by the military—these governments strove to dissolve or isolate civil institutions capable of protecting or insulating citizens from state power. The creation and implementation of terror, in turn, caused unprecedented levels of personal insecurity among citizens. A description of the depth, intensity, and multiple expressions of this personal insecurity, and of the innovative and courageous efforts made to overcome the effects of pervasive fear forms the core of this book.

The product of a long-term effort, this book was begun in 1980 under the sponsorship of the Social Science Research Council (SSRC) in New York. The central theme of what eventually became a collection of studies about political fear emerged from research conducted in Argentina in 1979, a period marked by widely disseminated reports of abductions, disappearances, torture, and random executions by the security forces in that country. The researchers, Argentine political scientist Guillermo O'Donnell and Brazilian psychologist Cecilia Galli, interviewed a broad range of primarily middle-class Argentines and found the results disturbing. Their assumption, based on past experience, was that most of their interviewees would be vocal in their opposition to the actions of the government or, at a minimum, would contest official versions of events. Instead, the individuals they questioned were generally uncritical and professed ignorance or lack of concern about reported government abuses.

Hypothesizing that Argentines had come to accept conditions that they ordinarily would have judged unacceptable because of pervasive fear rather than apathy, the researchers urged scholars to undertake studies that would shed light on the dynamics of what they believed to be a "culture of fear." Consequently, at regular intervals between 1982 and 1984, U.S. and Latin American scholars and human-rights activists met at the SSRC to present and discuss papers that described the dynamics of state terror, the nature of political fear, and efforts within civil society to counter the effects of terror and fear.

As the political situation in the Southern Cone opened somewhat, scholars in these countries, on their own initiative, began undertaking empirical and theoretical studies of the same topics. Growing regional interest in exploring the impact of authoritarian rule on civil societies led the SSRC to sponsor an international conference on "The Culture of Fear," which was held in Buenos Aires in June 1985. By this time, civilian government had been restored in three of the four Southern Cone countries. Only Chile still remained under authoritarian rule, but it too was to experience a transition to democracy by the end of 1989. In Buenos Aires, a number of the participants from the New York seminars joined colleagues from Argentina, Brazil, Chile, and Uruguay for a wide-ranging discussion on fear and society. The chapters in this book are the end product of this long process. They explore both past and present; they reconstruct the dynamics of fear by looking at its individual victims and its broad political, social, and cultural legacies; they examine both the creation of fear through systems of state terror and the means by which people managed to overcome fear in their everyday lives.

The complexity and multiple dimensions of a theme like "the culture of fear" required abandoning conventional approaches in sociology and political science to the study of authoritarianism and military regimes. Because the situation that developed in the Southern Cone in the seventies was unprecedented; because the military dictatorships that befell Argentina, Brazil, Chile, and Uruguay were quite different from the dictatorships in these and other Latin American nations in the past; because the depth and scope of repression (symbolized by torture and disappearances) were staggering, fear became a salient research theme and dictated a new turn in the development of the social sciences in Latin America.

Gruesome as the topic was, it nevertheless promised to yield important analytic dividends. In particular, the study of fear allowed researchers to bridge the gap between macrosocial structures and processes, on the one hand, and microsocial phenomena, like the interactions of everyday life, on the other. The problem of fear opened new vistas on politics and on the relations between state and society, and between power and its subjects. The aim of the collective research project—and of this book—has been to understand the experience of fear under these regimes in several dimensions: the structural and institutional framework of the experience, the forms for producing and overcoming fear in society, the social psychology of fear, the effects on the subjects and perpetrators.

Four major goals dominate our discussions about fear and society: first, defining and characterizing the culture-of-fear construct; second, examining the differences and similarities in the practices of repression in the different political entities where it can be said that a culture of fear was created; third, analyzing the differences and similarities in the stages and manifestations of fear and, perhaps most important, in the conditions under which fear is eroded and eliminated; and, finally, determining the legacies—political, social, economic, cultural, and psychological—of fear for the perpetrators as well as for the subjects once constitutional government has been restored.

In the first part of the book, a political scientist, Manuel Antonio Garretón, and a sociologist, Norbert Lechner, try to situate fear in relation to general political phenomena and, more particularly, in relation to the specific characteristics of the military dictatorships that prevailed in the Southern Cone in the seventies and eighties. Fear is intimately connected to what some scholars consider the political question par excellence—namely, the question of order. But the question of order prompts an array of alternative responses, depending on the culture within which it is posed. Thus, Lechner argues that in Latin America diversity is perceived not as plurality but as disorder. The consequence is overarching fear of the ubiquitous other ("chaos," "communism"), which is regarded as an invader and under whose rubric diverse social fears are subsumed. Authoritarianism "solves" the problem of order not by the suppression but by the manipulation of fear. Yet this appropriation of fear by authoritarian regimes, which eagerly seek the forceful integration of society, paradoxically promotes social disintegration. All social and political systems have to cope with fear, but authoritarian, as opposed to democratic, regimes fail to process fear in creative ways. From this perspective, democracy must be considered not only as the domain of substantive and procedural rules but also as a domain where the unpredictability of the other is not seen as a threat to the self, and hence as a source of fear, but rather as a condition and an opportunity for the self's own development.

In addition to covering general considerations about fear, politics, and culture, Garretón's opening chapter proposes a scheme for analyzing the nature and evolution of fear under the military dictatorships of the Southern Cone. It provides distinctions between fears (for example, those due to uncertainty and those due to certainty) and between the subjects of fear (for example, political winners and losers). It then applies these distinctions to the various phases that the military regimes underwent: an initial and predominantly repressive phase; a transformational phase; a critical phase; a terminal phase; and a phase of transition to nonauthoritarianism. In each case the predominant patterns of fear and of resistance to fear are examined. Garretón also discusses the legacy of fear and the steps taken to overcome that legacy.

Based on the analytical schemes developed in Part I, the second part of the book goes on to examine the specific means of instilling fear in each military regime and its impact on the victims and makers of terror. This part opens with Patricia Weiss Fagen's study of the apparatus of repression in Argentina, Brazil, Chile, and Uruguay. Drawing material from each of the countries, she describes the military justifications for seizing power and ruling above the law: that the nation was engaged in a war against an ideological enemy that, like a cancer, would destroy society if not extirpated. This theme persisted, as is dramatized by the fact that the most intense repression occurred when a significant armed opposition no longer remained. Fagen analyzes the ideology and the practice of internal war developed by the various military regimes. She discusses the transformation of state institutions and the exposure of civil society to state repression, with emphasis on military organization and security systems.

The chapters in Part II deal with the human cost of repression and fear-mongering. The authors explore the cultural, psychological, and even the gender dimensions of fear in situations of political repression. Sofia Salimovich, Elizabeth Lira, and Eugenia Weinstein bring to their chapter the experiences of the Fundación de Ayuda Social de las Iglesias Cristianas, an organization that has been working with exiles and with victims of torture in Chile. Their chapter describes fear in the face of arrests, torture, and exile. They discuss fear in an atomized, privatized society in which it was dangerous to be identified with the left, past or present. Their focus, however, is on the individual victims whose experience with repression caused lasting psychological damage. These victims often lost their ability to cope with or gauge reality, or to recover their sense of self. According to the authors, changes in Chilean society as a whole inhibited interpersonal relations, greatly augmented feelings of personal insecurity, and changed social values.

In Chapter 5, Juan Rial explores three themes: the vulnerability of Uruguayan society to the imposition of authoritarian power, the centrality of prisons in Uruguayan repression, and the factors that both engendered and counteracted the culture of fear. Political prisoners in Uruguay were generally not killed but held for years in total institutions whose primary purpose was to destroy their personality and individuality. Although the spiral of fear began with and was most strongly enforced in the prisons, the ultimate objective, as Rial elaborates, was to spread insecurity and apprehension throughout the population. The success of the Uruguayan regime in this regard was significant: it created a society that was silent, atomized, and, at times, without hope. Acknowledging this general sense of insecurity, Rial goes on to show why islands of resistance ultimately developed within the privatized society.

Jean Franco attempts to furnish the conceptual underpinnings of fear and repression, and to place the Southern Cone experiences within the wider sphere of what she characterizes as an ethical vacuum in postmodern society. She first develops the argument that current methods of social control by means of extermination have grown out of scientific experimentation. She goes on to examine the actions of victims and perpetrators of violence as manifestations of gender differentiation. Moving from testimony related to incarceration and torture in Argentina, Chile, and Uruguay, she examines the resistance of the mothers' movement. Franco states that the mothers' struggle, based on an ethics of survival, transformed gender-associated weakness into strength.

The third part of this book is the most extensive, for it deals with what, for the participants in the project, were perhaps the most engaging and fascinating questions: Who was immune to intimidation? What processes led some to conquer fear? What explains recorded instances of courage in the public and private spheres? What types of resistance developed?

A long tradition within sociology suggests that resistance to established orders of domination—including those that seem the most terroristic—is not a sporadic or exceptional occurrence but an everyday practice. Oftentimes, even the most spectacular successes of control are diverted and diffused by those who make use of the imposed system. Subdued populations are resourceful, even though their efforts may not always bring about the abolition of bondage.

Students of culture have often stressed the capacity of the arts to convert a dominant order through metaphor, transposing it to another realm of meaning. Art remains "other" within a system that it assimilates and that assimilates it. The chapter by Franco in Part II and two chapters in Part III, by Joan Dassin and by Beatriz Sarlo, highlight the importance of literature as an index of changes that take place in people living in fear. Thus, literature is both a topic and a resource in the study of the culture of fear. Among the issues that require examination, the following stand out: changes in genres, the relationship between official and oppositional texts and between official and unofficial discourse, changes in the social positions of the authors, the relationship between author and public, the impact of censorship and the importance of self-censorship, the comparison of literature under conditions of internal and external exile, the consequences of terror for literature (from the shipwreck of literary generations to the universalization of regional literature through the diaspora), and, finally, the implications of a high-risk situation for the intensity of commitment to cultural activities.

Other studies included in Part III remind us that similar processes also occur in the everyday "arts of living" and in other institutions. These practices amount to the invention of a poetics of resistance among women, students, workers, human-rights activists. Ironically, in the long run, the experience of repression may produce an increased understanding of, and appreciation for, an ideal of public life in a democratic society. Even at its most depressing stage, a culture of fear is not without paradox. Repressive, closed societies afford an opportunity to express and signal true intensities of commitment to certain values precisely because in them the manifestations of criticism, from the mild to the severe, carry some price tag or penalty. The sense of excitement and of participation generated under such conditions contrasts with the boredom often characteristic of political life in institutionalized democracies and, of course, with the hopelessness and despondency among those who have adapted to authoritarian regimes.

Therefore, an indispensable part of the study of fear is examining the processes whereby the sense of inevitability is conquered—that is, examining dynamic factors in culture, social structure, and personality that put iron in the soul. This is the gist of Javier Martínez's contribution. His study of the protest movement in Chile is a prototype of the kind of sociological research that we hope to encourage with the publication of this book. Readers will notice that Martínez's empirical research has a tight fit with the theoretical framework developed by Juan Corradi in the closing chapter.

In studying resistance to fear, two related tasks must be tackled: on the one hand, the examination of macrosociological processes, notably the study of failures, fissures, and contradictions in the sources of fear (especially state action), and, on the other, the study of resistance emerging from below, from minor challenges to full-fledged protest movements, with special attention to the mechanisms that insulate actors from fear and to their recipes for coping. Both case studies and comparative analyses seem indispensable for shuttling back and forth between the two levels, as shown by the sequence of chapters in Part III. What they reveal is that a basic human drive pushes us to find those moments when the tables are turned and justice is restored. Toward the end of the book, some of the chapters explicitly honor this impulse and, as in the case of Emilio Mignone's chapter on justice and compensation in Argentina, turn it into a topic. But beyond such sentiments, our goal is to determine those conditions under which genuine democratic power, which involves the ability to act in concert without fear, is renewed.

Hugo Fruhling's work explains how two Chilean human-rights organizations managed to provide partial alternatives to the Pinochet regime's policies of social control. These organizations, operating under Church auspices, created relatively protected institutional spaces within which adversaries of the government could work. Fruhling underscores the importance of these organizations' ability to break the monopoly of state-run communications, to provide legal and material assistance, and, most important, to support grass-roots efforts of resistance. Although these activities helped to undermine the legitimacy of the regime and facilitated the reconstruction of organized political activity in Chile, Fruhling concludes that the structure and mandate of human-rights organizations limit their capacity to bring about redemocratization.

Focusing on the Brazilian metalworkers of São Bernardo and Diadema, Maria Helena Moreira Alves describes how one sector of Brazilian society largely overcame atomization and fear through the process of building a democratic labor movement. Like all trade-union members subject to the repression of the Brazilian national security state during the 1960s and 1970s, the metalworkers were denied previously won benefits and prohibited from organizing and striking. Alves emphasizes the importance of two factors in the union's unequal battle against both government and corporations to regain these rights: the moral and material impact of widespread grass-roots support for the strikers and, more important, the commitment to participatory democracy and solidarity within the union.

Exploring the gradual loss of fear and the development of organized opposition in Uruguay, Carina Perelli analyzes the political trajectory of secondary school students. In contrast to the Brazilian trade unionists described by Alves, who were targets of repression under authoritarian rule, the secondary school students in Perelli's work were the objects of governmental resocialization and reeducation policies. She examines the situation in generational terms and in relation to the government's effort to transform the previously dominant ideology. Identifying three generations of actors: the "autistic adults," the "*marrano* youth," and the countercultural adolescents, Perelli describes the means they found to preserve or create forms of opposition. According to Perelli, the determination of the authorities to eliminate the old ideological order, combined with their own inability to create a new order, facilitated the students' ability to develop countermessages of their own. What began as a clandestine and symbolic opposition ultimately took the form of organized political militance.

As so many of our chapters indicate, the leaders of these repressive, terroristic states attempted to impose on citizens a certain type of social life. Did these fear-mongering regimes ultimately succeed or fail? In several cases, they succeeded only in destroying the existing social and

moral fabric without generating viable alternatives. As their own difficulties and failures drove them out of power, more "civil" societies
emerged. The success of democracy depends very much on outside
political and economic conditions. But internal factors are equally significant. Democratic societies will be the product of ongoing social conflicts. We must find out how, in the countries of the Southern Cone,
defensive reactions from the authoritarian period can be transformed
into social action within the framework of democratic institutions and
how such struggles can create a new public sphere.

Our book closes with a look ahead and beyond, seeking clues in
theories and historical events outside Latin America. It reflects on the
inevitability and the recurring cycles of fear in society, its ideological
roots, and the forms of social organization that are built under and
against fear. After rejecting absolutist modes of exit from fear, Corradi
surveys the dangerous political terrain that communities that have just
emerged from fear-mongering regimes must tread. On the one hand, a
symbolic cut between past and present must be made as a form of ritual
renewal. On the other hand, pressures build up to prevent such a collective catharsis from becoming itself a new source of insecurity. The
tension between punishment and reconciliation—the thorny issue of
political justice under successor regimes—leads us to explore new notions, such as that of transitional justice, and to recast, in the light of such
notions, the concept of democracy. A democratic system able to conquer
and contain fear must rest on a network of social relations that generates
moral convictions sufficiently strong to weather the deep economic and
institutional crises that lie ahead.

PART ONE

Fear and Authoritarianism

ONE

Fear in Military Regimes

An Overview

Manuel Antonio Garretón

Fear is inherent in human society. Fear underlies the precarious edifice of the human condition: we fear death, loss, society, the past, the future, pain, and the unknown. Just as death cannot be defeated, the essential battles with fear cannot be won; the conditions that produce it can be ameliorated, though, and the specific circumstances associated with it overcome.

Our subject is not the existential fear that is an integral part of the human psyche but politically determined fear, the fear associated with political regimes. Just as psychology looks at individual fear, the social sciences look at collective fear and the social conditions that produce it and allow it to be overcome. Because all societies and political systems consciously manufacture and then wrestle with fear, they can all be classified by their dominant fears. Although democratic regimes have not entirely dispensed with fear, they do generate mechanisms that discipline and overcome certain types of fear. Here, however, we shall focus on those historically regressive regimes in which the dominant fear is the primary fear of death. It is no coincidence that the positive theme in these systems is that of human rights, a historically and culturally determined extension of the right of life.[1]

We shall confine ourselves to the problem of fear in a particular type of regime, the military dictatorships that emerged in the Southern Cone during the 1970s. Because we define authoritarianism as a regime, as a type of relation between state and society, and not as a type of society, we will not be looking for any generic relation between authoritarianism and fear that might cover all social spheres and individual personalities. Rather, because military dictatorships are a historical type of authoritarian regime, we have to look at their distinguishing features and the particular consequences for fear.

For the purposes of this analysis we need to distinguish first between the dominant types of fear and second between the groups that experience them. There are two basic types of fear, which can be described in the context of infantile experiences: the "dark room," and the "dog that bites." The first is fear of the unknown, a sense of insecurity about something bad: we know the threat exists, but we do not know its exact nature. In classical sociological terms this qualifies as fear of an anomic situation; although the blow or harm is seen as imminent, we know neither whence it comes nor how hard it will strike. The second type of fear is stimulated by a known danger: the subject anticipates the harm he or she will suffer, and fear springs from a remembered experience with whose harmful dimensions the subject is completely familiar.

With respect to the subjects of fear, those who are afraid, we must distinguish between the losers' fear and the winners' fear within political regimes; the relations of these subjects are defined as asymmetric and normally conflictual or antagonistic. The losers' fear is pervaded by a sense of defeat, a perception of the overwhelming power of the enemy, a feeling of failure or weakness that cannot be blamed on others, and a sense of having lost the opportunity for personal or collective realization. It combines fear of terror or repression with terror of the future— namely, a new situation that will be fraught with unknown dangers.

The winners' fear stems from the trauma experienced before the victory, from their perception of how their victory has affected the losers, from their suspicion that the repressive mechanism unleashed might become an uncontrollable Frankenstein, from the sense that victory is ephemeral and that the tables might someday be turned on them and the losers will take their revenge.

These fears feed on one another despite the fact that they are independent of each other and have their own separate dynamics. Both fear of known and unknown dangers and the dialectic of the winners' fear and the losers' fear pervade the emergence, development, and end of the military regimes, and have significant bearing on the processes of democratic transition and consolidation. These regimes can be seen as systems that produce fear and that are challenged by processes and struggles to overcome it.

THE MILITARY REGIMES
OF THE SOUTHERN CONE

This chapter will not touch on the debate over the nature of the military regimes that were set up in Argentina, Brazil, Chile, and Uruguay. We shall take only a brief look at some of their characteristics, which are described elsewhere in more detail.[2] These regimes were at the same time institutional forms, a distinct phase of the development of capitalism in such societies, and the expression of a new type of militarism; they cannot be reduced to either one of these dimensions. These factors played into each other in various ways. First, the military regimes were associated with the denouement of a political crisis, itself a manifestation of the generic problem of hegemony, which has been endemic since the demise of the oligarchic state. This political crisis was characterized by the high degree of polarization between the active and mobilized popular sectors—whose political expressions had participated in power to different degrees—and the dominant sectors—who saw this situation as catastrophic, a zero-sum political crisis in which everything was at stake. The dominant sectors were able to instigate their fears in the middle classes. Second, however, these regimes can be seen as a part of the modernization, professionalization, and ideological homogenization of the armed forces in the context of their dependent position in the U.S.-controlled geopolitical system. Third, the military regimes under consideration were committed to restructuring their respective capitalist systems and then reinserting them into the global capitalist system.

The foregoing analysis allows us to understand the double logic, or two-dimensionality, of this historic type of regime. On the one hand, the regimes were reacting against something, be it populist society, the "state of compromise," or state-activated popular mobilization, and on the other they were attempting to construct something entirely new. Catalyzed by the political crisis—perceived by some sectors to be terminal or catastrophic, a clear threat to their social position—the regimes attempted to disarticulate the former society. The touchstone of this reactive logic was repression, whereby the regime relied on a powerful apparatus that employed vast quantities of resources and hitherto unprecedented techniques of brutality. The intensity of the reactive dimension varied by country, according to the nature of the crisis that preceded and provoked the military coup, the concomitant degree of radicalization and polarization of society, the level of activity and organization of the popular sectors or their political expressions, and the homogenization and efficacy of the military/repressive apparatus.

The process in the Southern Cone, however, involved more than disarming, disarticulating, fragmenting, or repressing the opposition. The goal of those military regimes, in contrast to that of more traditional dictatorships, was to transform society. Their plan was first to re-create the relations between the state and civil society in order to institute a nonredistributive, nonparticipatory brand of capitalism, and then to reinsert their respective economies into the world system. We shall call this the *foundational* or *transformational* logic or dimension of the process. Just because it failed does not mean it was not a basic goal of this type of regime. The main determinants of this dimension are, first, the capacity to constitute a hegemonic nucleus in the heart of the victorious coalition that induces part of the civilian sector (the bourgeoisie, technocracy, conservative intellectuals) to cooperate with the military sector in guiding and leading the attempt at capitalist recomposition. The second factor is the degree to which the society, or significant sectors within it, resist the state-induced transformations.

Different Southern Cone regimes placed emphasis on one dimension or the other and in some cases gave equal weight to both. The distribution of the emphasis allows us to differentiate phases in their development. Thus we can distinguish a reactive from a foundational phase, and a phase in which the transformational dimension predominates even while the reactive dimension remains.

Other phases are derived from these two. One, defined by recurring crises, comes about when the regime has exhausted its capacity to transform society or is having difficulties in the implementation phase; at this point the regime's principal problem is how to survive, not how to repress or to change the society. Another is the period of crisis accumulation, defined as a terminal phase when the main problem is how the regime is to withdraw or exit; it is, in other words, the final administration: the *administración de salida*. This phase either predates or accompanies the phase of transition between the military regime and the political regime that replaces it. The so-called dirty war is a good example of the reactive phase, while "economic miracles" or "booms" herald the foundational phase. Popular mobilizations against the regime illustrate the phase of recurring crises, while mobilizations and negotiations (direct or indirect) between the military and civilians, together with the resurgence of political parties, characterize the terminal and transition phases.

Although there is a high probability, historically speaking, that these phases will follow some sort of chronological order, there is no necessary sequence, and, apart from the terminal and transition phases, they can follow in any order: the process can jump about from one phase to another and then double back to a previous phase. Likewise, each phase contains, to varying degrees, elements of the other phases.

THE PHASES OF FEAR

THE REIGN OF TERROR

The object of the reactive phase, which usually follows directly after the installation of the military regime, is to deactivate and dismantle the previous sociopolitical system. Although it does not necessarily rely exclusively on repression, it is first and foremost a military phase; because the hegemonic civil nucleus has yet to be consolidated, the specific nature of the transformation remains undefined. The lack of a consensus within the governing bloc as to its future course leads to a consensus on the elimination of the enemy at all costs. This enemy is usually the sector that was overthrown by the military coup. It includes those who are defined as collaborators as well as political society in general; all those who are blamed for the "chaos" that originally gave rise to the coup are considered traitors and enemies of the state. Although technocrats and conservative intellectuals struggle to impose some direction on the concentrated power of the armed forces, they do not have a well-defined project that goes beyond the task of "order or stabilization."[3] Although the military coup implied the victory of one group over another, the winners still define society as being in a state of war; citing it as necessary and unavoidable, they justify the repression both to their supporters and to the silently complicit society as a whole. The predominant ideology is military and bellicose, and is defined by the so-called national security doctrine.[4]

Opposition in the strict sense of the word—a realm of forces comprising recognized intermediaries, adversaries, and alternative projects—does not exist in a society subjected to the culminating phase of state repression, the period when both tacit and explicit support for the coup is at its peak. The situation is still basic; primary concerns are resistance, physical survival, and, at most, organization. Therefore, subjects such as the right of life and human rights in general, which in turn highlight the role of national and international figures and institutions that speak this universal "metapolitical" language, are given priority. In some countries the churches are key, and in others the human-rights commissions.

At this time fear seems to pervade society as a whole. Each person seems to be facing the extreme Sartrian dilemma of having to choose whether to be a hero or a traitor. Everyone is afraid of everyone else. And this climax of fear is exacerbated by the official rhetoric, which activates the fear of the winners by showing how close they were to a catastrophe and that of the losers by demonstrating what the repression has accomplished. By denouncing the presence of the hidden enemy who has yet to be completely eliminated and by calling on society to collaborate in the final "clean up," such rhetoric stimulates fear within the society as a whole.

The losers experience a primary, existential fear: theirs is the terror of death and loss of physical integrity; they fear disappearance, torture, and destruction of the web of intellectual and affective meaning; they fear being uprooted, having to live in a darkened world. Fear of the known ("the dog that bites") combines with fear of the unknown ("the dark room"). Personal experience or the words of friends and acquaintances are the source of their knowledge. They have seen repression in the street, the torture cells, and the concentration camps. Sometimes, as part of the "war," the military even makes public and official threats. Moreover, there is rumor, uncertainty, surprise, and ignorance of all the variations of pain and suffering. The military tends to exaggerate this uncertainty and fear both by keeping the definition of the enemy or possible victims and the forms of punishment deliberately vague, and by insinuating that, as long as the enemy is still alive and active, excesses of repression will be inevitable.

When the state is omnipresent and the society is underground or submerged (when society actually *is* an "underground"), the struggle against fear tends to be individual and atomized, and people seek refuge in the most intimate nucleus, the primary group.[5] In some countries, institutions such as the Church play a double role in the process of overcoming fear. They provide a space to reestablish links and regroup, and they gather and diffuse information about what is happening in order to lower the levels of uncertainty.

The winners' fear is the residue of former fears experienced during the period of crisis that culminated in the coup; it reflects a sense of having survived a trauma or a perceived threat to their security. The relief that follows the coup transforms fear of the past into tacit or explicit complicity and, in some cases, acts of concrete vengeance. This fear tends to disappear as the new regime is consolidated; once the winners start to sense that "something is going on," that people have been executed, for instance, or that relatives have been victims of the repression, fear of what might have happened in the past becomes a hidden fear of what might happen in the present, fear of the Frankenstein they helped to create and that is now out of control. During the foundational phase this relatively secret fear will be sublimated in dreams of grandeur.

IMPOTENCE AND SUBLIMATION

The purpose of the transformational, or foundational, phase of the regime, which retains its repressive character, is to reconstitute society and usher in a new social order that matches the projected brand of authoritarian capitalism. This is the era of grand plans. It is when the military attempts to institutionalize various aspects of social life and implement policies that turn back the clock on the gains of former social actors, especially those in the popular sectors. It is a time of idealizations, "miracles," and "economic booms," superimposed plebiscites, and tri-umphalist *aperturas* (openings) that seek to incorporate the crushed sectors, albeit subordinated, in the creation of the "great power" or future "new democracy." During this phase, the hegemonic mili-tary/civilian nucleus that is to supply the guidelines and the substance of the project of capitalist reinsertion and recomposition is constructed within the dominant bloc. The governing nucleus, aside from its ambi-tion to open up the market and modernize some social spheres, is driven by a utopian vision of a society wherein politics has ceased to be either relevant or necessary. The imposition of a military regime is touted as the indispensable historic condition for the creation of such a society.

The program of the opposition tends to be social and cultural at this point in that the political structures, the parties, not yet having repaired the damage of the disarticulation, are attempting to reconnect with the social movement. Artistic and literary expressions that confine them-selves to human-rights issues begin to appear; these depict and criticize the new reality on the one hand and express resistance to the transfor-mations undermining the historic progress of the social movement on the other. Similarly, there is renewed activity in the trade-union and women's movements, and other sectors affected by the socioeconomic changes imposed by the regime begin to mobilize. To these movements is added the disenchantment of sectors that initially supported the dictator-ship: they begin to react to its longevity and excesses or express general unhappiness with the social and economic changes. Thus the opposition's task is both to reconstitute the relation between the political and social and to pit itself not only against the dictatorial nature of the regime but against the measures and policies it implements. Moreover, it must do so in a situation of fragmentation; it is more correct to speak of multiple oppositions than a single opposition because no such sociopolitical entity has yet been constituted.

What fears dominate society during this phase? To the extent that nothing has significantly changed in the repression, the losers' fear is, in part, an extension of the fear of physical repression experienced during the first phase. The transformation of society, which affects the losers most directly, brings with it also fear of the unknown, which results from the "transformed" material and cultural conditions under which the losers must live. Although this type of everyday fear can be partially mastered in the expanded spaces for meeting and communication that are available in the transformational phase, it cannot be completely overcome as long as society remains cloaked in illusion and triumphalism. This fear born of uncertainty, the "dark-room" type of fear, is also born of impotence vis-à-vis the all-powerful state, change, and a present and future that are beyond one's control. During this phase, the winners' fear is sublimated in an orgy of consumerism, in the illusion of a future that will preclude the possibility of returning to the past, in the recognition that, if there has been a price, "we're OK today, and tomorrow we'll be better." If the state and the underground society were the dominant factors in the previous phase, this is the era of the schizophrenic society: the miracle and euphoria, the underground and the fear.

HOPE AND UNCERTAINTY

The phase of recurring crisis, which is not necessarily one step away from a terminal crisis and a transition process, can drag on for a long time. Either the military regime fails to implement its foundational project, or the project falls apart. The regime is now concerned only with survival; having nothing left to offer the society, it has lost its ability to bring it together, however limited this ability might have been in the past.

Indicators of the crisis of the transformational or foundational project are, among others, disintegration of the hegemonic nucleus, isolation of the military from society, promulgation by the regime of erratic policies (many of which reverse the policies of the transformational phase), and incoherent official projects. Similarly, there is buildup of pressure in the corporate sectors that are fed up with the regime, and the popular mobilizations, which have been called "the resurrection of civil society," begin.[6] The intensified repression that is a response to these mobilizations and the occasional forced concessions designed to coopt destabilizing sectors are also features of the crisis phase. The opposition must now tackle the problem of how to transform the dissatisfaction and mobilization into a unified and balanced political force capable of converting the recurring crisis into a terminal crisis. This task involves unifying the sectors that are fed up with the regime and making a credible and consensual proposal for termination.

The widespread perception that the regime is weak, the massive mobilizations, the generalized criticism, and the forced opening of political spaces to channel this mobilization serve to lessen the losers' fear. The mobilizations and generalized criticism erode the barriers of atomization that have fed the fear. The presence of others reinforces one's personal security; private, everyday fear is transcended through collective action and becomes courage and heroism. The hope that things might change alleviates part of the ever-present fear. In that the results are uncertain and the source of trauma is still in place and might at any time unleash the repression, the alleviation is only partial. In other words, uncertainty is still present and, at times, is increased: it is often the case that after the first explosions of discontent, official rhetoric again feeds fears of the coup era, invoking memories of the "chaos." And this rekindled fear touches certain sectors that had begun to mobilize against the regime; once the initial euphoria dissipates they tend to withdraw in the face of uncertainty and threat. The fear of the winners, also a fear born of uncertainty and stimulated by the official propaganda warning of the "return to chaos," is rekindled during this phase.

The main issue for the opposition is how to reduce the level of uncertainty regarding the regime: faced with a shattered regime lacking a project, the opposition is seen as lacking concrete proposals for termination. Although there is no allegiance to the regime, there is fear of change.

REGRESSIONS, RESIDUES, AND EXORCISMS

The central problem of the terminal phase is devising the forms and mechanisms of exit—how the armed forces are to step down. The problem of the transition phase, which can coincide with the terminal phase, is to establish a replacement regime—in this case, a democratic regime. Essentially this political process combines regime decay, social mobilizations with political/institutional ends, negotiations between those in power and the opposition (as long as during these transitions there is no military defeat or insurrection), and mediation between the regime and the opposition by actors or agents not identified with any of the adversaries.[7] The nucleus in power and the dominant sectors in the regime seek to preserve the integrity and institutional immunity of the armed forces and as many established privileges and gains as possible. The opposition seeks to ensure rapid progress toward democratic elections and constitutional rule. Many opposition sectors will try to use the transition to promote social changes that reflect accumulated demands. This attempt at "deepening" the process is likely, however, to remain pending until the consolidation period, after the democracy has been inaugurated.

The winners' fear is dominant during these phases; they become the losers during the transition phase. There is growing recognition within society of the crimes they have committed, and demands for justice and punishment become widespread. They fear that the tables will be turned; they are aware that evil has been done. This fear drives the repressive apparatus to play its last cards: some try a preventative coup, others proclaim their innocence, others negotiate immunity so that there may be a fresh start.

Does the termination of the military regime and the transition to political democracy mean that the former losers and the victims will no longer be afraid and that a new society without fear is about to be inaugurated? The terminal and transition phases can be seen as periods when fear is exorcised. The triumphant mobilizations reinforce personal security and the individual's sense of being protected: the repressive apparatus is obviously collapsing; there is some assurance that crimes will not go unpunished. Objectively there is increased freedom, and the imminent demise of yesterday's winners occasions a sigh of personal and collective relief. Likewise, widespread knowledge of what happened and massive denunciation of the crimes provoke a catharsis and generate an antidote for the future (that it will never happen again). It is also the case, however, that many people do not undergo any such exorcism and that the survivors retain indelible scars. This legacy will affect not only their individual behavior and private lives but also their way of adapting to society, their confidence in others and in institutions, and their acceptance or rejection of politics. This point demands further research and reflection.

PRODUCING AND OVERCOMING FEAR

The Southern Cone military regimes, more than other dictatorships, were institutionalized systems that deliberately produced and spread fear. The system depended on the use of heretofore unknown structures of repression and propaganda. The generalized fear in the society was intentionally provoked in the losers by the military coup through diverse forms of repression and propaganda. Fear was aroused indirectly in the winners because they could never entirely eliminate the awareness of their crimes and complicity. And it was instilled both directly and indirectly in society as a whole through the combined effect of repressive policies, the absence of institutional protection, and the superimposed model of social transformation. All these features varied by degree and by country.

This system of fear combined fear of the known ("the dog that bites") with fear of the unknown ("the dark room"). Fear of the known was instilled through actual physical repression, threats, control of the society, propaganda, and the omnipresent power of the state. Fear of the unknown was instilled primarily through omission: disinformation, the absence of the defined rules for the "war," and the absence of spaces where people could meet and acknowledge the presence of one another. Likewise, the regime exaggerated irrationality and adopted an arbitrary and autocratic style of imposing change.

Although fear could never be eliminated, the struggle to overcome it constantly permeated the system of fear-mongering. The sublimation of the winners' fear in the consumerist euphoria and in the quickly dispelled illusions of "national grandeur" were inauthentic ways of overcoming fear. The losers and the victims, in contrast, and the institutions and the social, religious, and political organizations with which they identified, found authentic ways to overcome their fear. The struggle to gain civil liberties, to marshal resources for self-defense in a situation where the judiciary was essentially nonfunctional, to denounce crimes, and to mobilize against torture, disappearances, and the repressive apparatus in general, in an attempt to impose limits on state power, was nothing less than an effort to overcome or confront the known fear of danger or threat. The struggles for freedom of information, for the recognition of organized groups, for participation, and for the freedom and strengthening of such social and political organizations as could counteract the atomization of society were nothing less than efforts to shrink the frontiers of uncertainty and impotence, and thereby overcome the fear they produced.

What is the legacy of this experience of fear once the military regime is terminated? One possibility is that the processes of regime termination and democratic transition have prevented definitive exorcism of fear and that additional time is needed to absorb the process and overcome the fear. Notwithstanding, history seems to reveal that fear scares individuals and affects their behavior but that societies have a great capacity to absorb traumatic experiences and to look ahead to the future without making direct reference to memory. There is a dimension of the society that cannot be understood apart from its history, but there is also a creative potential that cannot be reduced to that history. Thus we are faced with an unknown. We do not know how much of the fear created by the military regimes will haunt individuals and stain collective memory.

Fear, as we said at the beginning, cannot be entirely eliminated. But if the new democratic societies are to free themselves from the traumas and ghosts that will inevitably manifest themselves, they must come to grips with the legacy of fear. The catharsis and exorcism of the transition period must be accompanied by a two-tiered process. First, the organization that produced the fear—the armed forces—must be subjected to strict controls by society and the political regime. The military must be cut back both in quality and in quantity, and training must be free from such ideologies as the doctrine of national security, which isolated the military from society and gave it the dominant role. The second tier involves strengthening institutions such as the judiciary in order to resolve the pending problem of exorcising fear. This process may be limited to exposing and publishing the truth about the crimes that were committed if there is no possibility of obtaining appropriate punishments and reparations. Effort must also be directed toward creating and strengthening institutions that confront the two types of fear produced by military dictatorships. To reduce fear of known threats, such institutions promote and ensure individual and corporate freedom, reform the judiciary, guarantee resources for individual and collective protection, and limit the power available to different agencies. Institutions that promote participation, different levels of social organization, and freedom of information and knowledge reduce fear of the unknown.

The challenge, given the ongoing threat presented by the existence of fear-producing organizations and the precariousness of inherited institutions, consists in constituting a political force with the power to create and sustain a consensus on the development of institutions that will structure not a society without fear but one able at least to bury past fears.

NOTES

1. M. A. Garretón, "En torno a la problemática actual de los derechos humanos. Derechos humanos y crisis social," in *Estudios*, vol. 1 (Santiago: Vicaría de la Solidaridad, 1978).

2. See, especially, M. A. Garretón, *Dictaduras y democratización* (ch. 1) (Santiago: FLACSO, 1984). English version: "The Failure of Dictatorships in the Southern Cone," *Telos*, no. 68 (summer 1986). We shall use the sequence of phases developed therein. The best-known discussion of these regimes is in D. Collier, ed., *The New Authoritarianism in Latin America* (Princeton, N.J.: Princeton University Press, 1979).

3. G. O'Donnell, "Reflexiones sobre las tendencias de cambio en el estado burocrático-autoritario," *Revista mexicana de sociología* 1 (1977). English version: *Latin American Research Review* 12, no. 1 (winter 1978).

4. M. A. Garretón, *El proceso político chileno* (ch. 4) (Santiago: FLACSO, 1983).

5. Paradoxically, humor becomes a defense against fear. This is the period when a lot of clandestine jokes about the military and the situation tend to circulate, as if to exorcise it. The following joke, which expresses this type of fear, was popular in Chile in the months immediately following the coup: A terrified bunny rabbit runs off to the border. The guard who stops him on the other side asks, "What are you running away from?" He answers, "They're killing all the elephants in Chile." The border guard soothes him, saying, "That's OK, you're a bunny." The bunny answers, "And how am I supposed to prove that?"

6. G. O'Donnell and P. Schmitter, *Transitions from Authoritarian Rule. Tentative Conclusions about Uncertain Democracies* (Baltimore: Johns Hopkins University Press, 1987).

7. M. A. Garretón, *Reconstruir la política. Transición y consolidación democráticas en Chile* (ch. 1) (Santiago: Editorial Andante, 1987).

TWO

Some People Die of Fear

Fear as a Political Problem

Norbert Lechner

Cities, like dreams, are built from desires and fears, although
the thread of their discourse is secret, their rules absurd, their
perspectives deceptive, and everything hides something else.
Italo Calvino, The Invisible Cities

Our subject is fear—defined as the perception of a threat that is either
real or imaginary—in the authoritarian societies of the Southern Cone.
Although different social groups have different perceptions, I propose
here to confine our inquiry to mortal threats (*peligros mortales*), which
are common to all. What is a mortal threat? First, it is a physical threat
(murder, torture, assault), and, second, it is whatever threatens the
material basis that sustains life (poverty, unemployment, inflation). The
perception that physical/material security is threatened does not account
in itself for a widespread, generalized feeling of fear, even though such
security is one's most immediate vital interest. Hidden fears—articulated
only with difficulty—are the handmaidens of these concrete fears. Fear
of physical harm and of economic insecurity is only the tip of an iceberg
whose bulk is obscured. The hidden mass is anxiety: diffuse, apparently
objectless fear that eats away at everything, crumbles hope, flattens
emotions, and saps vitality—a cold that invades and paralyzes. It is said
that a life not lived is a terminal illness. So we face death. Fear can kill us
before we actually die. People die of fear.

Authoritarianism creates a "culture of fear." The term, coined for
Argentina by Guillermo O'Donnell, refers to the wholesale, everyday
experience of human-rights abuse.[1] We experience the imprint of authoritarianism as a culture of fear. And the legacy will persist even after
the authoritarian regime has disappeared.

I wish to emphasize a paradoxical effect: a dictatorship increases the demand for security, which then feeds the desire for a *mano dura* (strong hand). Take the case of Chile. At the end of 1986, when the state of siege was at its peak, the population of Santiago feared an increase in the crime rate and in drug use more than a new wave of repression. Although the economic situation was cited as the primary national problem, crime was perceived as a greater threat than unemployment or inflation.[2] The fixation on crime and drugs, although startling, is plausible: it allows people to trace their anxiety to a concrete origin, maybe to a personal experience. When the danger is confined to a visible, clearly identifiable cause that has been officially stamped as "evil," the fear can be brought under control.

The operation is both simple and familiar. Differences are labeled "deviation" and "subversion" and are subjected to a process of "normalization"; because differences cannot possibly be abolished, they are treated as transgressions of the norm, which is then confirmed in the punishment of the transgressions. The emphasis placed on crime indicates the need to objectify unspeakable horrors, to project them onto a minority, and thus to confirm faith in the existing order. If citizens were certain of the basic norms of social intercourse, then the insecurity they feel could be treated as a technical/administrative problem and solved by police enforcement. But in an authoritarian regime, a focus on such solutions obscures the real problem.

To get to the bottom of this problem I propose instead (1) to distinguish between criminality—defined as the transgression (violent or not) of established laws—and violence—the violation (criminal or not) of a given order,[3] and (2) to relate fear to a violated order. Seen thus, explicit fear of delinquency is no more than an inoffensive way of conceiving and expressing other, silenced, fears: fear not only of death and poverty but also, and probably above all, of a meaningless, rootless, futureless life. Authoritarian power rests on this type of hidden fear, and having such hidden fears is the price everyone pays to survive.

So it is not enough to denounce concrete, human-rights violations and the dislocation they precipitate. Hidden fears are at once the product of authoritarianism and the sufficient condition for its perpetuation. Once collective referents have been lost, future horizons deconstructed, and the social criteria pertaining to what is considered normal, possible, and desirable eroded, authoritarianism will play on the vital need for order and present itself as the only solution. Fear, and particularly this "fear of fears," thus ultimately poses the question of order.[4]

THE DEMAND FOR ORDER

In Latin America, where differences rapidly turn into rebellion, fragmentation, and disaggregation, pluralism could not develop as it did in
North America.[5] Pluralism cannot exist without reference to a collective
order. In Latin America, the dominant conception, since colonial times,
is of a holistic society—a hierarchically structured organic order. This
compelling notion of community has even survived revolutions, subor-
dinating republican universalism to the nation-state. The young Latin
American republics are thus more grounded in the idea of the nation-
state (and, concomitantly, in the notion of community as a preconsti-
tuted unity) than in democratic procedures. Thus the question of order is
not posed as a political problem—as a collective and inherently conflictual undertaking.

The weak link in this quasi-ontological vision of order and politics is,
of course, the fact that large social sectors are excluded from it. The
counterpoint to such order has been a constant history of invasions:
invasions of the conquistadors and squatters as well as of Indians,
peasants, and various waves of "marginalized" sectors. Latin American
history is one of ongoing and reciprocal occupation. There are no stable,
commonly recognized boundaries. No one tangible frontier or social
limit affords security. So a transgenerational, ancestral fear of the invader—fear of the other, of that which is different (whether it comes
from above or below), of being expropriated by a landowner or a bank,
of being subjected to some sort of military occupation, of being overrun
by barbarians (the Indian, the immigrant, the ultimately dangerous
classes)—is born and internalized. The struggle for *tierra propia* (a place
to call one's own) extends, literally, to symbolic territory. Everyone is
concerned with preserving one's own against what is alien.[6] And this
danger of contamination, this generalized fear of being infiltrated, leads
to corporatist and even private withdrawal. The stronger the fear of the
intruder (of what is different), the higher the defensive barriers. This
context helps to explain the patterns of corporatist cloistering, veto, and
reciprocal blocking that characterize Latin American politics.

The social and ideological cohesion that Tocqueville identified as the
source of North American democracy does not exist in Latin America.
The development of capitalism—mercantilization of social relations,
industrialization, and development of an incipient welfare state—at
least in the Southern Cone, only deepened and complicated the existing
structural heterogeneity. In the absence of a collective referent that

allows a society to identify itself as a collective order, social diversity will not be perceived as plurality but will be experienced as increasingly intolerable social disintegration. Thence is born fear of difference and the suspicion and even hatred of the other. When no certainty is attached to collective references, social differentiation will be perceived as a threat to identity. Then one's own identity can be affirmed only by the negation of the other; the crucial defense of one's own self is identified with destruction of the other.

In that authoritarianism incarnates the desire for order in the face of imminent chaos, authoritarianism responds to this climate of total uncertainty. Interpreting social reality as a life-or-death struggle, order versus chaos, the dictatorship presents itself as and can be recognized as both defender of the community and guarantor of its survival. It seeks legitimacy in return for "restoring order," reestablishing clear and fixed limits, expelling everything foreign, preventing contamination, and assuring a hierarchical unity wherein everyone has a "natural" place. The result is a society that is under surveillance, under house arrest, and hence ultimately imprisoned.

These dictatorships promise to do away with fear. In fact, however, they generate new fears because they profoundly disrupt routines and social habits, making even daily life unpredictable. The sense of powerlessness increases as normalcy recedes. Even familiar surroundings are seen as harboring foreign and hostile forces. When people find that they are powerless to affect their situation, they deny responsibility for it, and a kind of moral apathy sets in. Above all, however, they get bored. Life under dictatorship is gray because people no longer get excited about anything.

When no one is committed to anything or anybody, people feel socially uprooted. Rootlessness is manifested in the mistrust that pervades social relations and leads to a process of privatization that drastically restricts the field of social experience. The resulting atomization, "me-ism," further shrinks learning faculties, which alters one's sense of reality. Isolated individuals have trouble verifying their subjectivity by testing it against the experiences of others. As a result, the limits between the real and the fantastic, the possible and the desired, become blurred. Under such conditions it is difficult to develop a realistic perspective. And lack of political realism—inability to perceive possible changes— ends up strengthening the artificial power of the powers that be. Discontent with the state of affairs becomes narcissism, self-satisfaction, and, finally, self-destruction.

We are thus led back to what seems to me to be the most serious political effect of authoritarian aggression: the erosion of collective identities. The distance between one's own reality and the official version, the difference between self-value and social value, is such that individuals are unable to recognize themselves in collective referents. Individual life remains frozen in the present moment; at most there is a sum of singular elements but no transcendent horizon (an imaginary community or utopia) whereby collective life can be conceived of and pursued as a common undertaking. Thus the propensity of authoritarianism to disorganize collective identities leads it to undermine its own legitimizing base. The promise of order leads to an acute experience of disorder. The same dictatorship that invoked the clamor for law and order itself poses the question of order. In Latin America, it remains to be seen whether democracy will also be able to satisfy the demand for order.

THE AUTHORITARIAN APPROPRIATION OF FEARS

One historical perspective interprets authoritarianism in the Southern Cone as the reaction to a long-term process rather than an isolated eruption. Systematic violation of human rights does not alter the fact that large sectors of the population greeted the installation of a regime that promised to restore law and order if not with enthusiasm at least with relief. The so-called authoritarian culture of the region does not account for this acceptance. It was a rational decision: dictatorship appeared as a "necessary evil" or a "lesser evil" compared with the insecurity provoked by the former period of changes and social mobilizations. Why do some people continue to justify a dictatorship even when they know about the death and violence it has brought? Because the dictatorship only deepens fear. The anxiety of losing one's identity, social rootedness, and collective belonging is exacerbated. Because of this fear, the authoritarian regime continues to rely on social support that, albeit that of a minority, cannot be explained simply as a means of defending economic privileges. There are other intangible "benefits"— concretely, a certain feeling of security. That this security seems to us to be completely illusory only underlines the political potential of fear.

Authoritarianism responds to fears by appropriating them. Existing fears are ideologized. A quasi-theological reassignment of meaning takes place that erases reference to the real threats, transforming them into demonic forces. The Church used to appropriate fear of plague or catastrophes and reinterpret it as fear of sin; now authoritarianism reworks concrete fears as fear of chaos, communism. Brainwashing becomes unnecessary when society internalizes this "reflected fear" that power mirrors back to it. The new authoritarianism neither mobilizes nor indoctrinates as fascism used to. It burrows under the skin; all it has to do is manipulate peoples' fears—that is, to demonize perceived threats so that they slide from our grasp.

The dictatorship reinterprets fear of an external threat as fear of the enemy within. Although sin is no longer the primary object of fear, the underlying principle is the same: to add guilt to fear. This process characterizes the authoritarian state: it exploits the fear of the citizens and makes them feel guilty.

Resurrecting an ancestral panic, the dictatorship domesticates and then infantilizes society. Accompanying the self-inflicted subjection, like a counterweight, power is sanctified as a redemptive agent. Faith in magic solutions replaces political participation as the feeling of power-lessness is reinforced. Citizens do not have to be excluded from the political realm; they exclude themselves because they feel incompetent in the face of such great danger. The social process appears as an Olympian struggle impervious to individual opinion. Desperately, dying of fear, people deliver themselves over to a superior agent that will decide for them. It is an act of faith based on the hope of winning salvation through self-abnegation.

The instrumentalization of fears is one of the principal mechanisms of social discipline. It is a strategy of depoliticization that does not require repressive means, except to exemplify the absence of alternatives. It suffices to induce a sense of personal and collective inability to have any effective influence on the public realm. Then the only alternative is to take refuge in the private realm in the hope (albeit vain) of finding minimal security in intimacy.

The strong desire for order stems from a real danger of chaos. People feel their sense of order—that which makes life in society and their place in it intelligible—threatened. They are afraid of losing a cognitive map that allows them to structure their possibilities in time and space. When everything is possible, when anything goes, the danger of chaos becomes imminent. The double-edged panic mounts: not only paralysis of the will but fascination. Power takes on a sort of divine splendor.[7] Violence is attributed not to the dictatorship but to chaos, the enemy that infiltrates and subverts the established order, the mortal danger that must be overthrown. By annihilating chaos—communist subversion—one defends life. The fideist act through which people cling to the dictatorship is, as such, a rational delivery.[8] People prefer authoritarian power in that it embodies life that struggles against death and disorder. The dictatorship appears as their savior.[9]

This "transubstantiation" of dictatorial violence into redemption is a key to understanding the deep roots of the authoritarian regime. In general, however, these roots have been undervalued or ignored by the democratic forces and, especially, by the left, whose rationalism leads to visualizing fear as coming from a distant past, a darkness that will dissipate with dawn. Moreover, its ideology of progress overemphasizes social changes at the expense of the question of order, which is then diluted as a practical question *hic et nunc*. The urgency of transforming unjust social conditions must not, however, blind us to a basic truth. Life in society must be structured in some form or other, and such structuring requires that there be institutions with rules, norms as to what is valid and forbidden, criteria to evaluate the normal, the possible, and the rational; it also demands that events be situated in durable time frames, and that public and private, individual and common spaces be defined. In particular, it demands that social limits be established—that collective identities be generated to organize the different experiences and options. Because the threads that bring people together are so tenuous, the process of change produces vertigo and anomie when such ordering does not take place.

Vertigo is frightening. People are unable to apprehend a reality with accelerated rhythms and increasing diversity. Then nothing is in its proper place, and the world seems out of control. In this type of situation, an anxious desire for normalcy arises. Even people who long for a democratic transition subordinate change to the maintenance of a certain level of normalcy, however precarious and illusory that may actually be. Because any information increases unpredictability and, as a result, uncertainty, people prefer not to know. A sort of sealing process takes place whereby people dry out their inner life, protecting it from the outside world.

I have already discussed the retreat into the private realm, the search for familiar ground that affords a certain degree of self-assurance. People rediscover everyday life. Perhaps everyday life becomes unusually significant because it is so affected by the authoritarian regime. To reestablish routines is to reestablish normalcy. And daily life is the means, because the framework of norms and habits on which it is constructed makes the course of the day predictable. Routine is indispensable; would we get up in the morning if we did not know more or less what was in store for us?

But this sort of expectation, because it is so repetitive, eventually locks us into a "perpetual present." In the words of Humberto Giannini:

> We keep hoping, but we do not search our hopes. Routine eventually anaesthetizes our ambitions because we are so afraid of sliding off the track. Psychologists call this "unfinished business," parasitic projects of a perpetual present. Thus the very same routine that fixes our identity by allowing us to circumvent the unexpected also fixes our buried ambitions; they are incorporated into our vision of the track and in the last instance identified with it. The future looks neither appealing nor threatening: a parasite of the present, it continually arrives, as softly as norm and normalcy. So also the past: what I always am, irremediably.[10]

The quote describes well how routine, a vital defense during periods of instability, becomes claustrophobic. Obsession with survival keeps people from living. In order to live, for our hopes to materialize, we must make ourselves vulnerable. And in this regard, Giannini stresses another aspect of everyday life: the street. The street as a symbol of the unexpected, of exposure to danger ("to stay in the street"), as well as a symbol of openness, of possibilities.[11] To what extent do the streets of our city make for new possibilities? Do they allow us to dream and experiment, to innovate and switch tracks, to explore new paths?

A traditional view of politics does not take everyday life into account. It is, nonetheless, an indispensable aspect of our effort to rethink democracy. Dictatorship itself has shown us how habits and daily routines condition shared meaning. Everyday experience teaches people the practical skills and knowledge that inform their social behavior. They learn fear and trust, egoism and solidarity—the social meaning of their situation. Unfortunately, the debate on democracy often fails to take into account this "life world." As a result, the inevitable distance between political discourse and everyday experience provokes boredom and, worst of all, growing disinterest in democracy.

In sum, no real democratization can take place unless we take responsibility for fear. Not that democracy will do away with fear: a society without fear is utopic. People can learn, however, to become less susceptible to ambiguous and threatening situations and to modify their perceptions. Concretely, to assuage their fear of the other, to be strange and different, and to accept uncertainty are conditions of freedom from the other. Democracy involves more than just tolerance; it involves recognizing the other as a coparticipant in the creation of a common future. A democratic process, in contrast to an authoritarian regime, allows us to learn that the future is an intersubjective undertaking. The otherness of the other is then that of an alter ego. Seen thus, the freedom of the other, its unpredictability, ceases to be a threat to self-identity; it is the condition for self-development. Through and with the other we determine the framework of the possible: the society that we wish to have and to create.

This proposal evokes the following objection: making the political system responsible for fear, we may overload it and contribute to the ungovernability of the democratic state. The argument is serious and difficult to answer. Actually, why does politics have to be responsible for fear? One could just as easily demand that it make sense out of death and pain. Does not our proposal also contradict the so-called secularization of politics, by identifying politics with salvation of the soul? We can be accused of erasing the modern division between politics and feelings (between authority and truth, power and love) that broadened the range of personal liberties. However, how are we to disentangle ourselves from fear and desire when these serve as the prism through which we construct the image of our city?

Reflection on an existential theme, fear, has led us to the core of democratic theory: the relation between political institutions and social experiences. Democracy entails formalization of social relations. The emotional and affective charge would overload the circuit, making the presence of the other unbearable, if we did not distance ourselves from one another. Formal procedures serve as a means of establishing distance. Distance neutralizes the subjective dimension; the validity of a vote or of a decision is independent of the personal considerations that motivate the activity. But we have so stretched the field of formal rationality that we have equated rational politics with the calculation of interests; for some, democracy is reduced to a cost/benefit analysis. These concepts reveal their inadequacy, however, once we attempt, in neoliberal style, to achieve a self-regulated political market at the expense of the values, ambitions, and feelings of the population. Its technocratic discourse notwithstanding, even dictatorship has not done away with the subjective dimension. On the contrary, it instrumentalizes it for its own purposes. The advent of formal rationality (progressive bureaucratization) did not, in fact, succeed in separating the world of the passions from that of politics. We may exclude subjectivity as a private affair, but sooner or later it will reappear in the political arena as rank irrationality. The subjectivity we repress returns to haunt us. In conclusion, if democracy does not accommodate our fears, they will get the better of us. Then we will succumb to the worse fear of all: fear of imagining cities that might have been.

NOTES

This chapter is based on a conference on urban cultures, organized by Jordi Borja and the Universidad Internacional Menéndez Pelayo in Barcelona, September 1985.

1. Guillermo O'Donnell, "La cosecha del miedo," *Nexos* (Mexico City) 6, no. 6 (1983).

2. In a survey carried out by the Facultad Latinoamericana de Ciencias Sociales in Santiago at the end of 1986, during the state of siege, of the 1,200 people interviewed, 82 percent said they were afraid of the rising crime rate and drug abuse; 77 percent were afraid of the increase in inflation; 61 percent of the increase in unemployment; and 64 percent of the increase in repression. In the same survey, 62 percent of those interviewed said that Chilean society needed drastic or radical changes, the economic aspects being the most urgent.

3. To my knowledge, only in Brazil has there been a systematic study of urban violence. The distinction belongs to Maria Victoria Benevides, *No fio da navalha; o debate sobre a violencia urbana* (São Paulo: CEDEC, n.d.).

4. The similarity between situations of fear described here and reflections on the postmodern condition is noteworthy. See, for example, Jean François Lyotard, "Une ligne de résistance," *Traverses* (Paris) 33–34 (1985), and Frederic Jameson, "Postmodernismo y sociedad de consumo," in Hal Foster, ed., *La postmodernidad* (Barcelona: J. Kairos, 1985).

5. See Richard Morse, *El espejo de próspero* (Mexico City: Siglo XXI, 1982).

6. Mary Douglas, *Purity and Danger* (London: Routledge & Kegan Paul, 1966). With respect to the historic tension between the real city and the symbolic city, see Angel de Rama, "La ciudad letrada," in Richard Morse and Jorge Enrique Hardoy, eds., *Cultura urbana latinoamericana* (Buenos Aires: CLACSO, 1985).

7. Jean Delumeau, *La peur en Occident, XIV–XVIII siècles* (Paris: Fayard, 1978), and his contribution, "A Historiographic Inquiry into Fear," in the interesting collection presented in *Debats* (Valencia) 8 (1984).

8. Pierre Bourdieu offers a brief description of fidéism in "Culture et politique," in *Questions de sociologie* (Paris: Minuit, 1981).

9. I am indebted to the reflections of Franz Hinkelammert in, for example, *Las armas ideológicas de la muerte* (San Jose, Costa Rica: DEI, 1977).

10. Humberto Giannini, "Hacia una arqueología de la experiencia," *Revista de filosofía* (Universidad de Chile, Santiago) 23–24 (1984): 54; my translation.

11. Giannini, "Hacia una arqueología," 23.

PART TWO

Constructing Cultures of Fear

THREE

Repression and State Security

Patricia Weiss Fagen

Military governments seized and held power in four Latin American countries in the late 1960s and early 1970s—first in Brazil and then in Chile, Argentina, and Uruguay. There were no historical precedents among the four Southern Cone countries for regime terror that would threaten and ultimately transform political, social, and cultural life. Although Argentina and Brazil had previously experienced authoritarian governments ranging from populist to dictatorial, Chile and Uruguay had maintained nearly unbroken records of constitutional government and orderly transitions of power throughout the twentieth century. The four countries had different political traditions and forms of economic organization, but, in all four, citizens had accepted means of expressing opposition and channels through which they could organize and enter the political arena to attain economic and social objectives.

This contemporary military rule in Latin America was reminiscent of the fascist regimes of Europe in that they all linked concepts of national well-being with justifications for the extensive, illegal repression of certain groups of citizens. In the 1930s and 1940s, the Nazis excluded Jews, Gypsies, and homosexuals from citizenship on racial and cultural grounds, and tried to exterminate them. Those in a far more nebulous social category, subversives, were similarly imprisoned, tortured, and murdered on political grounds from the 1960s to the 1980s in Brazil, Argentina, Chile, and Uruguay. The military rulers of Latin America, in terms reminiscent of those used by Nazis in Germany, openly proclaimed their intention to eliminate subversives from the body politic. To be sure,

the number of victims of the Latin American operations is hardly comparable to the number killed by the Nazis. Nevertheless, as will be seen, the
Latin American regimes generated widespread and pervasive terror.

An essential difference between the two historical experiences lies in
the role of popular support. Germans and the nationals of the occupied
countries mobilized extensively in favor of the new order and, thanks to
the collaboration of their own governmental agencies and civil institutions, ensured that the terror would be carried out. In several countries
the local populace, or what Hannah Arendt characterized as "mass
organizations of atomized, isolated individuals,"[1] directly assisted in
implementing the Nazi genocide by identifying and detaining the victims. So universally accepted was the regime terror that even the victims
participated in it. Frequently Jewish leaders were recruited to organize
and police the process that brought their own extermination.

There was no such broad-based participation in government repression in the Southern Cone. A large number of informants in Brazil,
Argentina, Chile, and Uruguay facilitated the work of repression by
accusing individuals of subversion. But government efforts to mobilize
mass support were reversed at an early stage. The public did not rally to
support state terror, and the military leaders readily acknowledged that
their economic policies and repressive methods were unpopular. The
purpose of state terror in Latin America, in addition to removing leftists
and identifying genuine subversives, was to discourage people from
organizing for any politically related motive. The Nazis punished those
found to have acted on behalf of victims, but at the same time they
realistically counted on large-scale cooperation with their political goals.
Their Latin American counterparts assumed, equally realistically, that
the general population would reject and oppose their continued rule if
given the chance to do so.

BACKGROUND TO MILITARY RULE

It is outside the scope of this chapter to review the process of democratic
breakdown in the four Southern Cone countries.[2] It is important, however, to underscore the similar chain of events that culminated in military
rule in all four, as well as to try to analyze how similarities and differences in the four military coups may have affected later outcomes.

Prior to assuming political authority, security forces in Argentina,
Brazil, and Uruguay substantially expanded their powers in the course of
defeating guerrilla armies that were attempting to wage social revolu-

tions. In Brazil, a new and enlarged military/police security system had been put in place throughout the country between the first and second coups (1964 and 1968); after 1968 there were no longer any meaningful legal restrictions on the functioning of this security system. In Argentina and Uruguay the military had already established full autonomy with regard to security operations before formally displacing the much weakened civilian governments.

In Chile, there were no guerrilla armies, and, prior to the coup, most parties of the left were cooperating in the Popular Unity government. There too, however, existing political structures were challenged during the 1970s by a minority revolutionary movement that rejected the institutional bases of the existing parliamentary system and sought rapid social transformation. Especially among the middle class, fear that continued rule by the left would culminate in just such a transformation undoubtedly contributed to later compliance when the military establishment rapidly dismantled Chilean democracy.

The revolutionary left throughout the region engaged in direct action against and confrontation with political and military authorities, hoping to mobilize exploited social sectors to overthrow ruling governments and establish socialism. Simultaneously, the polarization of the right encouraged direct action by openly antidemocratic paramilitary groups and political parties in each country. Their anticommunist rhetoric went well beyond condemnation of Marxist organizations and the organized left.

At first, military and police made abundant use of, and furnished much of the personnel for, the right-wing organizations and death squads. These groups rarely confronted the armed and revolutionary movements directly. Most victims of right-wing violence were leaders in the traditional political parties, the trade unions, and student organizations, as well as prominent figures in artistic and cultural circles and in the media. Although such individuals almost always defended democratic ideals, they also accepted and often insisted on the need for policies aimed at major economic and social transformations. Their opponents perceived their words and sometimes their actions as defending and extending legitimacy to the armed left.

Increasing violence, kidnappings, demonstrations of force and counterforce added to the ranks of both the armed right and the revolutionary left. Progressive polarization, in turn, inspired fear, confusion, and distrust and also generated public support for strong security measures. The military leadership in the Southern Cone capitalized on widespread doubts about the capacity of civilian governments to restore economic confidence or to end political violence. Indeed, the military and police credibly claimed to have a popular mandate as they bypassed the legal and constitutional restrictions that limited their methods of identifying and detaining terrorists.

Facilitating the military seizure of power was the collaboration of ideologically conservative sectors whose leaders anticipated that they would soon inherit the reins of government. As for the middle classes, feeling threatened not only by the armed left but also by the unarmed left and the increasingly militant grass-roots and popular organizations, they were largely willing to forgo political participation for a period of time. They had come to view the military as the only remaining institution able to redress the political balance and restore shattered economic confidence.

The military leadership, however, had another agenda. In each of the four countries the military took advantage of its enhanced institutional legitimacy to monopolize state power, giving even its closest political allies marginal political influence. In the economic realm, to varying degrees, the regimes deferred to civilian technocrats of the political right. The ensuing policies were themselves exclusionary and antisocial in character.

Although promising eventually to return to civilian rule, the military governments made clear their intention to prevent the democrats and populists of the past from returning to power. To legitimize continuing authority, the ruling generals conducted plebiscites or managed narrowly based elections. To institutionalize authoritarian rule, they promulgated new restrictive and exclusionary constitutions. The few remaining rights still contained in these constitutions remained largely inoperative because of continuing declarations of states of emergency. The political objective for the present and future was to preside over a state with few channels for popular protest and no systematic commitment to accommodate the material and social needs of the poor and middle sectors.

WAGING WARS AGAINST IDEAS

NATIONAL SECURITY THROUGH COUNTERINSURGENCY CAPACITY

Counterinsurgency doctrines developed logically from the nineteenth-century military ideology brought to the Southern Cone countries of

Latin America by way of German military training. In the twentieth century, military leadership remained largely isolated from what was viewed as the corrupting influence of civilian political and social forces and at the same time stressed professionalism and the military role in nation building. Strong moves toward military professionalism grew within a number of countries, particularly in Brazil, where this movement was combined with advanced theoretical formulations of the national security state.[3] Latin American leaders also paid keen attention to the French counterinsurgency methods developed in Algeria during the 1950s.

But, above all, U.S. influence became predominant. Thanks to U.S. military and police assistance and training programs, an entire generation of Latin American military officers and police were armed, trained, and "professionalized." During the 1960s, following the Cuban Revolution, U.S.-funded training featured counterinsurgency doctrines, and regional collective-security arrangements were redirected toward internal security. New programs and technologies prepared human and organizational resources for military strategies that bore little relation to traditional warfare against external enemies.[4] Since the 1950s, nearly every country in Latin America has participated in U.S. military assistance and training programs and in regional intelligence-sharing arrangements.

REPRESSION TO PURGE IDEOLOGICAL INFECTION

The first World War was a confrontation of armies; the second of nations; and the third is of ideologies.[5]

Military officers recognized that the revolutionary movements they confronted had been nourished by a variety of intellectual currents critical of the status quo. The breadth of later state terror owed much to their further assumption that groups and individuals advocating social change shared a subversive mentality, even if they had not engaged in subversive acts. The Argentine president, General Jorge Rafael Videla, said at a press conference in February 1978, "A terrorist is not just someone with a gun or a bomb but also someone who spreads ideas that are contrary to Western civilization."[6] And the Chilean president, Augusto Pinochet Ugarte, celebrating the first anniversary of military rule, told his listeners that minds armed with "envy, rancor and the irreconcilable struggle of classes" were more dangerous than guns.[7]

The wars against subversion quickly became wars against the social forces and organizations from which it was thought subversion might emerge. The theme of war was merged into the theme of illness, and the enemy came to be portrayed as a cancer to be surgically extracted and destroyed in order to restore social health. In these terms, for example, Rear Admiral Cesar Guzzetti justified the political assassinations carried out by the right-wing Argentine Anticommunist Alliance as a healthy response of the body politic:

> The body of the country is contaminated by an illness that corrodes its entrails and forms antibodies that should not be thought of as germs. I am sure there will be no more actions of the right in the coming months. . . . Theirs was only a reaction to a sick body.[8]

The language of illness combined well with the concept of contamination—those not directly part of the sickness might nonetheless be exposed to and become contaminated by its content. Hence the necessity to dismantle political and social organizations, prohibit private gatherings, and detain or otherwise punish people who impeded the operations of the security forces by assisting those destined for punishment. Concluding, finally, that the "sickness" was systemic and irrevocably rooted in democratic procedures, the military seized power.

Its leaders in all four countries proclaimed the intrinsic weakness and decadence of democracy. For example, in the Chilean Declaration of Principles, one of the few documents that attempted to explain the conceptual bases of military rule, the authors blamed Chilean democracy for the rise of the left and proposed:

> The right to dissent must be preserved, but the experience of recent years shows the need to subject it to acceptable limits. Never again must a naive democracy allow within its midst organized groups, acting under the guise of misunderstood pluralism, to foster guerrilla violence to attain power or, feigning a respect for democracy, to further a doctrine or morality whose objective is the construction of a totalitarian state. For this reason, Marxist parties and movements will no longer be admitted into our civic life.

The Declaration, published in 1974, appeared in glossy format for international as well as domestic consumption.

The material produced by Brazil's Escola Superior de Guerra (for advanced officer education and training) during the 1960s and 1970s provided perhaps the most comprehensive formulations equating ideas and their expression with revolution, associating social demands with subversion, and advancing the notion of total war against revolutionaries and social reformers. In the basic course manual of the school, students were warned repeatedly of threats to national security emanating from internal problems that gave rise to labor unrest, intellectual and artistic activity, and reform movements.[9] The most prominent ideologue of the Escola, Major General Golbery do Couto e Silva, elaborated:

> What is certain is that the greater probability today is limited warfare, localized conflicts, and above all indirect Communist aggression, which capitalizes on local discontents, the frustrations of misery and hunger, and just national anxieties.[10]

The image of the state as a human body suffering from the infection of subversion came to permeate the public statements made by Southern Cone leaders. They shared a perception of a weakened social order in which militarily and ideologically organized forces could easily spread Marxist poison. For example:

> Marxism is not a doctrine that is simply wrong, as many have been historically. No, Marxism is an intrinsically depraved doctrine, which means that everything that stems from it, however healthy its appearance, has been eaten away by the poison that corrodes its roots. . . . It is not only an intrinsically depraved doctrine, it is furthermore a permanent aggression which today is in the service of the Soviet imperialism.[11]

TOTAL WAR WITH THE LEFT

Latin American leftists have generally shared a Marxist orientation that, contrary to military characterizations, has been far from monolithic. The organizations and groups wholly or partially associated with Marxist tenets have always covered a wide political spectrum, sometimes coming together for common causes, often engaging in fierce debates. During the 1960s and 1970s the left was most divided over the question of the appropriateness of revolutionary struggle.

The traditional left had been engaged for decades in political action aimed at bringing about an eventual transformation from capitalism to socialism. In Latin America, as in Western Europe and North America, however, new groups developed during the 1960s and, fed on revolutionary ideology, convinced themselves and others that armed insurrection could succeed. The successful Cuban Revolution in 1959, in particular, had nourished hopes in many quarters of similar victories elsewhere in the hemisphere. The revolutionary groups attracted adherents, especially among the young, largely because of their optimism about their own powers to change the course of world history.

The expansion of armed leftist groups in the Southern Cone countries was clearly linked also to the systematic repression of legal leftist activity. Associating all forms of protest with subversion and insurrection, military and police repression turned would-be dissenters into armed revolutionaries. Chile was the partial exception. Prior to the coup in Chile, political groups on the left as well as the right legally opposed the elected socialist government. The revolutionary left in that country rarely engaged in armed confrontations.

In Brazil, Argentina, and Uruguay both sides in the military confrontations viewed themselves to be engaged in a total war of historic proportions. Revolutionary groups throughout the hemisphere imagined themselves to be the vanguard of a popular struggle. They represented themselves as fighting on behalf of the vast majority of downtrodden people and against domestic exploitation and foreign imperialism. It followed that the military and police, as the armed protectors of exploitation and imperialism, had to be confronted and defeated to permit the needed social transformation to occur. The military, for its part, made war against the left as a foreign enemy and claimed to be waging a third world war against subversion. Neither side would contemplate a society in the future in which the other would be free to operate, and both condemned frameworks of democratic pluralism as inappropriate for the societies they wished to bring about.

Though holding similar pretensions, the two sides were hardly evenly matched. The groups on the left were small, far less well armed than the military, and they largely comprised young, inexperienced militants. Their commitment, resourcefulness, and flexibility brought them pressworthy successes, particularly in urban areas. But in the long run they could never hope to achieve their goal of a Cuban-type victory. The military forces they faced had the advantage not only of superior numbers and arms but also of training in counterinsurgency, which had prepared them psychologically and technically for a war without quarter against internal subversion.

> [In wartime] the enemy may or may not have committed a military crime; . . . nevertheless, this enemy is arrested while the hostilities continue. . . . When the political authorities resort to the armed forces, in my view, this is a tacit recognition of war.[12]
>
> Wars are never fought with white gloves. . . . We have used the same drastic methods against the terrorists that they have used.[13]

The wars against the guerrillas became the vehicles through which the military leaders were able not only to seize power but also to establish the security apparatus that permitted them to hold absolute power. In Brazil, following the 1964 coup, the government enacted a series of Institutional Acts and decrees that banished individuals from political participation; curtailed political activities; outlawed political parties, student organizations, and trade unions; ended direct elections; and reduced Congressional powers. Each new restrictive act was met with an increasingly militant response, and each act of illegal resistance was met with greater repression and harsher measures. In the course of events, the broad political opposition was left without legal outlets for protest. Many turned to clandestine or armed actions (or both). These armed actions—ranging from the kidnapping of ambassadors to the mounting of rural campaigns—brought the so-called hardliners in the military to dominance in the government. In 1969 the hardliners removed the remaining vestiges of constitutional protections for suspected political opponents. By 1973 the guerrillas were defeated; they and thousands of Brazilians who had never formed part of any guerrilla operation had been imprisoned, tortured, exiled, and often killed. The military remained in power until 1985 and, despite a gradual détente, did not significantly dismantle the security apparatus until 1978.

In Uruguay in the late 1960s deteriorating economic conditions strained the resources of the welfare state. The government's economic measures imposing unpopular wage and price regulations were accompanied by political measures restricting public protest and strikes. These, in turn, gave rise to serious labor unrest and an expanding left that challenged the traditional party structure. At the same time, an urban guerrilla group, the Tupamaros (Movement of National Liberation), engaged in armed political actions against the authorities. During 1971 the Tupamaros gained strength. The civilian government, unable either to restore economic confidence or to control the political left, entrusted the military with the task its police had been unable to accomplish. Upon his succession in 1972, President Juan María Bordaberry introduced the Law of State Security and Public Order, which was followed by a declaration of the State of Internal War.

Using tactics of intelligence and interrogation that clearly overrode constitutional protections, but without interference from civilian authorities, the military had essentially routed the Tupamaros by early 1973. In June of that same year, however, the military took over the presidency and ruled directly. Constitutional rights were not restored, nor was Congress recalled. On the contrary, the country continued to be run by executive decree, as the legal left and many in the center endured

the same punishments as those meted out to the Tupamaros. Not until
1985 did the military, undefeated, return the executive office to civilian
politicians.

In Argentina two major guerrilla groups threatened the political order, the Ejército Revolucionario del Pueblo and the Montoneros, both of
which consolidated and became active around 1970. These groups undertook ambitious military actions with small forces of 100 to 200
combatants and suffered massive losses. The military not only outnum-
bered them overwhelmingly but responded with heavy artillery and
helicopters. Although the guerrilla resistance had the political support of
substantial numbers of Argentines, particularly young people, it never
constituted a serious military threat. Indeed, by 1975, the military had
vanquished its enemies in this so-called war (which critics subsequently
characterized as more of a "hunt" than a war).[14] Nevertheless, after the
1976 coup, a broad range of ideological opponents and general critics
were swept into military custody, where thousands died. Argentine society entered a period of unprecedented fear.

STATES OF EXCEPTION AND LAWS
OF NATIONAL SECURITY

Judicial protection, due process, and executive accountability were similarly undermined in all four countries. Legislatures were either abolished or disempowered. Military courts assumed jurisdiction over a
range of previously civilian offenses, including minor infractions and
formerly legal actions (for example, the so-called crimes of opinion in
Uruguay). Civil courts were unable (because of the removal of habeas
corpus) or unwilling (because of fear of reprisals) to investigate allegations of mistreatment, or even disappearances, at the hands of the military. Laws of national security, combined with states of emergency,
effectively removed access to due process from people accused of political crimes. Whether constitutions remained in force or were revised to be
more restrictive, they were rendered inoperative by continuing states of
emergency.

In all four countries, the military acted decisively, and immediately
upon seizing power declared states of exception (states of emergency,
states of siege, and, in Uruguay, security measures). Most Latin American constitutions provide for possible states of exception during which
some constitutionally protected rights may be abridged temporarily.
However, these states of exception, in all cases, are to be invoked only

during emergencies, to remain in effect only until authorities have restored order, and to be monitored carefully. The Southern Cone authoritarian governments, on the contrary, used more or less permanent states of exception to bypass legal limits on their power without ever departing from formal constitutional rule.

By a series of hastily promulgated decrees, laws, acts, institutional acts, and statutes—the legality of which rested on the questionable grounds that national constitutions had been declared no longer in force—the generals in executive office decreed themselves full ruling powers, independent of legislative structures and civil institutions. The new legal order, in reality an extralegal order, facilitated repression, as it exempted those meting out punishment for security-related activities from public accountability.

Attempting to legitimize the bases of military rule, the Chilean and Uruguayan governments eventually promulgated new constitutions that imposed institutional limits on any future democratic initiatives. In both countries the public voted on these constitutions through plebiscites in 1980. Although Chilean voters voted positively (for reasons that are still much debated), the Uruguayan public voted overwhelmingly negatively.

It is not possible in the space permitted here to review the process by which judicial protections were unraveled in each of the four Southern Cone countries. Detailed descriptions of the transformation of legal and juridical procedures in Argentina, Brazil, Chile, and Uruguay are found in the numerous reports of respected private and public international human-rights organizations (the Organization of American States, Amnesty International, the International Commission of Jurists) as well as of domestic human-rights organizations, especially in Chile and Brazil. By way of illustration, the following pages will highlight the legal frameworks that were promulgated in two cases: Brazil and Argentina. Brazil, considered the most "open" of the four authoritarian systems, saw the development of a strong civil opposition despite repression. Argentina, although less hermetically closed and controlled than Uruguay, sustained a vast system of secret terror, masked by a seemingly functioning judicial system. Elsewhere in this book (Chapters 5 and 7) are examinations of judicial processes in Uruguay and Chile.[15]

BRAZIL

The Brazilian coup of 1964 brought to power a coalition of military and civilian figures whose initial purpose was to purge the previous political leadership while retaining most of the institutional structures of the precoup state. A series of Institutional Acts assured that those political figures would be unable to compete again for power. Political leaders, dissident military officers, and other prominent individuals were banned from public office. Most also lost their political rights, including the right to vote.

The purges cut deeply into state and municipal bureaucracies, and the disbanding of previous political parties permanently changed the nature of political participation. Nevertheless, state security-force violence was not pervasive between 1964 and 1968, compared with the later period, and Brazilians who were so inclined still pressed for political change. In addition to the groups and organizations pledged to armed resistance that were already active during the mid-1960s, students, workers, journalists, peasant groups, congressmen, Catholic lay associations, and others openly opposed the military. However, the elaborate repressive apparatus already in place was centralized, rationalized, and further expanded after 1968. The subsequent rapid defeat of the guerrilla combatants left an elaborate repressive force still intact. The number of people arrested, tortured, and exiled grew.

For about a year after the April 1964 coup, most persons accused of political crimes still had recourse to civilian due process. The passage of the second Institutional Act (AI2), in October 1965, however, gave military tribunals jurisdiction in all crimes against national security or against the state. Thereafter, nearly all offenses deemed political in character were tried in military courts. These courts, like their civilian counterparts, were formally subject to procedural regulations that assured the rights of the accused. But such rights were either revoked by decree or systematically abridged in practice.

Finally, with the passage of AI5 at the end of 1968, the accused lost any recourse to civilian assistance or legal defense. The passage of this act began nearly a decade during which fairly large sectors of Brazilian society feared their lives might be threatened by actions of the state. That act, and the acts and decrees that followed in rapid succession, removed habeas corpus for all cases deemed to raise issues of national security and effectively terminated both the autonomy of the judicial branch and civilian oversight of security-force practices. Censorship was enforced in the media, the arts, and scholarship. Congress was suspended for a year and was reopened with restrictions intended to render it entirely subordinate to the executive branch. This time, among the new list of banned people were figures of the right, including Rio's ex-governor, Carlos Lacerda, who had actively promoted the military coup in 1964.

The major abuses occurred when suspects were apprehended. Prisoners held by the military security forces (whose practices are discussed in the next sections) remained incommunicado for varying lengths of time—nearly always beyond legal limits—and were systematically tortured during interrogations. After prisoners were passed from the military to the federal police for additional interrogation, the confessions obtained during this process became the legal bases for their sentencing. As an archdiocese-sponsored research team on torture in Brazil concluded:

> Without the right of habeas corpus, without the power to communicate his detainment, without a fixed time limit for the conclusion of the inquest, the political prisoner, once inside the security organs, was absolutely defenseless from the day he was abducted to the moment he appeared in military court.[16]

Between 1969 and the repeal of AI5 in 1978, the several groups targeted for repression lived with constant fear. Thousands of people were killed, arrested, and tortured. The post-terror investigations of human-rights violations turned up 125 persons who either disappeared or were killed and unaccounted for.[17] However, the majority of the victims, though denied due process and brutally treated, survived. They were sent into exile or later were held as recognized political prisoners.

More than any of the other Southern Cone governments, the Brazilian military preserved the formal institutions of the previous democratic order. Congress functioned, with an extremely restrictive mandate, and the government created two political parties, also with a limited range of allowed activity. The military imposed an electoral system that assured that members of Congress were virtually handpicked.

The other side of Brazilian military rule was its brief but impressive period of economic growth. For much of the period, apparent economic successes encouraged acceptance of the military, while strict censorship limited public awareness of the extent of its repression.

Congress could not be entirely subordinated. By the mid-1970s both Congress and congressional elections posed genuine obstacles to the military monopoly on power. Likewise, although the two political parties were postcoup creations of the government, they became increasingly independent. Ultimately, the government could not count even on the full support of the party it created to represent its own interests.

Although the passage of AI5 had represented a victory for the known hardliners, subsequent governments openly favored policies of détente and worked with civilian elites toward a political transition. For most of the transition period, during the latter 1970s and early 1980s, the government sought to control the process by electoral manipulations and limitations on the popular vote. Although AI5 was repealed in 1978, other national security measures remained in effect. Only in 1985 did open elections finally produce a fully civilian government.

ARGENTINA

Immediately upon taking power in March 1976, the military in Argentina dissolved Congress and provincial legislative bodies; it removed from office the president and vice-president, as well as provincial governors, municipal officers, the members of the Supreme Court and higher provincial courts, and the attorney general.[18] Declaring itself the "Supreme Organ of the Nation," the junta, through its appointed president, assumed the full powers formally held by both executive and legislative branches.

Whereas Brazilian authoritarian rule hardened gradually after the initial 1964 coup, the Argentine military already had achieved substantial power prior to its 1976 coup. Upon seizing power formally, the junta extended the state of siege that had been in effect since November 1974. It then assured itself extraconstitutional authority in the area of national security. With the Institutional Act of June 18, 1976, the military junta assumed "the power and responsibility to consider the actions of those individuals who have injured the national interest."[19] These measures notwithstanding, the Constitution remained in effect, to be applied in areas where it was not in conflict with new security provisions.

Military rule curtailed political activity from the outset. Many leftist political parties and associated groups were dissolved, while other groups (student associations, youth groups, labor organizations) were required to suspend all political activities. Political parties per se were not outlawed. Indeed the parties of the center and right, and the Communist party as well, were permitted to continue formal operations. But leaders and activists associated with the left were killed, arrested, or exiled; those of the center remained all but inactive in the face of deepening repression. By decrees, the junta prohibited the union activities of labor, business, and professional entities and suspended the right to strike or to effect other forms of work stoppage. In addition, the junta gave itself the discretionary power to remove individuals from professional positions and jobs, and to restrict the property rights of persons who had "facilitated an increase in disruptive subversion."[20] In reviewing the postcoup acts and decrees relating to political activity in Argentina, the Inter-American Commission on Human Rights concluded:

> On March 24, 1976, all political activity in Argentina ceased, and the democratic system of lawmaking through elected representatives, with the free participation of the press and citizens in support of, or in opposition to, any project, was replaced by a system in which, in the final analysis, only the will of the three commanding generals of the armed forces . . . count.[21]

The realm left to the independent judiciary was extremely small. Any crimes or activities remotely political in character came under military jurisdiction. To handle the expanded caseload, the government created special standing military tribunals throughout the nation—an extraordinary procedure the Code of Military Justice provided for in times of war. Civil courts were purged and their judges intimidated. Hence, although the accused could sometimes appeal to civil courts, these rarely challenged either the decisions of military courts or security-force practices. The security forces and the courts treated defense lawyers as accomplices of the accused.

The Institutional Act of June 18, 1976, defined "failure to observe basic moral principles in the exercise of public, political, or union offices or activities that involve the public interest" as injurious to the national interest. Within the framework of this act, a number of laws were enacted that greatly altered the nature of crimes and the relation of crimes to punishments. Persons could be taken into custody and sentenced to long prison terms or to death for a broad range of new "criminal acts." The death penalty could be imposed for illegal association, and prison terms of fifteen years to life were required for violent actions against military personnel, police, security agents, or prison officials. Alternatively, persons accused of political crimes could be detained without charges under discretionary executive power (the Poder Executivo Nacional, or PEN) for indeterminate lengths of time. Most political prisoners, in practice, were PEN detainees.

The security forces far exceeded their extensive powers. The armed forces, security forces, and police had obtained the authority to arrest and interrogate suspects, and to submit the evidence obtained in summary military proceedings. However, they were not permitted by any codes or regulations to kidnap people, torture them in secret places, and cause them to disappear. Yet between 15,000 and 30,000 Argentines reported to have been detained, disappeared afterward.[22] Time and again witnesses to disappearances testified and people presented evidence to Argentine courts, only to be told that nothing could be done. There were no effective judicial sanctions to check the military's criminal practices; nor was there legal recourse to obtain the release of kidnapped victims.

Unlike the Brazilian military government, the Argentine junta did not remove the right of habeas corpus. Indeed, the families of the disappeared filed thousands of writs of habeas corpus, often several times for the same case. But they failed to obtain a single release. In these cases, typically, relatives did not know which of the security forces had done the kidnapping; hence a judge who received a writ of habeas corpus requested information from the police, armed forces, and various armed-forces command posts. Almost invariably, these authorities replied that the individual was not in their custody. Rather than pursue further investigations as permitted by law, the judge then simply denied the validity of the writ on grounds that the person was not listed as detained.

When families were able to appeal these denials to the Federal Court, it almost always affirmed the initial decisions. Further appeals to the Supreme Court for the most part were thwarted by the Federal Court. In the few cases where such appeals could be made directly, the Supreme Court upheld the Federal Court. In a few instances, the Supreme Court asked that there be additional investigation[23] or complained that its jurisdiction had been unreasonably limited by the government's failure to provide information.[24] The military response to pleas for greater respect for the judicial system was to further tighten access to habeas corpus.[25]

In reality, the members of the Supreme Court had no authority to enforce the few independent rulings they chose to make. For example, the Court twice ruled that there were no grounds for the continued detention of newspaper publisher Jacobo Timerman, and on both occasions the military overruled the decision and vetoed the release.[26] Whether or not one justifies the timidity of the judges on grounds of their vulnerability, clearly the judicial system offered no meaningful recourse to victims of gross human-rights violations. On the contrary, the Argentine National Commission on the Disappeared concluded:

> [The system usually] recognized the discretionary application of the powers of arrest under the State of Siege and accepted the validity of secret reports from the security services as justification for the detention of citizens for an

indefinite period. At the same time, it turned the writ of habeas corpus into a mere formality, rendering it totally inefficient as a means of combating the policy of forced abduction. . . .

Our conclusion is that during the period in which large numbers of people disappeared, the judicial process became almost inoperative as a means of appeal. Furthermore, it could almost be said that . . . the right to life, security of person, and individual liberty had little to do with the decisions of the judges; the sole arbiters of these decisions were the members of the state's repressive apparatus.[27]

ESTABLISHING PROFESSIONAL ANTISUBVERSIVE FORCES

Effective counterinsurgency methods imposed new institutional mandates. Well before the Southern Cone coups, the military leaders who eventually seized power had begun to reorganize and redirect military and police structures, thanks in large part to the arms, organizational advice, and counterinsurgency training provided by the United States and Western Europe. Counterinsurgency provided the rationale, as well as the techniques, for military involvement in social control. Toward this end, the military overthrew the existing governments largely to permit greater institutional independence and freedom of action than was possible under civilian rule.

REORGANIZATION OF THE SECURITY FORCES

The challenge facing each of the authoritarian Southern Cone governments was to create security forces willing to engage in extralegal activities who were also to be unquestionably loyal to the regimes in power—whose legality was questionable. To this end, each government created new security forces, either within or parallel to regular military and police units, responsible for identifying and removing sources of opposition and implementing regime terror. Torture and other forms of intimidation became professionally accepted techniques, widely perceived as essential to the military's domestic operations.

Each repressive tactic was tailored by some logic to the needs of large-scale, extralegal repression. Paramilitary operations were found to have the advantage of allowing police and military personnel to carry out acts that, in uniform, would be prohibited and might have had to halt. But using paramilitary entities had drawbacks in that the members were not subject to centralized control or discipline, and at any time might cease to be loyal to those in power. The parallel structures of repression through military and police units in Brazil, Argentina, and Uruguay implicated the entire military and police in illegal repression and murder. The objective, aside from the broadest possible "coverage," was to assure that no one sector of the armed forces could emerge unsullied by the process, and that all became beholden to the system. However, as with paramilitary groups, the risk with decentralized models of repression is that individual units may act independently of official policy. Indeed, the Brazilian political leadership is believed to have dismantled its security apparatus after 1978 largely because of the unbridled power of the Second Army Command.

The traditional armed forces and police were neither adequately trained nor ideologically and psychologically prepared to undertake these tasks, however hostile they may have been toward Marxism and the left. The military rulers criminalized political dissent and most forms of economic demands. To deal with the new class of "criminals," the armed forces and police were mobilized to take on functions well beyond their traditional roles. Recruited to protect the nation against threats of invasion from outside, they were ordered to wage war against citizens within the country, for ideological and political reasons.

In effect, the military had to take on the functions of the police, locating and capturing subversives. Or, as was more frequently the case, soldiers were ordered to identify and punish individuals who were not engaged in subversive activities but were characterized as ideological accomplices of subversion. In doing so, the military devoted themselves, essentially, to the interrogation and torture of persons known to have committed no subversive acts, even as defined under military law. The police, theoretically the keepers of law, charged to protect civilian rights and security, also found the nature of their work transformed. The Southern Cone authoritarian regimes required police as well as the military to turn their professional skills to the task of identifying subversives.

Unquestionably, police in democratic societies as well as those in military regimes have abused suspects. Nevertheless, in democratic societies there are rules, however weakly enforced, that differentiate the professional use of force from barbarous excesses, and there are channels of appeal when force is abused. Both the armed forces and police of the Southern Cone authoritarian regimes inflicted punishments that civilized societies generally consider cruel and degrading. Unlike their counterparts in civilian societies, they did not have the option—except at great risk—of refusing to go beyond what the law permitted or eventually of seeking alternative employment.

Three factors assured their loyalty. First, they themselves were as much subject to capricious and arbitrary exercises of power as were those they were paid to repress; second, to the extent that they became involved in acts for which they might expect retribution from civilian society, they grew increasingly isolated from their communities and acquired a vested interest in continued military rule; and, third, they were materially rewarded for the services they performed.

Security forces in none of the four countries were accountable to public officials outside of the ruling executive. In organization and specific techniques, the security forces in each of the four countries were different. All were involved in extralegal repression and secret punishment but conducted these by different means:

- by civilian paramilitary death squads (Argentina before 1976; Brazil and Chile in the immediate postcoup periods)

- by special units in the military and police, dispersed throughout the country (Brazil and Argentina)

- by specialized, centralized intelligence agencies (Chile)

- by repression and torture in numerous military barracks and police stations throughout the country (Uruguay and Chile, 1973–74).[28]

Brazil.   In Brazil, prior to the 1964 military coup, retired and off-duty police founded the Esquadrão da Morte (death squads), which undertook to kill petty criminals among the so-called marginal population, or *marginais*. Sectors of the middle class at first welcomed the death squads, viewing them as more effective than the regular police. In the late 1960s and early 1970s, without changing their methods (torture murders), the death-squad members devoted their major energies to killing political enemies. (In the 1980s, death squads returned to killing the *marginais*.)

Almost immediately following the coup, in June 1964, the Brazilian military government created a nationwide intelligence system, the Sistema Nacional de Informações (SNI). Its task was to coordinate and supervise all intelligence activities pertinent to national security in all the ministries, as well as in the armed forces and police. The military director of the SNI had ministerial rank and was directly tied to the executive through the National Security Council.

By the 1970s, Brazil had developed an elaborate repressive apparatus

within the military that eclipsed the death squads. In 1969 the commander of the Brazilian Second Army launched the Operação Ban-
deirantes (OBAN) to assist the armed forces in its ongoing antisubversive work, particularly in obtaining information. Brazilian business
interests and multinational corporations reportedly assisted in financing
OBAN. In the 1970s the work of OBAN was largely taken over by the
Centro de Operações de Defesa Interna (CODI), an administrative body
that coordinated the various military departments of the Operações e
Informações (DOI). Each army command had its own CODI, supervis-
ing the DOI in each military region. Political suspects, typically, were
interrogated and tortured by these entities or in the equivalent Navy
intelligence center, the Centro de Informações da Marinha. Then, they
were passed on for formal interrogation to the police Departamento de
Ordem Politica e Social.[29]

Argentina. The Argentine Anticommunist Alliance and similar paramilitary organizations dedicated themselves to eliminating ideological
enemies. They were especially active during the interregnum between the
death of Juan Perón and the 1976 coup. As the members of these groups
were either former police or military personnel themselves, or persons
with strong police connections, they were able to obtain arms easily.
Often, they had access to the police dossiers of the people they sought.

With the 1976 coup, military and police units took over the management and implementation of repression. Each of the military battalions
and police units had a parallel, clandestine structure responsible for
illegal acts such as disappearances. The spread of responsibility for these
acts throughout the security forces expanded complicity, hence loyalty.
Noting the consistent patterns of arrests, kidnappings, and detention
practices, the members of the Argentine National Commission on the
Disappeared rejected the contentions of military leaders that human-
rights violations had been caused by the excesses of some field commanders. Instead, they concluded, human rights were violated systematically as a matter of official policy. The information confirms, the
commission wrote, "that this diabolical technology was employed by
persons who may have been sadists but who were carrying out orders."[30]

Chile. Immediately after the 1973 Chilean coup, all the branches of
the military and police took suspects, tortured and imprisoned them, in
what seemed to be random and arbitrary violence against the left. By
mid-1974, however, the military presence was less obvious and repres-

sion less arbitrary. Chile centered its intelligence-gathering and security operations in a single agency, the Dirección de Inteligencia Nacional (DINA), which from 1974 to 1977 appeared to have primary responsibility for arrests and torture and full responsibility for disappearances. In 1977 the DINA was dissolved and replaced with the Central Nacional de Informaciones (CNI). The terms of reference and operation of the CNI differed little from those of the DINA, but the CNI engaged in more targeted repression, characterized by less gratuitous violence. By 1978, the Chilean disappearances had practically ceased. Nevertheless, previous disappearances (620 fully documented disappearances and at least twice this number reported) were neither acknowledged nor punished, while political arrests and incidents of torture persisted and, during the 1980s, increased. Unlike the repression in Argentina, Chile's repression followed evident phases, aimed first at the political leadership of the left, the press, the trade unions, and other organizations, and subsequently at middle-level cadres of specific political parties.

In the mid-1980s, when Chile was the lone remaining military dictatorship in the Southern Cone, there were almost daily protests, strikes, and demonstrations of opposition from a wide range of the Chilean population. Hundreds were arrested in broad military or police sweeps. Although most were released within a short period, nearly all were mistreated. A favorite punishment in the mid-1980s was to "banish" protesters and dissenters to "internal exile," sending them to remote locations where they were left to survive on their own. By this period, the military and police responses no longer derived solely from the CNI. To this day, Chileans do not know precisely how the state security forces were coordinated.

Acting with greater autonomy than before, the security forces continued to repress all forms of opposition, especially in poor neighborhoods, where, in any case, repression had always been most pervasive. People taken into custody were often killed in what officials referred to as "shootouts with security forces." One or another branch of the security forces was believed to have murdered specific individuals and to have attributed these murders to unofficial death squads or to have blamed other sectors of the security forces.

Uruguay. Uruguayan police and military officers questioned and invariably tortured political suspects in barracks or police stations throughout the country. No single agency or branch of the armed forces had specific responsibility for interrogating those suspected of political offenses. The distinctions between military and police repression were blurred because military officers headed all the police departments, as well as local and national governmental offices.

The military legal system had jurisdiction over all national security offenses. Few cases were transferred from military to civil courts. Military judges, in turn, overwhelmingly, sentenced Uruguayans suspected of opposition activities, or even with opposition sympathies, to long terms in military detention facilities. Relatively few Uruguayans were executed.[31] Rather, the government used torture and long-term detention as its principal repressive tactics. The detention centers were organized to dehumanize and break the spirit of the prisoners. Close to 50,000 people were estimated to have been detained, often several times, between 1972 and 1983 (total population is under three million), and some 5,000 were convicted of national security crimes.[32]

TRAINING THE MILITARY FOR SOCIAL CONTROL

The Brazilian Escola Superior da Guerra is credited with having provided the most comprehensive elaboration of the theory of the national security state, the French military with having demonstrated the practical necessities of counterinsurgency methods, and the United States with a major role in training for counterinsurgency action.

The Southern Cone coups of the 1960s and 1970s were largely the products of technical and ideological preparation that had characterized military training for more than a century. Nevertheless, the steps taken to implement the new military mandates and the military/civilian relationships that subsequently developed were largely the fruits of U.S. ideological influence and counterinsurgency training.[33]

Until 1973, the United States operated and funded three parallel training programs: one for police forces, to train them in crime control as well as in antisubversive actions and interrogation techniques; another primarily for noncommissioned officers, to train them in conducting antiguerrilla operations; and a third for the higher ranking military leadership, to advance their theoretical understandings of geopolitics, economics, and ideology. There has been much controversy about the extent to which U.S. military schools may have trained Latin Americans (and others) in illegal practices or fostered antidemocratic orientations. Most concern has focused on the antiguerrilla training provided in U.S.-operated military schools in Panama. Without question, the curriculum in this and other facilities stressed an anticommunist ideology that encompassed hostility to leftist ideas and movements.

The Agency for International Development operated a police training program through the Office of Public Safety during the 1960s. The program fit President John Kennedy's interest in supporting "local police forces for internal security and counter-insurgency purposes."[34] Working closely with the Central Intelligence Agency, accused of directing torture training in Brazil and Uruguay, the Office of Public Safety and its activities eventually proved so controversial that its programs were terminated in 1973.

POWER AND CORRUPTION

Clearly, giving the armed forces a free hand to inflict social terror had a profoundly corrupting impact. Stories of venality, corruption, and scandal circulated widely in the four Southern Cone countries. Military and police professional standards deteriorated in daily practice and so did the definition of their role: in all four countries, but with particular abandon in Argentina and Uruguay, security-force personnel customarily stole their victims' possessions, calling these "war booty." In 1975, Uruguayan military leaders, through the Council of State, legalized the confiscation of victims' property, and relatives could not even sue for illegal possession of the motor vehicles or real estate registered in their names.[35] In 1976, an anonymous Uruguayan officer addressed a letter to the Vatican describing the torture he had witnessed and also noting:

> Not only the army tortures; the police, the navy, and the air force torture the same or worse. Breaking and entering also make up part of the barbarity. I have seen them ransacking houses like savages, destroying whatever is left, fighting over a TV set or a coat—and this under the pretext of undermining the bases of Communist support.[36]

The Argentine National Commission received testimony from members of the military "task forces" expressing resentment that they had risked their lives while their superior officers enriched themselves.[37] These officers, not surprisingly, proved utterly unprepared to manage— much less fight—an external war against an armed enemy force. The defeat of the Argentine armed forces in the Malvinas (Falkland Islands) produced shock and scandal as the public became aware of the extent of military corruption and incompetence.

REORGANIZING SOCIETY FOR REPRESSION

The dictatorship is still here. It is present day after day, year
after year, invading even our most intimate moments. It affects not only those who suffer cruelty or censorship directly
but also those who are indifferent to dictatorship, and even
those who support and justify it; because they too are caught
in a system that determines what we can and cannot do, what
we think, what we create, what we dream, and what we sup-
press.[38]

Military rule in Brazil, Chile, Uruguay, and Argentina profoundly
transformed civil society. The pervasive state violence and the psychology of fear caused citizens to turn inward, avoiding public contact. Not
only were people likely to abandon overt political activity, but they also
grew wary of social interactions that might have a political content and
fearful of joining with others to make economic demands. Deprived of
information, unable to predict who might be suspect, and aware that to
be suspect oneself could carry dreadful consequences, most citizens
feared to complain or protest. This phenomenon was no accidental
outcome of the widespread violence. It was the intended outcome of
regime terror designed to inhibit collective action, diminish support
networks, and depoliticize social interactions.

Political and economic policies were mutually reinforcing. Military
rule brought markedly new directions in policies related to economics,
finance, and development. The "neoliberal" economic models that were
introduced affected most peoples' lives in quite direct ways—their wages,
their buying power, and their access to work, goods, and services. These
models favored the international and domestic interests most supportive
of military rule. At the same time, in abruptly reversing the populism of
prior regimes, they were most detrimental to the quality of life of the poor
and sectors of the middle class. The military governments, lacking political legitimacy and support, imposed unpopular economic measures by
means of repression and force.

SUSTAINING TERROR SECRETLY AND PUBLICLY

While for political reasons and to preserve international legitimacy, the
Southern Cone authoritarian governments denied official involvement in
terror, they also considered it essential that the terror be widely known.
The methods of repression adopted by authorities were intended to

humiliate, demoralize, and terrify a broad population beyond the particular persons detained for punishment. The persons detained were subjected to treatment designed to remove their dignity and sense of self. On the one hand, government officials would deny that prisoners were mistreated or subjected to torture and would deny that disappeared persons ever had been prisoners. The survivors and their families, on the other hand, were likely to communicate these abuses in one form or another—with the intended effect of augmenting fear.

Whatever relief Uruguayan prisoners must have felt when transferred from torture centers to detention centers, detention centers proved to be virtual laboratories of personality destruction. The prison regime was designed to produce behavior modification by generating permanent anxiety in the prisoners.[39]

There were relatively few disappearances in Brazil and Uruguay. Brazilian and Uruguayan security forces—and Chileans as well after 1978—routinely tortured suspects while holding them incommunicado, sometimes for quite long periods. Eventually, in most cases, the authorities registered the arrests and allowed families to write and occasionally to visit. For these reasons, prisoners and their families were spared much of the uncertainty and pain suffered by the relatives of those who disappeared. Nevertheless, these practices generated fear on a massive scale and discouraged protests.

In Argentina victims were often kidnapped with a public show of force and then made to disappear with no public acknowledgment of their existence or whereabouts. According to the National Commission, it was not unusual for several vehicles—automobiles, trucks, vans—as well as a helicopter to surround the victim's home.

> The intimidation and terror were employed not merely to forestall any possibility of response by the victims. [They were] also intended to terrorize all those living nearby. Traffic was frequently brought to a halt; loudspeakers, searchlights, bombs, and grenades were used in an excessive show of force.[40]

The neighbors awakened in this process undoubtedly knew that after this spectacle they would not see the victim again. They probably did not know that the person would be taken to one of the secret detention centers, from which few returned.

> [These centers] had been specifically conceived for the subjection of victims to a meticulous and deliberate stripping of all human attributes, rather than for their simple physical elimination.
> To be admitted to one of these centers meant to cease to exist. In order to

achieve this end, attempts were made to break down the captives' identity; their spatiotemporal points of reference were disrupted, and their minds and bodies tortured beyond imagination.[41]

For this reason they had to be secret.

The magnitude of the operations put in place for the purpose of causing 15,000 to 30,000 Argentines to disappear was enormous. This tactic of terror and extermination required the construction of the 340 clandestine centers in which victims were housed; the preparation of mass cemeteries where they were secretly buried; the organization and training of hundreds of "task forces" that carried out the operations; the training of the people who staffed the detention centers and who punished the victims; the connivance of military and police officials not directly involved in the operations; and the cooperation of legal, medical, and other personnel who came into contact with victims and their families.

The apparatus of disappearance was a top priority in military strategy. So important was its secrecy that the rare guard, nurse, or officer who broke discipline and delivered a letter or gave information to a family was almost certain to be subjected to the same fate as the victims. Like many journalists, newspaper editor Jacobo Timerman recalled dreading the visits of desperate relatives asking that he publicize their stories:

> I could anticipate this woman's story [of the disappearance of her two children] and therefore didn't receive her. I receive some, others not. . . . How can I tell this woman that if I published the story about her children, it would most likely amount to a death sentence? How can I tell her that the government will never tolerate the assumption that a newspaper article can save a life? To permit this would mean losing the power of repression, the utilization of Fear and Silence.[42]

Timerman lived this ambivalence until he was arrested in April 1977, perhaps because—among other reasons—he wrote stories about such women's children. Hundreds of journalists, lawyers, and clergy suffered for complicity in subversion because of their efforts to make public the secret terror.

But, one way or another, the news was disseminated, by families and neighbors, or by means of the testimonies published by respected human-rights organizations. Perversely, the same denunciations that brought international attention to and condemnation of disappearances—and ultimately probably did save lives—also confirmed for the public the reality of their worst fears. These fears were further intensified by the knowledge that the bearers of the terrible news not only were powerless to help but might become the next victims. The fact that a few people were spared and recounted their experiences augmented both terror and, consequently, acquiescence.

Why did the Southern Cone governments punish their citizens with seemingly unprecedented cruelty, totally outside national or international legal norms for the treatment of any kind of criminals? The phenomenon of disappearing prisoners has raised the question with greatest poignancy because it combined cruelty to the prisoner with punishment to presumably innocent families and loved ones, even children and babies.

Clearly, making suspects disappear isolated them from possible legal interference, assistance, or rescue. Disappeared prisoners remained entirely in the power of captors who considered their information possibly useful and their lives entirely expendable. For the governments who authorized and organized the policies, the disappearances served additional purposes. With the victims invisible, the governments could invent a facade of normalcy. That facade made it possible for domestic and international apologists, and the uninvolved, to interact with ruling officials in familiar and accepted ways. One could ignore the facts that the disappearances had been publicized and that official denials of accountability had ceased to be credible. As for those who undertook to search for the missing, they were obliged to enter a fearsome and unfamiliar world of criminal activity at the highest levels. Fearing reprisals, many gave up the search.

ECONOMIC INDIVIDUALISM

The Southern Cone military governments inherited economies in crisis. Indeed, the postcoup leaders, in countless speeches and declarations, claimed to have seized power at least as much to restore economic health as to curtail leftist politics.

The Brazilian leadership, in particular, linked economic development to the military mandate. The generation that took power in Brazil in the 1960s was made up of nationalists who thought in terms of merging national security and national development.[43] The Brazilian economic model was coherent, and the economy maintained an impressive growth rate for nearly a decade. Both the military itself and the civilian economic leadership considered economic growth to be the sine qua non of military rule. And, in fact, acknowledging that the economic situation had deteriorated by the late 1970s, sectors of the military, under strong civilian pressure, moved toward a transition to civilian rule.

The architects of the Brazilian miracle had associated the economic demands of organized social groups with insurrection and subversion. These groups were allowed no voice in economic decisions. In addition, the regime pursued forms of capital accumulation and investment that excluded many salaried workers and the poor from economic benefits. Thus, the Brazilian economic miracle was accompanied by significantly increased inequality in the distribution of wealth.

Like their Brazilian counterparts, the Chilean, Uruguayan, and Argentine military leaders believed populist policies and grass-roots organizations had opened the door to subversive influences as well as to economic inefficiencies. Hence, they repressed and disenfranchised those sectors of the population whose fragile economic security had been gained by the collective pursuit of their interests. But, contrary to their Brazilian counterpart, the three regimes saw little use in fostering autonomous national development. Instead, all three embraced rigid free-market theories. By means of these they hoped to be found worthy of substantial international economic loans and credit.[44] The policies, at least for a time, seemed to produce some economic growth, thanks largely to foreign borrowing and high commodity prices.

But outside Brazil, where the middle class enjoyed a period of prosperity, all these economic measures required painful adjustments throughout society. In all four countries, the poorest sectors bore the major brunt of the required adjustments. The new policies also quickly undermined national enterprises, both urban and rural, thereby greatly augmenting social distress. Nor did the economic growth prove enduring. When the military leaders left the presidential palaces in Argentina and Uruguay, they left their countries in far worse economic straits than they had found them.

As for Chile in the late 1970s, the government proclaimed the success of the economic "shock" plan it had put in place in 1975 to conquer inflation. Officials recognized the enormous social costs of this plan but blamed the previous government for having created the economic distortions that made it necessary. The economy minister, Pedro Baraona, assured Chileans in 1977 that the sacrifices would produce a stronger economy:

> In this country everybody was educated in weakness. To educate them in strength, it is necessary to pay the cost of temporary unemployment and bankruptcies.[45]

Eventually, the Chilean economy showed considerable strength in the export sector, the trickle-down effects of which have been limited.

The new civilian democratic governments in Uruguay, Chile, Argentina, and Brazil, like governments elsewhere in the hemisphere, have been unable to acquiesce to the wage demands of long-suffering workers. Nor have they reestablished most of the state subsidies and supports for programs that once benefited middle- and working-class sectors. They have found it necessary, to some extent, to continue following the austerity programs of their predecessors. This policy derives, in part, from the generally difficult situation in which most Third World countries find themselves. It also derives, unquestionably, from the economic damage done by the preceding governments and from the enormous debt with which three of the four new governments have been saddled.

PRIVATIZING SOCIAL LIFE

Restrictions on social gatherings, on elections in social and sports clubs, and censorship of press, television, and popular songs all conspire to draw people away from public life into private spheres. Fears about talking freely in front of neighbors and colleagues, suspicions about strange people in unaccustomed places, reluctance to pursue friendships with new acquaintances follow. As people turn inward, there is less contact or communication among different social sectors, fewer possibilities for collective action, and greater personal frustration. The public sphere shrinks, and the private sphere is strained.

The bureaucratic authoritarian state in the Southern Cone substituted technocracy and apathy for political and social-class support.[46] Sociologist Guillermo O'Donnell has elaborated on this phenomenon. He concluded that the removal of institutions that mediate between citizens and state and channel demands of the citizens to the state, the economic exclusion of major social sectors, the hierarchical organizations, and the pervasive censorship were, in effect, the fatal fragilities of the bureaucratic authoritarian order. He noted prophetically:

> The silence of the excluded and coerced sectors generates a very special situation: that of a state that, from the apex of its institutions, loudly proclaims the importance of the tasks it is performing and announces a future greatness, and yet does not receive in return even the echo of its voice.[47]

None of the military regimes succeeded if measured by their own objectives. The repression brought suffering and fear, distorting the social order without creating a new social consensus. None of the four military regimes remains in power. Although the military remains powerful in all four countries, political parties of the left and center have reemerged. Labor, student, professional, and cultural organizations also have regrouped, and new human-rights groups have come into being.

In none of the Southern Cone countries can politics be conducted as if the military takeovers had not occurred. Despite a revival of political culture, there remain deep psychological and social scars caused by repression, exile, and fear. Unhappily, the most lasting change brought about by—or at least catalyzed by—military rule may be the wreckage of once-viable national economies and the seemingly unsurmountable indebtedness that civilian rulers now face. This and the legacy of unpunished crimes against tens of thousands of citizens are what remain of the decade of terror.

NOTES

1. Hannah Arendt, *The Origins of Totalitarianism* (San Diego: Harcourt Brace Jovanovich, 1973), 323.

2. See Juan Linz and Alfred Stepan, eds., *The Breakdown of Democratic Regimes in Latin America* (Baltimore: Johns Hopkins University Press, 1978); and, within that series, Arturo Valenzuela, *Chile* (Baltimore: Johns Hopkins University Press, 1978). See also Peter H. Smith, *Argentina and the Failure of Democracy, Conflict among Political Elites* (Madison: University of Wisconsin Press, 1974); Marcelo Cavarozzi, "Political Cycles in Argentina since 1955," and Charles Gillespie, "Uruguay's Transition from Collegial Military-Technocratic Rule," in Guillermo O'Donnell, Philippe Schmitter, and Laurence Whitehead, eds., *Transition from Authoritarian Rule* (Baltimore: Johns Hopkins University Press, 1986); and Charles Gillespie's paper, "Unravelling the Breakdown of Democracy in Uruguay," presented at the Conference on Democracy and Uruguay, Woodrow Wilson Center, Smithsonian Institution, Washington, D.C., 12–15 September 1984. See also part 1 of Louis W. Goodman, Johanna S. Mendelson, and Juan Rial, eds., *The Military and Democracy* (Lexington, Mass.: Heath, 1989).

3. Works treating these themes include Goodman, Mendelson, and Rial, *The Military and Democracy;* Alfred Stepan, *The Military in Politics: Changing Patterns in Brazil* (Princeton, N.J.: Princeton University Press, 1971); Alfred Stepan, *Authoritarian Brazil: Origins, Policies and Future* (New Haven, Conn.: Yale University Press, 1973); Alfred Stepan, *Rethinking Military Politics: Brazil and the Southern Cone* (Princeton, N.J.: Princeton University Press, 1987); Peter Flynn, *Brazil, a Political Analysis* (Boulder, Colo.: Westview Press, 1978). Also Augusto Varas, Felipe Agüero, Fernando Bustamante, *Chile, democracia, fuerzas armadas* (Santiago: FLACSO, 1980); Augusto Varas, ed., *Hemispheric Security and United States Policy in Latin America* (Boulder, Colo.: Westview

Press, 1988); Rosendo Fraga, *El ejército argentino* (Buenos Aires: Editora Planeta, 1987); Robert Potash, *The Army in Politics in Argentina, 1945–1962: Peron to Frondizi* (Stanford, Calif.: Stanford University Press, 1979); Brian Loveman and Thomas Davies, *The Politics of Antipolitics: The Military in Latin America* (Lincoln: University of Nebraska Press, 1978).

4. Books and articles about the national security state and techniques and training for counterinsurgency abound. Among the works specifically focused on these issues are: Maria Helena Alves, *Estado e oposição no Brasil, 1964–1984* (Petrópolis: Vozes, 1984), English version: *State and Opposition in Military Brazil* (Austin: University of Texas Press, 1985); Michael McClintock, *The American Connection: State Terror and Popular Resistance in El Salvador,* vol. 1 (London: Zed Books, 1985); Victor Marchetti and John Marks, *The CIA and the Cult of Intelligence* (New York: Dell, 1974); A. J. Langguth, *Hidden Terrors: Truth about U.S. Police in Latin America* (Toronto: Pantheon, 1978). The operation of military repression within the framework of the national security state is the underlying theme of the post-terror accounts of human-rights violations in Brazil, Argentina, and Uruguay: Archdiocese of São Paulo, *Brasil: Nunca mais* (Petrópolis: Vozes, 1985), English version: *Torture in Brazil,* trans. Jaime Wright, ed. Joan Dassin (New York: Random House, Vintage Books, 1986); *Nunca más: Informe de la Comisión Nacional Sobre la Desaparición de Personas* (Buenos Aires: Editorial Universitaria, 1984), English version: *Nunca Más: The Report of the Argentine National Commission on the Disappeared* (New York: Farrar, Straus & Giroux, 1986); Servicio Paz y Justicia, *Uruguay, nunca más, informe sobre la violación a los derechos humanos, 1972–1985* (Montevideo, February 1989).

5. General Leopoldo Galtieri, quoted in *La prensa,* November 1981.

6. Quoted in Stephen Kinzer, "Argentina in Agony," *The New Republic* 23 and 30 December 1978, 18; the original Spanish appeared in *Clarín,* 18 December 1977.

7. Quoted in *El mercurio,* 12 September 1974.

8. Quoted in Daniel Frontalini and Cristina Caiati, *El mito de la guerra sucia* (Buenos Aires: CELS, 1984), 21–227.

9. Estado Maior das Forças Armadas–Escola Superior de Guerra, Departamento de Estudos, *Manual básico da Escola Superior de Guerra* (Rio de Janeiro, 1976). See also Alves, *Estado e oposição,* 36–46; and *Brasil: Nunca mais.*

10. Quoted in Stepan, *Authoritarian Brazil,* 56.

11. Quoted in *El mercurio,* 11 September 1976.

12. Uruguayan Subsecretary of the Interior Nestor Bolentini, May 1972; quoted in *Uruguay, nunca más,* 64, from the *Diario de Sesiones de la Asamblea General,* vol. 56, 130, 601–3.

13. Argentinian Minister of the Economy José Martínez de Hoz; quoted in Frontalini and Caiati, *El mito de la guerra sucia,* 34. The speech appeared originally in *La prensa,* 21 September 1978.

14. Frontalini and Caiati (*El mito de la guerra sucia*) devote a whole chapter to this point, see ch. 3; see also the book's prologue by Emilio Fermín Mignone.

15. In addition to the human-rights reports already cited, see the articles in *Symposium on the State of Emergency and Human Rights in Uruguay* (Paris:

International Secretariat of Catholic Jurists/International Federation of Human Rights, 1978), especially the articles by Robert K. Goldman and Hans Thoolen; Robert K. Goldman, "Critique of the State Department's 1978 and 1979 Reports on Human Rights Practices in Uruguay," in *Reports on Human Rights Practices for 1979* (New York: Lawyers Committee for International Human Rights, 1980); Lawrence Weschler, "The Great Exception, I: Liberty," *New Yorker,* 3 April 1989, 43–85. A full elaboration of Chilean law and the operation of the judicial system is found in Inter-American Commission for Human Rights, *Report on the Situation of Human Rights in Chile,* OAS/Ser.L/V/11.66 doc. 17 (Washington, D.C., 27 September 1985). For Chile, an important volume by Hernán Montealegre, *La seguridad del estado y los derechos humanos,* makes a case for the criminality of a government that violates the security of its citizens (Santiago: Academia de los Derechos Humanos, 1979).

16. *Torture in Brazil,* 149. This review of the years of repression was the result of a project sponsored by the Archdiocese of São Paulo.

17. The names of the disappeared are listed in the appendix of *Brasil: Nunca mais.*

18. Inter-American Commission on Human Rights, *Report on the Situation of Human Rights in Argentina,* OAS/Ser.L/V/11.49 doc. 19 (Washington, D.C., 11 April 1980), 16.

19. Ibid., 19.

20. Ibid., 20.

21. Ibid., 247.

22. The Argentine National Commission on the Disappeared fully documented 8,960 cases, but virtually all human-rights sources agree on the higher estimates.

23. Case of Inés Ollero.

24. Case of Perez de Smith.

25. Details concerning these and numerous other cases are found both in the Inter-American Commission for Human Rights report and in *Nunca más.* The Argentine National Commission on the Disappeared was created by President Raúl Alfonsín in 1983 to investigate military repression with particular focus on the disappeared.

26. Jacobo Timerman, *Prisoner without a Name, Cell without a Number,* trans. Tony Talbot (New York: Knopf, 1981), 128.

27. *Nunca más,* 387.

28. The security apparatus of each country is elaborated on in previously cited works by Alves, Goldman, and in reports of the Inter-American Commission for Human Rights and Amnesty International. For Argentina, see also Emilio Fermín Mignone, "Desapariciones forzadas: Elementos básicos de una política," *Punto final,* supp. no. 194 (June 1981).

29. Alves, *Estado e oposição,* 175; *Torture in Brazil,* ch. 7.

30. *Nunca más,* 2.

31. *Uruguay, nunca más,* tallied seventy-eight deaths in detention and fifty-three street confrontations. Seventeen Uruguayans were killed and nearly two hundred disappeared in Argentina. Most of those who disappeared later reappeared in Uruguayan jails (293–94, 419–21, 425–30).

32. *Uruguay, nunca más,* pt. 2, ch. 1, p. 4 (figures on p. 116); Lawyers Committee for International Human Rights, *Uruguay: The End of a Nightmare? A Report Based on a Mission of Inquiry* (New York, May 1984), 15–16; see also previously cited works by Goldman, Gillespie, Weschler, and frequent reports of Amnesty International, the Washington Office on Latin America, and the International Commission of Jurists.

33. A comprehensive review of the issues and debates associated with U.S. training and military assistance programs and a summary of the literature are found in Lars Schoultz, *Human Rights and United States Policy toward Latin America* (Princeton, N.J.: Princeton University Press, 1987), ch. 6.

34. Quoted in McClintock, *The American Connection,* 54. The Office of Public Safety is discussed on 61, 68–69. See also Langguth, *Hidden Terrors.*

35. Alejandro Artucio, "Violation of Economic and Social Rights of Political Prisoners," in *Symposium on the State of Emergency and Human Rights in Uruguay,* 55–58.

36. This letter is quoted in "Uruguay, an Imprisoned Democracy," an Infor Act bulletin of the New York Circus, no. 3 (n.d.).

37. *Nunca más,* 241, 272–73.

38. From the preface of Patricia Politzer, *Fear in Chile: Lives under Pinochet* (New York: Pantheon, 1989), xiii.

39. Lawrence Weschler, "The Great Exception"; and *Uruguay, nunca más,* pt. 2, ch. 4.

40. *Nunca más,* 12.

41. Ibid., 52.

42. Timerman, *Prisoner without a Name,* 43.

43. As elaborated in Stepan, *Authoritarian Brazil,* 47.

44. See, for example, Adolfo Canitrot, "La disciplina como objetivo de la política económica, un ensayo sobre el programa económico del gobierno argentino desde 1976," *Estudios CEDES* 2, no. 6 (1979); Pilar Vergara, *Auge y caída del neoliberalismo en Chile* (Santiago: FLACSO, 1985). David Pion-Berlin, *The Ideology of State Terror: Economic Doctrine and Political Repression in Argentina and Peru* (Boulder, Colo.: Lynne Reinner, 1989).

45. Quoted in Vergara, *Auge y caída del neoliberalismo,* 96–97; originally in *Cosas,* no. 10 (17 February 1977).

46. For an analysis of the policies that characterize authoritarian rule in the Southern Cone, see David Collier, ed., *The New Authoritarianism in Latin America* (Princeton, N.J.: Princeton University Press, 1979).

47. Guillermo O'Donnell, "Tensions in the Bureaucratic-Authoritarian State and the Question of Democracy," in Collier, *The New Authoritarianism,* 311.

FOUR

Victims of Fear

The Social Psychology of Repression

Sofia Salimovich, Elizabeth Lira, and Eugenia Weinstein

Fear has always been widespread and deeply felt among the poor in Latin America, where it is rooted in the uncertainties of life and individual and family survival. The fears of the poor emerge from the threat of disgrace, destitution, disaster, and ruin, and from dread of the future.

The repression suffered by the poor has been long and painful. But with the rise of military dictatorships the experience of fear emerged forcefully in other social groups as well. It altered peoples' sense of continuity and achievement in their lives. The direct victims of repression have suffered personally, as have their families, from the traumatic aftereffects of violent experiences such as torture, disappearance, the execution of relatives, arbitrary arrest, intimidation, unemployment, and exile.

This chapter approaches fear as a psychological phenomenon provoked by specific social situations. We understand fear to be a subjective experience whose effects are initially on the individual but which, when occurring simultaneously in thousands of people within a society, can have unforeseeable repercussions for social and political behavior. Thus, fear can be described as an experience that is collective and observable as well as individual and denied, and one that acts on and shapes the forms of collective behavior.

Fear is a behavioral phenomenon and a complex human experience that needs to be examined at different levels. We describe how fear becomes pronounced in specific situations and elaborate the consequent psychodynamic and psychopathological responses. The analyses are based on our clinical experiences in Chile and on the preventative mental-health work we have done with the social groups affected by political repression.

The term *traumatized* is commonly used to describe persons suffering the long-term consequences of an event defined as traumatic. In such persons the fear reflex expands well beyond its original life-serving adaptive function to become an unknown force in an individual's subsequent political and social life. The subjective experience of fear does not disappear as soon as the causes that provoked it have ceased to exist. Hence, in the context of efforts to build democracy, we believe it necessary to study and discuss the impact that fear has had on social behavior and political participation. We believe that psychology can contribute to an understanding of the subjective social effects of fear and can explain the difficulties inherent in overcoming it.

CONCEPTUAL FRAMEWORK

Fear, anxiety, anguish, terror, panic, fright, and *horror* are words that have been used to describe the response set off by a perception of clear or undefined danger. A situation is perceived as dangerous when the individual becomes aware of the magnitude of a threat and of his or her own powerlessness to confront it. The perceived danger may be real or imagined and can come from within the individual or from the environment. Its presence leads people to experience situations as life-threatening. The certainty or high probability that the real or imagined threat will occur and the resulting feelings of biological helplessness and social vulnerability transform initial insecurity into fear. The perception of the threat as imminent converts the fear into terror or panic. Panic occurs when the dangerous situation provokes a spontaneous and disorganized reaction in an individual or in a community.

The inability to identify the precise content of the threat to one's own life or to pinpoint when it will occur has been called anxiety. Anxiety, as Freud noted, is related to anticipation. At the point when the person suffering anxiety is able to identify the content of the threat, the phenomenon is called fear.

Insecurity and anxiety often arise when there is a change in the social and physical environment or an imagined change in the patterns of everyday life. Reality and fantasy can generate different kinds of insecurity, which can vary in intensity. The experiences may be expressed as difficult-to-specify concerns about change or as life threats involving many different factors.

The life threat may be perceived in several ways. First, it may be perceived as a physical threat: of death, of being attacked, beaten, raped, or tortured. Second, it may be perceived as a threat to one's livelihood— that is, to the loss of a means of subsistence or to an inability to earn enough to fulfill basic needs. Third, it may be felt as a threat to one's values, something that prevents one from living in accordance with one's own beliefs and premises.

Unquestionably, political events that result in significant changes in the lives of individuals or social groups generate fear in those affected, and their feelings clearly affect their behavior. Their responses may vary from aggression and violence to apathy and resignation, depending on the social and political circumstances.

PSYCHOLOGICAL PROCESSES GENERATED BY FEAR

Political repression can be described as a multifaceted phenomenon whose principal goals are to destroy the individual as a political being and to affect the individual as a person by severing links with family and other valued groups. To gain an understanding of the fear generated as a consequence of repression, it is necessary to analyze it in the context of the specific situation in which it occurs and to examine it from the perspective of the different psychological processes to which it relates. Fear provokes specific behaviors that can be described as adaptive responses. However, fear can become permanent, especially when the circumstances are perceived as life-threatening. Finally, fear, as well as other experiences, can affect emotional stability and psychic functioning, thus generating specific psychopathological processes.

The psychological characteristics of the processes generated by fear can be classified into four groups. First, a sense of personal weakness emerges in the face of a life-threatening situation, a feeling of vulnerability. The individual perceives himself or herself to be "labeled" or "persecuted," or to have lost the sense of privacy. This feeling places one at the mercy of arbitrary events beyond one's control.

Second, with an interpretation of the situation as life-threatening, the senses remain in a permanent state of alert, with no possibility of rest. This state is later expressed through different symptomatologies.

Third, a feeling of powerlessness results from the acknowledgment that one's own resources are useless in the face of adversities. One feels no control over one's own life and believes that decisions about the future lie outside one's hands. Feelings of helplessness and defenselessness are expressions of this powerlessness.

Fourth, one's perception of reality becomes distorted. One of the goals of intimidation is to inhibit action by violently depriving individuals of their capacity to act, thereby interfering with the psychological process of reality testing. The impossibility of testing subjective experience against reality causes the boundaries between the real, the possible, the fantasized, and the imaginary to become blurred. Reality then becomes confused and threatening, without clear boundaries, and is no longer able to fulfill its role as guide of the subjective process.

THE REPRESSIVE EXPERIENCE AND THE PSYCHOLOGICAL EFFECTS OF FEAR

Repression disrupts social practices and fragments of social relations (job-related, familial, political). Individuals are at risk of interpreting these losses as irrevocable and surrendering to defeat. In Chilean legal indictments and in the press, the words *enemy* and *unpatriotic* were used to refer to individuals with ties to the former regime. The definition of the enemy was broad, ultimately based on ideological allegations and not on concrete, committed acts. This definition, combined with constant encouragement to denounce those who fit the description, constituted for many people an ongoing life threat. Furthermore, retroactive definitions of crimes placed people in highly threatening situations beyond their control. They could face punishment not only for present or future acts known to be legal or illegal but also for actions taken at a time when they were legal.

Chileans had been convinced that their civil rights were protected by the prevailing rules. This conviction was deeply rooted and widespread, particularly among the middle class. As individuals internalized the possibility that their lives might be threatened and experienced continuing feelings of vulnerability and constant assaults on their civil rights, their faith in personal protection was undermined. They began to experience their society as one that lacked civil liberties.

At the early stage of individual repression, the use of threats is tied to two fundamental conditions: to be significant the threats must impinge on what the individual values, and to be effective they must subjectively and symbolically affect a large number of people. Another contributing factor to the development of fear is the promulgation of laws that prohibit individuals from gathering in groups and organizations. These laws splinter social and public ties, while press censorship keeps the majority ignorant of the processes in which they have been immersed.

Repressive violence is intended both to annihilate the active opponents of the regime and, gradually, to dominate the whole population. Such domination is accomplished as people internalize life threats and therefore engage in a self-regulatory process of learning socially approved behavior. The lack of clarity as to what kind of political activity is permitted to the opposition, what the retributions might be, and what the dangers are provides fertile ground for subjectivity, fantasy, and irrationality. The fantasies can be extremely frightening because the possible horrors have never been objectively or publicly observed. Thus, fantasy functions as internalized self-repression.

The persistent difficulties and risks involved in making a living, performing small tasks, and facing daily life affect the individual internally. Either one's identity as a political being and one's desire to participate are disrupted, or one's self-perception and affective relations are altered.

HOUSE SEARCHES

Police in Chile routinely carried out house searches when looking for suspects or for the proof needed to indict them. After 1973, and especially between late 1984 and 1986, they made frequent mass raids in poor neighborhoods. These raids were designed to intimidate the poor as well as to search the houses.

The procedure typically involved a massive deployment of police and soldiers, who surrounded certain communities. The action included destruction of property, ransacking of homes, and violent intimidation of family members. This experience was always traumatic for the family. Not only were household effects and furniture usually destroyed, but family privacy and the signs and symbols of intimacy and attachment were also violated.

The analysis and the testimonies transcribed below describe the massive searches that took place in November 1984.

> Some people have trouble defining fear. They affirm that it is "the lot of people who live here" and something you "get used to." Women more often admit to fear: they still feel the panic they experienced. But, in general, everyone is aware of an ongoing anxiety and worry. The daily ration of misery, the

constant search for food, and the worry about the future of their children are now intensified by an unwelcome sense of vulnerability. The humble wooden dwelling which, in spite of everything, had become a refuge for their sufferings, is no longer even that.

I happened to be at the door when they took all the men out of their houses. I saw them tearing up the mattresses, throwing clothes on the floor, and turning everything upside down. They woke my two-year-old son by pulling out the mattress he was sleeping on. The poor thing opened his eyes to the sight of uniformed men and weapons. Now he lives in terror. He hears a helicopter and runs to hide.

(Nicolas, Campamento Raúl Silva Henríquez)

I can still remember my children crying from fear as I tried to comfort them as best as I could. I felt tremendously powerless when I saw they were taking my husband and there was nothing I could do. They had no reason to come into my house. . . . Now I feel bad here, and in the Camp as well. If I could I would leave here tomorrow because I don't feel safe. I'm always afraid they will come back or go to a neighbor's house. I was not this way before, even though we are very poor. We have one wooden room. Everything we own is there: the kitchen, our beds, everything. They broke into our houses, they got into everything that is ours. . . . I am not only scared. I have been humiliated.

(Marta, Campamento Raúl Silva Henríquez)

ARRESTS

Many Chileans were arrested in their homes, in front of their families, by a large contingent of police who ransacked their houses. At other times the arrest took place in the street, either in the presence or absence of third parties, at work, or during social activities or union-related meetings. Often the individuals feared they would be arrested; they were aware of being followed and watched. Yet, even if the arrest was no surprise, its violent nature always produced a response of fear, panic, or anxiety. The emotional reaction of those who were arrested for the first time of course differed from that of those who had been detained before.

In countless cases, the period following arrest was characterized by three events. First, there was a lack of information about the prisoner's whereabouts for periods of from five to twenty days. During this time the responsible authorities would not acknowledge that the arrest had occurred. The family, therefore, feared for the victim's life and worried constantly about the detained person's physical and psychological condition. Second, the authorities used television and newspapers to accuse the victims of serious crimes that impugned their honor and that of their families. Although the accusations were usually unfounded, the media's

failure to refute them caused predictable consequences for the victim's
social life and employment. Third, the authorities used torture (illegal
coercion) as a routine method of interrogation.

TORTURE

Torture produces extreme psychological trauma in the victim because of
the intensity of the physical and psychic aggression that is suffered, the
dire threat to life that is experienced, and the degree of passivity or
impotence (or both) that the victim necessarily feels. Torture is used for a
number of purposes related to the individual and the broader society.

Torture as a Political Phenomenon.   Against an individual, the goal
of torture appears to be to secure information by confession, but equally
or even more important it is intended to destroy the victim as a political
being. The aim is to shatter the will, beliefs, loyalties, affective ties, and,
as a result, the social and political involvement of the victim.

At a broader level, the goal of torture is to intimidate third parties,
thereby ensuring responses of fear, inhibition, paralysis, impotence, and
conformism throughout the society. Torture is first and foremost a political phenomenon and should not be characterized as the disturbed, aberrant, or out-of-control behavior of the torturers. It is a routine practice
employed in a sophisticated and systematic way. Its methods are widely
taught and are adapted locally by repressive governments, which use
torture to control and destroy individual adversaries and their organizations.

Torture operates in the following sequence to produce the double
effect of both individual and social trauma. Torture is applied to selected
individuals identified as representatives of, sympathizers with, or collaborators of specific social groups such as political parties and organizations and unions. The victims respond to the psychological and physical
pain with their own internal resources. The individual physical and
psychological harm, however, acts as a psychological mechanism of
control over their respective social groups and organizations, and over
society as a whole. This mechanism works because intimidation, fear,
and pressure force would-be opponents to give in, as the only way of
avoiding punishment.

Torture as the Ultimate Experience of Defenselessness.   The ordeal of
being taken to a secret place to be tortured takes the victims to the limits

of endurance by subjecting them to violence and the most absolute sense of powerlessness. Handcuffed, blindfolded, and deprived of any means of self-defense, victims are faced with situations in which their lives and integrity are in dire danger.

Torture is a prolonged and massive assault on the person. Direct physical methods (such as electric shocks, beatings, asphyxiation, hanging, and burning) are its most extreme and concrete forms, but these are by no means the only ones used. Psychological techniques are also used to break people. These seek to transform time and space, and to turn the cell itself into a source of constant torment, in order to perpetuate the victims' sense of powerlessness and prevent recovery.

Torture as a Cause of Severe Psychosomatic Stress. The psychosomatic strain that accompanies any severe trauma becomes extraordinarily acute in the case of torture. This result is actively sought by the torturers, who systematically and continually refine their methods. The insecurity about one's own future and that of family members, the arbitrary and unpredictable behavior of the guards, and the total absence of schedules or points of temporal reference keep the torture victim in a state of perpetual expectation and alert. The result is a weakening and stifling of emotional self-control.

The overwhelming nature of the torture experience affects mental health in a variety of ways. Its precise consequences depend on such variables as the history and psychological resources of the victim, the characteristics of the torture itself, and the impact on the family.

The experience of torture alters the internal framework of the victim. It influences the way of interpreting and codifying not only external situations but also internal events, feelings, and the way these relate to the outside world. Because of its intensity, torture may lead to a break with reality. It can provoke feelings of generalized anxiety as well as specific fears, such as the fear of another torture, of subsequent physical or psychological harm, of being threatened again through family members, of death, and of suffering any one of a number of important losses (prestige, housing, employment). Sexual torture generates other specific fears, such as that of losing the reproductive capacity. All of this fear may be aggravated by lack of steady employment and social instability, by expectations of personal failure, and by the permanent sense of insecurity that usually accompanies repressive situations.

We have described the specific psychological trauma of torture in order to analyze its aftereffects. We are particularly concerned with how the experience is processed psychologically in a society that does not guarantee that the same person will not be tortured again. The experience is usually followed by the development of psychopathological and other long-term mechanisms.

It may be impossible for the victim ever to forget the torture, but it is not necessarily the case that the individual will renounce beliefs, plans, and political projects. Like all experiences of trauma, the torture experience needs to be worked through in the context in which it occurred by reconstructing and reliving it in all its horror and thereby coming to terms with its personal and social meanings.

THE SEARCH FOR A DISAPPEARED RELATIVE

After 1973, many Chileans were arrested but not placed in public detention. Government authorities denied having ordered the arrests, and legal recourse was useless, even when there were witnesses.

Disappearance was a particularly cruel form of political repression against the opposition. Beyond the horror experienced by the direct victims, it caused incalculable psychological harm to the victims' immediate relatives. Disappearances not only were inconclusive, uncertain, chronically harmful, and indefinitely prolonged, painful experiences for the relatives but also had repercussions in the workplace and society, which rebounded again on the individuals affected. The experience is described here.

First Stage: The Search. After an arrest, family members devoted most of their energies to the search. They clung to the hope that the prisoner might be alive. This was a time of much activity, high expectations, and hope. The arrest was emotionally processed as a temporary absence, not a loss. During this stage, substantial fear arose from uncertainty about the harm that the disappeared prisoner might have suffered and from the possibility of repercussions on the family group.

These fear responses correspond to those experienced by relatives of political prisoners. Uncertainty as to the whereabouts of the prisoner was combined with fear about his or her condition and fantasies about physical and psychological torture that might have been inflicted. Members of the family visualized the prisoner as being defenseless and vulnerable. The family members felt unprotected as well. Repeated searches of their homes raised fears of new and violent intrusions and the arrests of other relatives. Fears also arose as a result of economic insecurity. The prisoners were often the family breadwinners. Other members of the family had to assume that role, thereby disrupting the family organization.

Children began to exhibit intense fear reactions. Their normally protected world and their parents underwent abrupt changes, and they themselves felt extremely vulnerable. The children's feelings were related to the harm inflicted on those who represented their security and protection. Their world no longer contained defenses against or limits to the threats from outside. Children observing their parents' helplessness in the face of danger also felt defeated and defenseless. Moreover, the closest adult figure, generally the mother, could not appropriately explain the circumstances to her children. Her own insecurity and her fear of hurting or frightening them led her to give confused and contradictory explanations. Such explanations further increased the children's uncertainty.

Second Stage: Acceptance of the Disappearance. The frustrated efforts to find the relative, the lack of concrete responses from the authorities, the passage of time, and feelings of desperation ultimately led the family to begin to accept that a relative had disappeared. Having accepted the disappearance, the family then was beset by fantasies of torture and abuse and images of the deplorable physical and psychological state in which the loved one must be. The situation could still be defined as contradictory because the victim had been arrested by security forces that did not admit to having done so. The family therefore felt both loss and blame; accompanying the memories and the hopes of finding the relative alive were painful speculations about the relative who was suffering under torture.

Although family life began to reorganize itself around the reality of the disappearance, the situation itself remained inconclusive, uncertain, and fraught with contradictions. Feelings of fear and insecurity, accompanied by a sense of guilt and disloyalty, would invade all efforts to plan for the future. It was not possible to incorporate the loss and to mourn it.

Within their fantasies, the children continued to be tormented by and inundated with speculations about the fate of the disappeared parent. Their fantasy world was rooted in a concrete situation that was unresolved and always changing, and in which new facts caused meanings and interpretations to vary. The fantasies were the expression of an internal state of anguish and fear.

In adults, the impossibility of dealing with contradictory feelings and the fear of falling apart emotionally produced a fear of feeling itself, which was accompanied by a sense of guilt and disloyalty. Family ties were altered as members closed themselves off in response to a situation that was uncertain and prolonged.

Disappearances were rarely spoken of. The fear and insecurity provoked by social stigma generated even greater isolation and suffering, especially in the children. The resulting concentration of frustration and desperation in the family had serious repercussions for interpersonal relations and family stability and development. At times, feelings of profound despair about the meaning of life without the disappeared person could diminish fear, despite possible life threats. This despair was experienced in different ways depending on the individual's relationship to the victim.

In the late 1970s organized protest and group actions in Chile demanded public acknowledgment of the existence of the disappeared. The fact that the relatives organized and participated in these actions brought changes in the way they experienced fear. The intense fear of the initial period, which was associated with feelings of isolation and vulnerability, of confusion and chaos, diminished in proportion to the extent that the problem could be shared with others and be understood. Participants in the protests discovered their ability to share and to act on their own. Nevertheless, the capacity of the regime to continually reinstate the state of siege demonstrated its ability to survive the popular protests, thereby reinforcing fears.

Third Stage: The Possibility of Death. After long years of group protests about the disappeared with no response from the authorities, the first evidence that some of the disappeared had been killed came to light with the findings of their remains at Lonquen, Yumbel, and Mulchen in 1978–79. These findings had a significant effect on the connotations of disappearance, and fears about the deaths of relatives resurfaced with increased force.

For the family members, a disappeared prisoner was both alive and dead. On the one hand, keeping the person alive meant maintaining the memory and the hope, but it also implied prolonging the fantasies of agony, isolation, deterioration, tortures, and all the imaginable sufferings associated with situations of such extreme vulnerability. This alternative becomes unbearable. On the other hand, the family might consciously decide to assume the disappeared person to be dead, in order to bring uncertainty to an end. In this case, if the relevant authorities refused to recognize the arrest, much less the death, of the loved one, the idea of death was the family's own invention; in effect the death was their decision and not one that could be attributed to political repression. Self-responsibility for the death, with the attendant self-blame, was also intolerable.

Thus, relatives of a disappeared prisoner found themselves on the horns of a dilemma, unable to undergo the normal periods of bereavement and healing. The fear that their loved one might be dead and the denial that this was possible became an incessant refrain in their minds.

GRIEF IN THE RELATIVES OF EXECUTED PRISONERS

Many people were killed in Chile, and most of the deaths were related to their political activities. Given the unexpectedness and arbitrariness, such deaths usually had a traumatic effect on families. The relatives of executed persons all testified to having experienced feelings of sadness, horror, astonishment, disbelief, and helplessness on learning of the death of the loved one.

The immediate response on becoming aware of the irreversible loss of the relative was one of shock. The anxiety, degree of suffering, and sense of internal emptiness resembled a nightmare. The horror and injustice associated with the events made it impossible to accept the death as a fact. Relatives were torn between grief and rage, and between active denial and paralyzing impotence. Their imaginations filled repeatedly with images of the defenselessness of their loved one, recognition of their own inability to help in any way, attempts to reverse time so as to gain back the loved one, and the bitter disillusion of being unable to find him or her. A common reaction was a state of alienation, which acted as a defense mechanism. Sometimes a kind of stupor, later transformed into hyperactivity, characterized this phase. A feeling of emptiness that became chronic flooded the person.

The grieving process commonly occurs in sequential phases following a loss. First comes acceptance of the death, and, second, adaptation to a reality that no longer includes the loved one. In the families of executed persons, the repressive situation tended to profoundly alter the grieving process, preventing its normal unfolding. Time did not become an ally; the habitual defense mechanisms broke down, and it became difficult for individuals to release negative feelings. Therefore, the wound stayed open, refusing to scar, and the sharp pain of the first moment became chronic. A profound feeling of disgrace and an ongoing sense of loss lingered.

In contrast to other grief situations, bereavements in Chile took place in the context of multiple losses—for example, loss of the political project that the person executed was involved in, of other friends or relatives, of stability, or of housing. The stigma involved in society's attitude toward the death took on special connotations generating negative and contradictory feelings.

Fear was present from the first moment. In many cases, families were unable to carry out the usual funeral rites and ceremonies. Sometimes they did not even receive the corpses of their loved ones or were forced to abandon their homes with short notice. Besides being paralyzed by fear, many family members sought to minimize social stigma by attempting to pass unnoticed, to avoid mentioning what happened, and, therefore, not to express their pain in any way. They did so partly because they believed this behavior was what was expected of them and partly out of self-stigmatization generated by fear. The Chilean media fed into such attitudes by making disparaging references to the dead. These references prevented the family from restoring the public image of their relative and further inhibited the grief process.

Thus, grief remained trapped within by the feelings of fear and vulnerability, and death was kept hidden for the sake of protecting those who remained alive. The results were feelings of guilt and self-blame. Families constantly confronted the contradictions between the socially transmitted negative images and their own determination to restore the public and private integrity of their loved ones. Within the family, it proved difficult to share the sadness because each member feared harming the others. Members withdrew from one another to deal with their loss in a private way.

The relatives of executed persons were fearful and insecure about resuming everyday chores as the threats to the family and the searches and raids of their houses persisted. Moreover, returning to everyday life meant accepting the loss, which seemed intolerable.

THE IMPACT OF GRIEF AND FEAR ON CHILDREN

The fears of the adults produced a self-censorship that prevented them from openly discussing the events with their children. To avoid new problems, they kept details from the children and, when they finally disclosed the truth, told the children to keep it secret.

During the dictatorship, our attempts through psychological treatment to retrieve the experiences of the period following the loss evoked strong sensations of fear and bewilderment. In some cases many years passed before children could express their reactions to a parent's death or cry about it. Even to think about their parent made them relive all their chaotic and violent sentiments. The repression of fantasies of terror resulted in an overall impoverishment of their creative and affective lives.

Fear about death, their own or that of other members of their family, remains as a long-term psychological consequence in these children. The persistent fear common to children who have suffered such a loss is exacerbated by the perception of continuing threats against people whose activities resemble those of their assassinated parent.

Within the families fear was experienced in different ways. The adults found it difficult to understand and accept what was happening. The children, for their part, sensed the climate of threat and insecurity but were unable to identify its source. Many worries or phobias arose in their efforts to define the object of the fear.

At first, children's fears did not seem related to the political situation. For instance, they became fearful of thieves or of their parents becoming ill. Underlying their fears was a sense of family vulnerability. In play therapy we observed such children repeatedly constructing solid houses, with large walls, alarms, locks, and guard dogs.

Once children began to associate their fears with the political conditions, their phobias receded, but the worries persisted. They began to pay attention to the newspapers and radio. They needed to know exactly what was going on. They waited in vain for some reassuring news.

Sometimes fear persisted because it fulfilled a function for the family members. An adult may reason, "If my child is scared, I can protect him or her; therefore I'm not so vulnerable." The child may contend, "If I, a child, am afraid, my parents can take care of me; therefore I feel better because we are discussing my own fear and not that of my parents, which, in the long run, is what scares me most."

SOCIAL EXCLUSION

Exile and Return.   Social and political circumstances in Chile and in Latin America gave rise to large-scale exile. The experience of exile had a major impact on the individuals and their families. It interfered with the development of affective ties because it separated people from their children, relatives, and friends; it almost always posed formidable challenges. Forced to build a new life, political refugees had to contend with the disruption of their previous equilibrium, as they were not able to function by using previously learned behaviors. They had to abandon their homeland and material belongings, relinquish their inner world, and rethink their sociocultural identities. They continually had to renounce objects and roles that were highly gratifying. Additionally, because circumstances in the host country were not always conducive to psychological recovery, individuals had to deal with the incongruity between their experiences and the reality that surrounded them.

Many of the exiled Chileans have returned to live in their country. The road to their reintegration has also been complex and contradictory, sometimes becoming painful and upsetting if they do not find an adequate welcome. And even when they do, the welcome has not been without problems. Often, the contradictions experienced by the returnees unleash equally conflicting feelings in those Chileans who stayed. They observe the deterioration and decay of many aspects of their culture reflected in the surprise and rejection demonstrated by the new arrivals.

The decision to return implies a full spectrum of longings, needs, and expectations. In many cases, a key motivating force is the possibility of reinvolvement in the social and political projects that were interrupted by the exile. To survive while in exile often means denying the fear experienced before departure. But as the decision to return home is formalized, the feelings are revived. Those who returned prior to the fall of the Pinochet government often had fantasies of persecution and destruction. One factor that inhibited the process of reintegration was the resurgence of these intense feelings of fear, which conflicted with their need to act, to settle in, and to feel at home. Isolation was another factor that contributed to feelings of fear. Isolation was the product not only of the returnees' lack of employment or of social and political nonparticipation but of society's failure to validate their difficulties.

Returning exiles were already informed about the important events and activities that took place during their absence. Ignorance was not a problem. On the contrary, the former exiles often had more information than did those who remained in the country. Once home, however, the exiles were unable to fit the ongoing events into the intellectualized or idealized contexts into which they incorporated information outside the country. Therefore, they were likely to be somewhat unrealistic. The years of absence from a country that had changed so profoundly made it difficult to recognize what was once known and to interpret the physical, social, and cultural signals of the environment. It was also difficult to measure the risks associated with political participation, so individuals often alternated between paralyzing fear and impulsive actions.

Returnees often continued to be intimidated. They received threatening telephone calls and were followed and persecuted in other ways. That the mass media depicted returnees as criminals or terrorists who had participated in "armed clashes" served to exacerbate their feelings of fear and insecurity.

To confront fear and begin to cope with it, the returnees had to learn how to integrate information, emotions, and practices into a reality that—even though previously known—did not feel like the familiar one. They had to work through former experiences of repression. Otherwise, once they were back the old fears would reappear, making the adjustment to the new reality harder.

Unemployment. Unemployment is perceived as life-threatening because it generates a sense of vulnerability and of uncertainty about one's ability to maintain access to the means of survival. With the high unemployment rate in Chile, any sort of protest or demand for improved working conditions (salaries, contracts, hours, or vacations) could be overcome by firing the protesters. Hence, wages remained at inadequate levels. There was a small—almost nonexistent—margin for collective bargaining. Anything was better than losing one's job.

Furthermore, because of political restrictions, the workplace became the space of social integration. To lose it led to social, political, and economic marginalization. Unemployment, therefore, amounted to an individual and family trauma; the characteristics of this trauma varied according to social sector. Paradoxically, it was more feared by the middle classes and comfortable sectors, where more material resources had been accumulated to meet basic needs but where there may have been fewer emotional resources to cope with catastrophes. The lack of emotional resources probably stemmed from the belief common in the middle class that their level of education, ownership of property, and social position would protect them.

Unemployment continues to affect a large group of people who remain excluded from the economy and the society. The consequences of unemployment have been felt in the economic, social, and psychological spheres. At the economic level, unemployment has meant that adults cannot fulfill their role of providing the basic necessities for themselves and their dependents. Therefore, they contemplate a future of poverty and significant material limitations. Socially, their ties to others and to society are often broken. Psychologically, this situation affects the identity of individuals and their personal projects. At the emotional level, if the situation becomes permanent, frustration, anxiety, and depression become the norm.

Unemployment is experienced as a loss of status and a negation of the possibility of becoming fully integrated into society. Creativity, which is a product of interactions with a reality full of viable possibilities, decreases. A process of withdrawal begins because the supports that once made the individual's connections with society meaningful seem to be shattered.

The initial crisis originates from the breakdown—provoked by unemployment—of the established ways of relating to society, to the family, and to oneself. Social participation becomes difficult as there is no way of being integrated into society, and the impact is felt within the family structure. Increased efforts are required to satisfy basic needs. The problems accumulate. Individuals continue pursuing other possibilities in the very social and economic system that caused the unemployment. They seek alternatives, contact friends and acquaintances, read ads in the papers. Though failures mount, they keep trying. But they start to feel insecure.

At this point, it is common for them to become irritable, anxious, and insomniac, moody and intolerant of everyday or unforeseen situations. Almost any change is perceived as a new problem in a rising tide that threatens to destroy everything. Nobody knows what is going to happen or how it will all end. The waiting and the uncertainty about the future provoke anxiety.

Repeated failures lead to despair as time passes and the situation remains the same or deteriorates further. Outward symbols of identity begin to change. For instance, household effects are sold; the family moves; the state of their clothes, shoes, food indicates that conditions have changed.

Change has also taken place within. Feelings of inferiority, humiliation, shame, and devaluation proliferate. Individuals begin to blame themselves for what is happening. As the anxiety grows, they feel nervous and aggressive. Debts pile up and communication within the family deteriorates further. They then begin to isolate themselves. Ultimately, they adapt pathologically to an intolerable situation. Exhaustion, deterioration, sadness, a sense of inferiority, shame, hunger, dissatisfaction, family disorganization, lack of sleep and hope, anxiety, fear, and depression become pervasive. Eventually, individuals lose touch with the outside world. The process culminates in resignation, fatalism, and apathy.

FEAR AND REPRESSION

The fear and paralysis that result from experiencing repression can be described as a political reality with personal consequences. Many Chileans who led active and participatory lives suffered such overwhelming horror and loss that their attitude became one of waiting for their own catastrophe. Many lived in the expectation of being arrested, tortured, or executed, even though their level of participation did not necessarily warrant such an outcome. The constant anxiety tended progressively to confuse the analysis of real risks and of the threat to personal security. People devoted a major portion of their time to the attempt to control fear or to feel secure. With this goal, personal activities and social participation became limited. Avoiding thoughts of past and future, people developed a form of social amnesia.

Thus, for many, fear became the organizing structure of life. They feared to think about a past that had meaning and hope; they feared being identified as one of "them" and therefore to suffer their fate. At the same time they did not want to be seen as fearful people. Indeed, they became afraid of fear. Fear associated with anxiety and guilt interfered with the perception and analysis of reality. Such people emerged in what we may describe as a state of numbness. The future social and political consequences of the amnesia and numbness that we believe exist on a massive scale are incalculable.

This chapter was edited and translated by Patricia Weiss Fagen and Elena Cohen.

FIVE

Makers and Guardians of Fear

Controlled Terror in Uruguay

Juan Rial

STATE AND CIVIL SOCIETY: FROM CONSENSUS TO COERCION

Uruguay began to develop a welfare state early in the twentieth century. Even though this "caring" state benefited only the people of the capital city of Montevideo, its appearance produced the myth of a "Happy Uruguay."[1] This satisfied self-image extended well beyond the middle classes, which were both the product and the main beneficiaries of the state's policies. To a significant extent, state policies anticipated social demands and thus contributed to a sense of collective euphoria, to the spread of typical middle-class values, and to a peculiar mixture of utopian expectation and conservative conformity.

The hegemony of middle-class values in Uruguay as a whole dampened the reality of class conflict and domination, and promoted instead the role of the state as the economic and political caretaker of civil society. The outcome of this political project, based on the preemptive fulfillment of popular demands—which later became the basis of consensual politics—was the effective Battlistization of the population. By Battlistization I mean neither the political dominance of the faction led by José Battle y Ordóñez within the Colorado Party nor even Battle's imposition of his style of development over an entire period of Uruguayan politics, but rather the internalization by a great number of people (particularly by the middle classes that Battle supported) of a universalistic, tolerant, and lay ideology favorable to state paternalism.

By the late 1950s, Uruguay's prosperity—based on agricultural exports—came to an end. A protracted period of social and economic crisis ensued. Thereafter, the paternalistic state failed to fulfill its customary role as "protector of the people." It was forced to abandon its function of mediator and arbiter of social demands, and it frustrated the expectations of the poorer sectors of society. Class conflicts erupted over the calm surface of politics, and as these conflicts became increasingly visible, they prompted the gradual abandonment of consensual policies in favor of defensive and repressive measures.

The de-Battlistization of the state—though not of the Uruguayan people's worldview—intensified between 1968 and 1973. In hindsight, this period appears to have been a preparatory stage for authoritarianism. During this time administrative/repressive mechanisms replaced the former consensual relations between the state and civil society.

This devolution was perceived by part of the population, which still regarded the state as "the legal expression of civil society," as a contradiction between the performance of the state and the expectations of society.[2] In other words, there was a growing dissociation of the new functions of the state and the residual attitudes of society, a sort of cognitive dissonance that made the state appear no longer as the familiar extension of society but as a threatening "other." The estrangement of the state from society had as an important consequence the breakdown of traditional limits to what was considered politically permissible in Uruguay. The result was a collective feeling of insecurity coupled with a collective feeling of freedom from traditional legal and institutional constraints.

The breakdown of the old abiding certainties signaled the loss of the collective feeling of security and the start of a collective fear in civil society. It would be a mistake to regard the new situation as a mere episode: it was a historic turning point. Different social groups adapted to the new situation according to the various material and symbolic resources at their disposal. Migration for socioeconomic reasons was one of the early responses to the new framework of uncertainty. In just one decade the country lost 10 percent of its total population and nearly 20 percent of the economically active population.[3] It is impossible to gauge the number of potential leaders among this highly qualified young group that left Uruguay.

Other people sought a way out through radical action and radical ideologies. As a result, a number of political and social movements appeared that challenged the state and attempted to restructure it so as

to reduce the dissonance between reality and expectation. This radicalism with strong utopian undertones was particularly attractive to the
middle sectors. To them, the crisis of the welfare state meant the loss of
the basis for reproducing their material and social interests. Eventually,
this radicalism crystallized in the armed struggle undertaken by the
Movimiento de Liberación Nacional, the Tupamaros. As a response to
the Tupamaros a different kind of radical action also developed, this time
spawned by the armed forces and colored by their political culture. The
armed forces set out to defend their own idea of the state—a state that
was their source of income and also the source of their corporate identity. In pursuit of their respective faiths, each of these antagonistic groups
violated the very dogmas that they sought to preserve. The victors,
however, would turn their heresy into a new dogma. The struggle between these two groups of zealots—one in quest of utopia and the other
in defense of the status quo—contributed to the loss of the liberal
democratic freedoms enshrined in the Constitution. In this sense, an
anomic and frustrated modernity gave way to a perverse postmodernity
in Uruguay.[4]

The institution of a long series of repressive measures (tantamount to
a protracted coup) on the part of the authorities culminated in the
dissolution of Congress in June 1973. This political event signaled the
eclipse of the public sphere that had developed in Uruguay throughout
most of the century. And without an open public sphere, the private
sphere so cherished by the bourgeoisie was left unprotected. The blurring of the public/private distinctions that characterize democratic society left each of these spheres vulnerable to an invasion by the other.[5]

The authoritarian regime installed in 1973 went through different
political phases. The first stage was characterized by intense political
repression. The second was a "foundational" stage, a period of deepening changes in the role and the ideology of the state. The arbitrating role
of the state was abandoned, and *battlismo* was blamed for its failures.

The national-security state attempted to substitute for the old (vertical) clientelism—a grouping of dependents under the social and economic patronage of power holders—a new horizontal type. It sought to
redefine political certainty as military security. In contrast to the Battlist
state, the new dictatorial state did not seek to maintain a tutelar relationship with the middle sectors or with the organized working class. Instead, it opted to protect some marginal sectors of society—the lum-
penproletariat that had been a traditional reserve pool for the
recruitment of military personnel. These political pariahs henceforth

found a voice through the spokesmen of the armed forces. Thus, a great number of new soldiers were recruited,[6] and there was a marked improvement in the welfare benefits of military personnel and their families.[7] As Marx's analysis of French politics had anticipated, in Uruguay marginal social sectors were used to impose a new Bonapartism on radicalized middle classes. The new system projected an image of a paternalistic and popular army and beamed this image at marginal sectors of Montevideo and provincial cities, which now replaced the traditional middle sectors as the main beneficiaries of state policies. The middle class was left bereft of state protection and was forced to seek new channels of influence. It found these channels in limited clientelistic practices that paradoxically perverted the original designs of the armed forces, so much so that the armed forces were forced to publicly disavow the expectation that civil service jobs or state contracts required the prior sponsorship of high-ranking officers.

Hence, the combination of terror and rewards gave a different meaning to welfare traditions. It was no longer the state as a whole but the apparatus of the armed forces that became the point for both material and symbolic dispensations. A new signifying order emerged; a new map of hopes and fears was drawn.

THE LOSS OF CIVIL LIBERTIES

By the late 1960s the use of the Medidas Prontas de Seguridad (Prompt Security Measures), a sort of limited state of emergency, began to increase as a result of the government's failure to manage conflict. These measures, envisioned by Article 168 of the Constitution, allowed the government to detain people without trial. The detainees were given the option of leaving the country.

Repression entailed a significant degree of arbitrariness and "creativity" on the part of the police.[8] In 1970, after a wave of left-wing violence, the government resorted to another emergency measure, Article 31 of the Constitution. It allowed the executive, with prior approval of Congress, to carry out arrests and household searches without court warrants, to censor the press, to open mail, and to wiretap communications. Gradually, the barriers erected against the intimidation and abuse of citizens by the state were removed.

Three important measures prepared the ground for the establishment of an authoritarian state based on fear. On April 15, 1972, as a result of attacks by leftist urban guerrillas, Congress declared the State of Internal

War. Thereafter, acts of sedition were tried by military tribunals, which were not organized as true courts of justice. A new State Security Act passed in July 1972 further restricted the civil rights of individuals. In early 1973, the Law of General Education was passed; it imposed repressive measures in primary and secondary schools. Despite its stern intentions, this law was regarded as insufficient by military hardliners.

A harsh new phase of authoritarianism began in June 1973. Soon after the dissolution of Congress, the main labor federation, the Convención Nacional de Trabajadores, was declared illegal. This measure was followed by an attempt to pass legislation regulating union affairs. Then the state university was taken over by the government on October 28. In attacking the labor unions and the university, the dictatorship sought to neutralize two crucial centers of opposition.

The regime combined a number of devices in order to impose its views. The armed forces and the police launched a propaganda campaign vaunting the defeat of guerrillas, of communism, and, in the end, of any opposition.[9] A government office with the Orwellian name of National Center of Public Relations sought to project a positive image of the regime and to portray it as revolutionary. It declared 1975 the Año de la Orientalidad (something like "the year of Uruguayanhood"), and the government sought to whip up popular enthusiasm, but the campaign was met with silence and apathy.

The National Security Doctrine enforced in Uruguay was a package of military, police, and economic measures that greatly increased the uncertainty and vulnerability of the population. For instance, a decree issued in 1975 centralized all educational policy in the hands of a single ministry, which imposed strict ideological control over the content of courses and also dismissed large numbers of teachers.

In 1977, an institutional act allowed the arbitrary dismissal of public employees, who had hitherto been protected by an elaborate tenure system. It also instituted a special Certificate of Qualification for Public Employment, which was extended to the private sector as well. These certificates classified the entire population according to ideological positions.

An extensive spying and information network undergirded the police state. It involved the close surveillance of certain people, such as activists, detainees, their relatives, and their acquaintances.[10] The reputation of this network was more formidable than its actual extent and performance.

THE FRAMEWORK OF FEAR

By executive decree dated August 15, 1972, President Juan María Bordaberry commissioned the army high command to transform a former "model" prison into a detention center for those convicted of crimes of subversion. The establishment was ironically known as Libertad (after the name of a small village nearby). Its official designation was Military Detention Center No. 1. In February 1973, a second detention center was created to house female political prisoners. Shortly before its establishment, the army high command had created the Women's Military Police as the force in charge of female inmates. These two prisons became the emblematic centers of a new system of administered fear.

The detention centers were "total institutions" of a special kind.[11] The treatment of political inmates differed from that of ordinary criminals. As Michel Foucault has pointed out, ordinary criminals are negatively integrated into the system, whereas political dissidents seek to replace the established order with a new and different one.[12] For this reason, Uruguayan dissidents were isolated. The decision to isolate them was important because, in the past, mixing political with ordinary prisoners had resulted in the political conversion of some ordinary convicts.

The special prisons were part of a larger network of institutionalized repression and intimidation aimed at specialized publics and at the population at large. Fear functioned like a complex architectural construct—like an edifice with mutually supporting vaults and arches, foundations, reinforcements, and crowning points.[13] On the one hand, there were measures designed to terrorize dissidents, to neutralize and destroy them.[14] On the other, the regime attempted to manipulate the fear of marginal sectors of the population and to draft them as guardians of the dissidents. The special military prisons brought all these tactics together in a universe of discipline and punishment that radiated out toward the population at large.

The special prison had several functions, of which the prime one was to destroy the inmate as an individual. The second was to experiment with new forms of punishment. The third was to train the staff of guardians. The last and perhaps the most important function was to disseminate fear among the general population.

To destroy the prisoner as an individual meant making him or her a person different from the one who entered the institution. It was not just a matter of driving prisoners to madness or of seeking from them the most abject of submissions—collaboration. In fact, such a goal was hard to attain with captives imbued with strong values and commitments and was successful in only a limited number of cases. In the end, what was effective, from the standpoint of the agents of repression, was the "annihilation of the enemy" through the perversion of their own mechanisms of defense.

The task that all prisoners had when entering the institution was to keep themselves unchanged—that is, to keep intact their ideas, interests, and ways of life. This process was favored by the prison: it made the prisoners remain suspended in time, fixed in their own identities, which became crystallized and sclerotic. This tactic was a perverse but efficient device to isolate them from life outside the prison. If prisoners were eventually set free, their behavior would be different and abnormal and would serve as an intimidating example to fellow citizens. In those years, a common popular expression was "Fulano salió muy rayado" ("So-and-so came out nuts").

How was this process carried out? The prison regulations[15] were to a large extent those applicable to soldiers,[16] while others were drawn from ordinary prisons. The regulations also mixed rules designed for maximum-security prisons with those developed in concentration camps.[17] The treatment of political prisoners was often not very different from that of ordinary inmates. But the difference in their social backgrounds made the whole situation more painful for the political prisoners. The military forms of treatment sometimes applied to civilian political prisoners involved a high degree of degradation in areas such as service and food privileges.

Torture was widely used. This fact is well documented in numerous denunciations.[18] Torture took the form of continual harassment of prisoners,[19] of special punitive treatment of some of them (the "hostages"),[20] and, above all, of a systematic attack on the individual psyche. A journalist who had himself been a former inmate wrote in the Colorado Party weekly *Opinar* during a visit to a military prison at the moment of its closing in March 1985:

> A visit to this place cannot give an idea of what was going on here. The buildings are functional, the prison cells well ventilated, and the flower beds are in bloom. The main thing for the prison authorities was to keep the inmate in a permanent state of insecurity. He was periodically forced to move from cell to cell and was sanctioned regardless of his being at fault. . . . The regulations were enforced with complete arbitrariness and the inmate was never certain of what constituted an offense.[21]

Defined as a psychiatric prison, Libertad was, according to statements by former inmates, not a place of confinement and rehabilitation but a center for psychological destruction.

Fifty inmates died in prison or shortly after being released, several of them by committing suicide. About a third suffered from digestive disorders. The cancer rate among inmates was extremely high. Eighty percent resorted to tranquilizers. These consequences and the fact that the prisoners were used as guinea pigs for dangerous drugs clearly indicate that the regime's main objective was the destruction of prisoners, especially their psychological breakdown. In the words of a former inmate:

> The mechanisms for destruction are subtle. They are masked behind the appearance of satisfactory physical, material, and hygienic conditions of the prison. That is why it is difficult for the delegations of the International Red Cross to understand what repression was like—that is, the inhuman conditions of the prison. They consist mainly of a systematic and prolonged psychological pressure sustained over many years. It is the same effect as that of the drop of water hollowing a stone. It is difficult for someone who did not have a direct experience to imagine to what extent a person can deteriorate by being insulted, humiliated, and by the repeated banging of your cell window day and night over ten years.[22]

The aim of such treatment was to induce a state of permanent insecurity and hence a continuous tension and mental instability. The prisoners were made to lose all temporal and spatial references to the outside world. This fact reinforced a view widely held outside the prisons that many of the inmates were "completely crazy." Such alleged craziness served in turn to "explain" their previous behavior.

The prisoners' resistance to this treatment was to safeguard their psychological and physical integrity as much as possible. Their strategies varied according to their social background, their previous experience, and their past political activities. The struggle to maintain an identity in the face of repression was conveyed by such acts as painting birds' eyes when birds, regarded as a symbol of resistance, were a forbidden motif.[23] Those who had a clear vision of their lives after release resisted better than those who did not have such a vision.[24]

The use of new, experimental forms of repression (the second function of special prisons) deflected the international bad press that would have been provoked by a policy of purely physical punishment. Such open and brutal forms of repression had been carried out and even publicly defended by the authorities in Argentina.[25] As a result, the Argentine regime was condemned and isolated. By contrast, statements such as the ones uttered by the former head of repression in the province of Buenos Aires, General Ramón Camps, in which he adamantly defended extreme repression, have no equivalent in Uruguay, even though the agents of repression were ready and willing to act in a similar fashion.[26] Traditional "hard" methods like murder were occasionally used, but the number of disappearances was low in Uruguay: no more than twenty cases have been documented. However, 200 Uruguayan dissidents disappeared in Argentina as a result of the joint operation of the repressive forces of both countries.

In a country where the armed forces had been an isolated segment of an otherwise tolerant society, the treatment of civilians as low-ranking military personnel were normally treated was a humiliating experience. The combination of such treatment, outright torture, and the imposition of punishment usually reserved for repeat offenders facilitated the neutralization of individuals deemed dangerous by the regime and intimidated the rest of the population through the more-or-less intentional publicity that was given to these practices.

Because political prisoners had a higher-than-average intellectual level, it was possible for the jailers to impose severe hardships on them by withholding information and preventing them from studying. For the common criminal and the army private these are generally matters of little significance and would hardly be considered harsh punishment or torture. But, like the victims of Nazism, many of the jailed dissidents would rather have chosen "a terrible end" than face what they considered an "endless terror."[27]

The third important function of special prisons was to train the military personnel to deal with the enemies of "national security." At the entrance of Libertad prison a sign stated, "You are here to obey" (which was reminiscent of other notorious slogans from the past, like "Work liberates," which were posted at the gates of German concentration camps). The goal was to transform not only the inmates but the guards as well by making them aware of their capacity to destroy people who ranked higher on the social scale than they did. This goal was achieved without resorting to specialized personnel. Instead regular military cadres were trained in the punitive management of political prisoners. As a sign inside Libertad prison stated, "The task is to keep the inmates in security," which meant not to protect them but to maintain a state of constant alert against them.

The guardian soldiers thus learned to carry out police functions with a marked political character. They were taught not to observe and enforce the law but to keep their victims outside the protection of the law and to make the rest of the population aware of this terrible power. In this limbo where prisoners were kept, arbitrariness was the only norm. The need to motivate soldiers to be ready for action made it necessary to produce "visible" enemies, and these were the prison inmates who, in addition, were available for experimental "treatment."

The intentional leak of information on life inside the prisons served the fourth, and perhaps most important, function of repression—namely, to make the rest of the population afraid of the authorities, whose power seemed to have no limits. In this instance, perhaps the regime's success was more significant than many are willing to concede today, after the end of the dictatorship. As Senator Hugo Batalla put it: "People have to get used to living in democracy. Do you know which is the worst of all jails? Fear, and I feel that many people act with fear still today, even though they tell themselves they have lost it. Their incidental radicalism has not erased the fear they have carried inside for so many years."[28]

Every night at eight o'clock a joint communiqué from the armed forces was issued, preceded by martial music. It made everyone aware of the authorities' extensive powers of surveillance and repression. As time went by, this technique of propaganda was used only sporadically. Also, from early on, news was leaked about the condition of some political prisoners, confirming their "madness." This was a way of making the population pass a retrospective judgment on the Tupamaros, which could be summarized in expressions such as "They were all crazy" and "I didn't have anything to do with it." In the same way permission to collect bags of food and clothing for prisoners helped disseminate frightful information about conditions in the prisons.

Fear affected each social group, each class, in a different way. In varying degrees, it reached everybody and made people aware of a state that had ceased to behave as a welfare system and had become a dreadful leviathan instead. The culture of fear spread outward from the prisons by at least two different class channels. For the lower and marginal classes, army privates were the main conduit of information about conditions in the prisons. People of higher social status, from industrial workers to the educated middle classes, were kept informed by relatives of the inmates. These communications conveyed knowledge of what could happen to those who opposed the regime. They were intended to convince potential opponents that terror had no limits and that for them there was a fate in store that could be worse than death.

In March 1985 the military prisons were closed down by an amnesty bill passed by Congress. The prisoners had not defeated the military. Neither had a popular struggle released them from jail. What produced their liberation was a pact negotiated by the elites. Popular mobilization influenced the tempo and the modalities of their liberation. But it was clear that the heart of the culture of fear would disappear only with a genuine transfer of power and the restoration of democracy. The system of prisons was only the most important link in a whole network of practices and institutions that supported a culture of fear.

THE EXTENT AND LIMITS
OF CONTROLLED TERROR

The culture of fear imposed by the authoritarian regime involved extending the hitherto recognized limits of fear as a normal effect of socialization to the individual and society. In particular, reference should be made to the collective feeling that was produced by the extension of those limits.[29] The combined effect of news censorship, economic exploitation, physical repression, and tight political control, which prevented any kind of collective activity, was the crystallization of three basic components of the culture of fear.

In the first place silence became the expression of profound and general distrust. As Ximena Barraza put it: "Silence is a kind of self-defense: it conceals murder, it conceals knowledge. Silence is a strategy of survival in a repressive society."[30] Although there were only a few explicit norms regulating the written press, radio, and television, "suggestions," pressures, and certain events or deeds acted as effective agents of censorship. Indeed, self-censorship was more effective and insidious than censorship. The majority of the population was forced into neutrality, as expressed in statements such as "Don't get involved," "I didn't have anything to do with it," and even the harsher expression recalled by Guillermo O'Donnell, "What the ——— do I care?"[31]

Silence was an effective form of self-protection, but it imposed a heavy toll on everyday life. It required isolation and privacy, which were the second components of the culture of fear. The suppression of political activities was accomplished through direct repression and also through devious, clandestine means, completely outside the law. Judges acted no longer as arbiters but as punitive agents. Repressive law became a sham legality, ad hoc and retroactive. The only rule of thumb for survival was "from home to work and from work to home in silence."

Three conditions of isolation had to be met for a dictatorial regime to endure: a weakening of social solidarity, the depoliticization of the state and its transformation into a technocratic entity, and the establishment of a monopoly on political discourse. However, at this very point, the limits of terror became apparent. The enforced privacy and confinement of social activity to a small nucleus of family and friends allowed these circles to become barriers against terror. Despite the fact that it held a complete monopoly on public discourse, the repressive state failed to promote new forms of identity. Although it controlled the ideology of education, it failed to promote the production of knowledge. As a result of these purely negative strategies, citizens were able to create pockets of resistance.

For a majority, the authoritarian years were a period of nonexistence as citizens. In Bruno Bettelheim's terminology, it was "social autism" as generalized behavior.[32] Adaptation to extreme repression required people to show a complete lack of will. At the same time, it required a certain degree of schizophrenia, a selective loss of memory about risky events of the past. An impoverished personal and social life was the price of survival. The citizenry learned to live on probation. Simulation and dissimulation were rampant. Through the pedagogy of terror people learned to classify themselves according to various gradations of shame for past beliefs and actions. The process has many parallels in historic cases of enforced religious conversion such as that which took place in Spain at the end of the fifteenth century.

Those citizens who did not emigrate became internal exiles, the permanent victims of witch-hunts. Internal exile became a phenomenon as important as exile itself.[33] Real expatriates could overcome fear in distant lands. For the internal exiles, fear was ever present.

In addition to silence and privacy, the third component of the culture of fear was a sense of hopelessness. It involved the feeling of being trapped in time, with no possibility for action, a feeling that there was room for only inadequate individual solutions to collective problems, a feeling that not even those who belonged to the dominant in-group could be safe.

With the passing of time, hopelessness would recede because of weaknesses and mistakes on the part of the regime. The plebiscite of November 1980 allowed the population to express its rejection of the government and started a process of reversing the terror.

In general, hopelessness was not so much a function of violence as a consequence of the loss of a clear perception of the limits of fear.

Hopelessness affected certain social sectors more than others, as did the belief that hopelessness could be reversed. For instance, the middle sectors were the first to engage in campaigns to overcome fear.

Despite the thorough nature of control and intimidation, terror was limited for several reasons. In the first place, a capitalist society requires a minimum of secrecy and inviolability in order to operate, and this requirement creates some sanctuaries for potential opposition. Second, the armed forces lacked a long-term project for the organization of society—that is, a sense of genuine alternatives to the status quo. Third, the armed forces, although they were the main agents of repression, had a tradition of deference toward civil society. And finally, the cost of maintaining the authoritarian regime in a hostile international environment became high. These processes acted as brakes on the spread and consolidation of terror. True, after years of repression, many Uruguayans internalized fear and have since lived with it as a new part of their existence. This sequel represents a certain triumph for the authoritarians, the makers and purveyors of fear. In the end, direct fear—intimidation on the part of the authorities—was brought to an end. But its memory lingers as the fear of fear itself.

NOTES

1. See Carlos Real de Azúa, *El impulso y su freno* (Montevideo: EBO, 1964).

2. Ibid., and Carina Perelli, *El proyecto ideológico battlista. Notas* (Montevideo: CIESU, 1985).

3. Cesar Aguiar, *Un país de emigración* (Montevideo: EBO, 1983).

4. See chapter 14.

5. For discussion of a similar development in Argentina, see Juan E. Corradi, "The Mode of Destruction: Terror in Argentina," *Telos* 54 (winter 1982–83).

6. Official figures show an increase in personnel attached to the Ministry of Defense, from 21,269 in 1970 to 38,545 in 1978, and an increase in military and police personnel attached to the Ministry of the Interior, from 20,854 in 1970 to 25,718 in 1978. See *Anuario estadístico del Uruguay*, 1970–78, fasc. 10.

7. Benefits were dispensed through the health services of the armed and police forces, which covered some 300,000 persons, or 10 percent of the population.

8. See Walter Benjamin, *Para una crítica de la violencia* (Mexico City: Premia, 1982).

9. On this offensive, see Ministerio del Interior, *Siete meses de lucha antisubversiva* (Montevideo, 1972), and Junta de Comandantes en Jefe, *Las fuerzas armadas al Pueblo Oriental,* especially Vol. 1: *La subversión* (Montevideo, 1976). A summary version appears in R. Burgueno and J. J. Pomoli, *La experiencia uruguaya,* 2d ed. (Montevideo: Centro Militar, 1984).

10. See Edison Rijo's column in *El día* (Montevideo), 31 March 1985, p. 5.

11. In the sense described by Erving Goffman, *Internados. Ensayo sobre la situación de los enfermos mentales* (Buenos Aires: Amorrortu, 1971).

12. Michel Foucault, *Vigilar y castigar* (Mexico City: Siglo XXI, 1979).

13. See R. Ruyer, *L'utopie et ses utopies* (Paris: PUF, 1950).

14. See Bruno Bettelheim, *Surviving and Other Essays* (New York: Random House, Vintage Books [1952], 1980).

15. Decree 686/972 of 24 October 1972 and Decree 503/973 of 3 July 1973 established norms for the control of prisoners in two of the most important detention centers.

16. Reglamento General de Servicio 21 of the Uruguayan Army.

17. See Decree 686/972, articles 89 ff.

18. See the testimony of Daniel Rey Piuma and others in H. Garcia Rivas, *Los crímenes del Río de la Plata: Memorias de un ex-torturador* (Buenos Aires: El Cid, 1984).

19. Documented in the journal *La hora*, nos. 220 through 223 (23 March 1985).

20. See *Informe de madres y familiares de procesados por la Justicia Militar*, April 1984, reprinted in the weekly *Las bases* (Montevideo), no. 20 (17 March 1985).

21. *Opinar*, no. 206 (March 1985), 15.

22. Testimony of J. Nieto, in Madres y Familiares de Procesados por la Justicia Militar, *Las cárceles militares del Uruguay. Informe de salud* (Montevideo, 17 August 1984). See also "Cuando la salud es luchar," interviews of prisoners, in *Las bases* (Montevideo), no. 23 (7 April 1985).

23. *Los ojos de los pájaros* is a film directed by Gabriel Auer in 1982; it portrays the situation in Libertad prison.

24. See *Las bases* (Montevideo), nos. 20 (17 March 1985) and 22 (31 March 1985).

25. See Juan E. Corradi, *The Fitful Republic* (Boulder, Colo. and London: Westview Press, 1985), and Guillermo O'Donnell, "La cosecha del miedo," *Nexos* (Mexico City) 6, no. 6 (1983).

26. Ramón Camps, *El caso Timerman. Punto final* (Buenos Aires: Tribuna Abierta, 1982), and Ramón Camps, *El poder de la sombra* (Buenos Aires: ROCA Producciones, 1983).

27. E. K. Bramstedt, *Dictatorship and Political Police: The Technique of Control by Fear* (New York: Oxford University Press, 1945), passim.

28. Quoted in *Jaque* (Montevideo), 15 March 1985, p. 7.

29. See Jacques Le Goff and Pierre Nora, *Faire l'histoire. Nouveaux problèmes* (Paris: Gallimard, 1974).

30. Ximena Barraza (Paulina Gutiérrez), "Notas sobre a vida cotidiana numa ordem autoritaria." *Araucaria* (Santiago de Chile), no. 10 (1980): 28.

31. Guillermo O'Donnell, *¿Y a mi qué mierda me importa? Notas sobre la sociabilidad en Argentina y Brasil* (Buenos Aires: CEDES, 1985).

32. Bettelheim, *Surviving*.

33. See Carina Perelli, "Sobreviviendo. Memoria del inxilio" (Montevideo, 1985, mimeographed).

SIX

Gender, Death, and Resistance

Facing the Ethical Vacuum

Jean Franco

In her book *The Body in Pain: The Making and Unmaking of the World,* Elaine Scarry argues that pain destroys the sense of self and world and is "experienced spatially as either the contraction of the universe down to the immediate vicinity of the body or as the body swelling to fill the entire world."[1] Intense pain not only "unmakes" the world but destroys language: "As the content of one's world disintegrates, so the content of one's language disintegrates as the self disintegrates, so that which would express and project the self is robbed of its source and its subject."[2] For Scarry, pain has no gender, and it is incommunicable. Yet the "unmaking of the world," certainly as it was experienced in the Southern Cone in the 1970s, had different implications for men and for women. In this chapter, I explore these differences by examining both the process of "unmaking" and the reverse—the creative "remaking" of the world both in literature and art and in movements such as that of the Mothers of the Plaza de Mayo.

THE END OF THE HERO

What distinguished the military governments that came into power in Brazil, Uruguay, Argentina, and Chile in the late 1960s and early 1970s was not simply repression but a more ambitious project—that of extirpating revolutionary politics and abolishing heroic charisma. To this end, thousands of people were killed, imprisoned, placed in death camps, and tortured. This project was remarkable not only for its scale but also for the behaviorist ideology that underlay what was virtually a project of population and mind control.

The notion that personalities could be altered by modifying behavior was not, of course, confined to the Southern Cone; it informed the treatment of patients in psychiatric wards in the Soviet Union, and during the 1960s in the United States brain operations (lobotomy) and electrical stimulation were used to alter the behavior of criminals who were supposedly unredeemable by other means. Experiments in mind control, such as those of José M. R. Delgado, perhaps gained some currency because of CIA interest in their political application.[3] Delgado himself affirmed that it was "accepted medical practice to try and modify the antisocial or abnormal reactions of mental patients" and advocated electrical stimulation of the brain as a selective and powerful way of achieving this goal.[4] These experiments were well funded during the 1960s but met with widespread opposition in the United States.

The use of electric current as a technique for breaking down resistance and altering behavior in a radical and permanent way links the torture methods used in the 1960s and 1970s to mind-control experiments. Faced with the problem that large sectors of their populations supported revolutionary politics, the military governments of the Southern Cone embraced a politics of repression that depended not only on large-scale slaughter but also on the application of powerful deterrents to the resurgence of revolutionary politics. The usual police methods of beatings and brutalization were replaced by a far more systematic apparatus of secret camps and torture by electroshock, sometimes in the presence of doctors and psychiatrists. This apparatus was accompanied by an attempt to destroy the prisoners' sense of self by referring to them by number rather than by name, by denying all access to and communication with the outside world, by keeping prisoners chained to their beds or in confined spaces, and by using a variety of disorientation techniques—blindfolds and hoods, mock executions.[5] The *picana*, or electric prod, was used for extracting information, for making the prisoner betray his or her comrades. But it did not replace other forms of brutalization and terror. Women prisoners were raped, and their children were put up for adoption by military families. In the camps, there were systematic beatings and constant petty humiliation.

In such circumstances, there were no opportunities for exemplary heroism or grand gestures. In Uruguay confinement was often solitary;

for years prisoners were denied any human communication.[6] In Argentina and Chile every effort was made to reduce the prisoner to a helpless, cringing mass dependent on the torturer for survival.

Although each country had its distinct methods, a certain similarity of techniques throughout the Southern Cone lends credence to the fact that methods were taught, routinized, and exported. We refer here to techniques of psychological as well as physical torture. Electric prods, first extensively used in Brazil, became an essential part of the torture routine in both Chile and Argentina. The rounding up of prisoners who then "disappeared" into secret camps created, among those left behind, an intolerable sense of uncertainty and anguish.[7] Sometimes the mutilated bodies of "terrorists" appeared on the streets and spread fear among the population.

The death camps were governed with a curious mixture of bureaucracy and sadism. The sordid bloodshed and torture were systematized, and euphemistic language that referred to various aspects of torture gave the barbarous proceedings a certain routineness and legitimacy. In Argentina, the torture chambers had their "managers" and "assistant managers." One victim described how the torturers outlined the rules before proceeding, explaining the exact voltage that would be given and assessing the possibility of permanent injury.[8] In Chile, torture was referred to as "a job"; an informer requested a transfer from the air force security force to the Dirección de Inteligencia Nacional because he hoped for better pay and a new car.[9] Prisoners were referred to as if they were merchandise. They became *paquetes* (Chile) or *trasladados* (Argentina). Jacobo Timerman perceptively noted the element of fantasy in this process, remarking that although torture sessions were conducted in sordid basements, the torturers "try to create a more sophisticated image of the torture sites, as if thereby endowing their activity with a more elevated status. Their military leaders encourage this fantasy, and the notion of important sites, exclusive methods, original techniques, novel equipment, allows them to present a touch of distinction and legitimacy to the world."[10]

In Nazi Germany, Aryanism provided the "religious" element that justified extermination of the Jews. In Chile and Argentina, the dirtier the methods employed, the more high-flown and "Christian" the public rhetoric became. Admiral Emilio Massera, for example, once stated that "we all act out of love, which is the basis of our religion."[11] There was even a torturer who offered his victim a medal of Our Lady and, on her release, sent her a copy of a torturer's prayer. Among other things, the prayer requested Our Lord to make the torturer's hand "accurate so that the shot will hit its mark and put charity in my heart so that I fire without hatred."[12]

GENDER AND TORTURE

Though pain has no gender, sexual difference became important in the torture chamber. Men were deliberately feminized; they were taunted about their manhood, about the size of their penises, or, if they were Jews, about circumcision. Electric current was applied to the testicles. The "masculinity" of the torturers was affirmed by their absolute power to inflict pain. This power was often reinforced by the totemic use of animal nicknames—tiger, jaguar, puma, gorilla—and by initiation ceremonies of induction into the group. One of the few descriptions of this initiation is a Chilean document, *Confesiones de un agente de seguridad,* in which an ex-agent describes how a selected group was taken to see the torture of a woman prisoner. His description is laconic: "They applied the current, and she cried out. She was the fiancée of a young man who was a militant in the MIR [Movimiento de Izquierda Revolucionaria]. I don't remember exactly what current [was] used. They were testing us to see whether we would be taken on permanently in the service."[13] The most important ritual of incorporation was, however, the "blood pact"—that is, participation in violent actions, typically disemboweling or mutilation.

During torture sessions in Argentina, there were jokes, laughter, music, and sadistic excitement. One prisoner described one such orgy of violence: "It was a Dantesque scene since we were handcuffed and blindfolded, and we had no idea where the blows were coming from. We fell one on top of the other, hearing cries of pain and horror. I was aware that others hit and kicked us and lifted us by the hair when we fell to the ground."[14] There are many such accounts of these moments of exaltation, when the torturer felt as if he were God. This situation of absolute power has been explored in literary texts, notably Griselda Gambaro's play *El campo* and Elvira Orphée's novel *La última conquista de El Ángel,* although both were written before the military government came to power.[15]

Is there something about the social construction of masculinity that accounts for the fact that the torturers were male, or is it simply the possession of certain kinds of power (in the military and the police) that makes them engage in these activities? The answer does not lie in some essentialist opposition between the aggressive male and the caring female. Rather, it has to do with long-standing social practices that contribute to male and female identity.[16] The military governments inherited a long tradition in which the power to inflict pain was taken as proof of masculinity. The rituals that bonded many male groups (whether boarding-school rites of passage, military drills, or group sexual experiences) traditionally reduced the other to the status of passive victim, to a body to be acted on or penetrated.

Hundreds of literary accounts from all over the world associate such rituals with an evil other who must be eliminated—a tribal enemy, a ferocious animal, or simply an effeminate schoolfellow or a misfit in the regiment: Robert Musil's *Young Törless,* Rudyard Kipling's *Stalky and Co.,* Mario Vargas Llosa's *Time of the Hero,* to name only a few. These casual rituals of cruelty, which have marked the adolescence of many young men, even in liberal societies, were formalized and institutionalized in the death camp. Hernán Valdés's *Diary of a Chilean Concentration Camp,* which is one of the most eloquent accounts of day-to-day prison life, again and again stresses the macho rituals of the camp personnel. An ex-soldier, describing the way his brother was tortured for not being an obedient soldier, commented, "He came out half crazy, the fucker, but we've all got to learn what it takes to be a man." A prisoner who had been reduced to passivity by torture was still subjected to ritual sexual humiliation, which included electric charges applied to the anus. When Valdés was taken to be tortured, one of the first questions was "Are you a queer?" There were constant sexual references during the torture, both to Valdés's alleged homosexuality (which the torturers associated with the fact that he was a writer) and to the supposed unbridled sexuality of his girlfriend. When Valdés emerged from the torture chamber, having been subjected to electroshock and beating, he was first of all concerned with his sexual organs. "I didn't dare look at my penis. I was scared to."[17]

The polarization of masculine/feminine, active/passive was taken as natural not only by the military but by other armed groups fighting the military government. Interviews with women of the Tupamaros movement in Uruguay make it clear that women were never completely accepted as militants; if they proved themselves in combat, they were referred to as butches.[18] Thus the militant was defined as masculine in the socially constructed sense of the word, and women militants became pseudomales. Manuel Puig's novel, *The Kiss of the Spider Woman,* eloquently explores the confrontation between an ascetic and puritanical male militant, obsessed with maintaining his bodily and spiritual integrity, and a homosexual prisoner who lives in a fantasy world. In this novel, the militant's primary obsession—to withstand torture like a man—blinds him to the pleasures of play and fantasy so much that he cannot understand that personal emancipation is an important part of political emancipation. The fact that his opposite is a homosexual and not a woman underscores the fact that fear of the feminine extends to men who supposedly adopt the female attributes of caring and feeling.[19]

The supreme model of the male hero was undoubtedly Che Guevara, whose Bolivian diary prescribes an ideal of asceticism and exemplary behavior.[20] Clearly such behavior was effective only if it was publicly known, yet publicity for heroic exploits was precisely what the death camp was designed to eliminate. The supreme horror for the militant was that the death would go unnoticed or would simply become fodder for the enemy propaganda mill. Those who did talk (but were not full-fledged informers) became literally abject—that is, they were thrust out of any possible community, having betrayed their friends or group.

For prisoners whose whole life structure had been attacked, suicide or madness seemed the only alternatives. Timerman longed for madness while recognizing that it would mean definitive impotence and a humiliation "greater than a kick on the behind from some voiceless, faceless stranger who leads you blindfolded, from your cell, stands you flat against the wall, gives you a kick in the ass, always in silence, then has you return to your cell with one of those delicate gestures suggested by the bejeweled hands of an El Greco painting." For Timerman, it was his Jewishness, "the mother tongue," that enabled him to resist, confirming his sense of identity and community and allowing him to express his pain without feeling emasculated.[21]

Yet abjection often forced male prisoners to live as if they were women, so that, for the first time, they came to understand what it meant to be constantly aware of their bodies, to be ridiculed and battered, and to find comfort in everyday activities like washing clothes or talking to friends.

Whereas the torture of men often presented them with the challenge to behave like a man and die or to become like a woman to survive, the treatment of women prisoners was rooted in sadistic fantasies. Some were raped; but more often women were beaten, stripped naked, and tortured with the *picana*. If they were pregnant, they were often beaten or given electroshock on the abdomen in an attempt to harm the fetus.[22] Women prisoners felt ashamed of speaking of their torture, and literary accounts of the torture of women do not always avoid crossing the fine line between description and pornography.[23] One example is Omar Rivabella's *Requiem for a Woman's Soul,* which, though structured as an exposé of the Argentine death camp, is in reality a sexual fantasy. The novel narrates the agony of a priest who has received some documents smuggled out of a death camp that turn out to be a first-person account written by one of his female parishioners of her torture and rape. Even though the narrative is obviously based on documentary sources, the author uses language that contributes to sadomasochistic fantasy. For example, the woman writes, "And I have seen the tender look in the eyes of my torturer as he talks about his daughter's poems while fondling my genitals." The giveaway here is the word *fondling,* which would hardly occur to a woman undergoing rape and torture or even remembering it.[24]

A rather different but equally misleading use of torture is encountered in Isabel Allende's popular novel *The House of the Spirits,* in which one of the women protagonists is tortured. One of her torturers is a perverted illegitimate offspring of her grandfather who is savoring revenge on the family.[25] The use of torture as a device that mystifies rather than illuminates is at best questionable.

In contrast, first-person accounts by people who underwent torture and rape are often laconic and euphemistic. Women in particular seemed to be ashamed of talking about their experiences; when recording the experiences for commissions on human rights, they merely stated that they were raped without attempting to describe the event.[26] In this light, texts that convey the horror of torture either for men or for women tend to be exceptions. Valdés's account is extraordinary for the detailed manner in which it records the alteration of personality through humiliation and beatings in the camp and for its description of what it is like to experience the *picana.* What Valdés describes is indeed a loss of manhood.

The other major testimonial is Alicia Partnoy's *The Little School,* which, in many ways, is strikingly different from Valdés's account. Valdés was a solitary person who was only occasionally able to empathize with other prisoners. Partnoy, however, found herself imprisoned with comrades, both men and women, and to the very frontiers of death she refused to allow herself or her fellow prisoners to be dehumanized. Forced to strip naked and sit under a leaking roof, Partnoy "felt as if the guards did not exist, as if they were just repulsive worms." Unlike Rivabella's narrator, she refuses to be a passive victim and constantly uses imagination to "remake" the world that the torturers are bent on destroying. When a comrade is hung upside down and naked in the same room, the naked body becomes the object of compassion. "Poor little Benja! Now he looks so helpless, naked, his ribs sticking out. I'm sure he's hungry. . . . I wish I could protect him. Just a kid!" Such metaphors of motherhood constantly pervade Partnoy's text, and her own resistance to torture is strengthened by constant reference to the baby daughter she had to leave behind when she was arrested. Her experience of motherhood also allows her to speak not only in her own first-person voice but in that of a pregnant woman who gave birth in the death camp before becoming one of the disappeared.[27]

Valdés's experience forced him to live like a woman, conscious for the first time in his life of every bodily function. Partnoy, however, clearly derives her strength and effectiveness from mothering. It sustains her during her torture and allows her to empathize with her fellow prisoners. Under torture, she reverts to childhood and hangs on to her identity by remembering a nonsense rhyme that she had once recited to her daughter:

> *Nobody know where he hides / nobody's seen him at home / but we hear him all the time / Rib-bit rib-bit Little Frog.*
> Daughter, dear, my tongue hurts and I can't say *rib-bit rib-bit;* even if I could, you wouldn't hear me. This little poem soothed you when you cried; you went to sleep listening to it. . . . I've repeated it for a whole day, but I still can't sleep. *Rib-bit rib-bit he sings on the roof.* . . . I won't see you again. . . . The electric prods on my genitals. . . . Trapped, like the little frog . . . *but we hear him all the time.* I told the torturers if they took me to the meeting place I would point to him; then, when I saw him I didn't do what I'd promised. Afterward, the electric prod again, and the blows, . . . harder: "Where is he?" But my child . . . *Rib-bit rib-bit.* . . . Where are you, my little girl?

After the torture, she is convulsed with fear of repetition.

> But when they come for me . . . to kill me next time. . . . No, please don't come. . . . I'm not an animal; . . . don't make me believe I'm an animal. . . . But that's not my scream. . . . That's an animal's scream. Leave my body in peace. I'm a little frog for my daughter to play with; . . . she'll soon be two years old and she'll learn the whole poem. . . . *We all hear him / Rib-bit rib-bit when it rains . . . rib-bit rib-bit.*[28]

Scarry declares that pain destroys language. Partnoy's account does not contradict this observation. The torturers reduce her speech to a babble, to a children's poem. Yet it is clear that the family (including the extended family of her comrades) provides her with the model that allows her both to survive and to maintain a sense of her own humanity and that of others even while experiencing pain.

SOCIAL DEATH

Despite the fact that the military constantly appealed to family values— the family, indeed, being one of the central concepts in their ideology— the holy war was carried out as an act of destruction against families. For the "terrorist family," there was no quarter and nobody—grandparents, children, mothers, priests, and nuns—could claim immunity. Moreover, the military governments were determined to wipe out the historical memory that allowed the idea of resistance to be passed from generation to generation. In many Latin American countries the family has tradi- tionally provided a protective network even to its politically aberrant members.

The military recognized that the family did not always reproduce the dominant values but also reproduced dissidence, hence the severity of their attack. Parents were tortured in front of children; children were put up for adoption by military families, where they could be brought up as proper patriots; the bodies of the disappeared were either destroyed or mutilated so that there would be no chance of the family's commemorat- ing its dead. In Chile prisoners were thrown into an unused furnace in Lonquen and buried alive. People seized by anonymous forces simply "disappeared"; their very existence was denied. And when relatives tried to claim them, they were told that they had fled the country or run off with somebody. In other words they became fictions without civil exis- tence or history. Yet, significantly, out of this massive "unmaking" came an imaginative remaking in which women were major actors.

As Michael Taussig has shown, the space of death (which is also the space of immortality, communal memory, and connections between generations) is particularly important as a site of struggle in the colo- nized areas of the world, and this struggle is of necessity ethical.[29] By attacking the family and destroying the home as a region of refuge, the military unwittingly unleashed powerful elements of resistance. The relation of mother and child proved far stronger than the threat of death. Meeting one another in fruitless visits to government offices, the mothers and the families of the disappeared constituted a space of memory that also became a counter to the public sphere. Movements such as the Mothers of the Plaza de Mayo in Argentina and the Families of the

Disappeared in Chile brought women to the fore at a time when political parties and political action were in abeyance, when there were few or no institutions that could mediate between the state and the individual. The lack of mediators was particularly evident in Argentina, where the Church, unlike the Chilean Church, did not stand up to the regime.

The loss of their children ejected these women from the protected circle of the home and threw them into a confrontation with the state, which had hitherto represented itself as the protector of women and children. A Chilean woman describes how disappearance changed her image of society from a relatively benign one to that of a "gray, dark fortress with closed doors and people who laconically replied, 'He hasn't been detained. There's no record of him.'" And she goes on:

> I had lived until then like any other Chilean from a family that had been useful and respectable, hard-working and honest members of society, and therefore felt entitled to appeal to the police or to the system of justice if anything happened to one of its members. I soon discovered that those who wore uniforms were enemies and that the judges administered justice in order to uphold "the established order."[30]

The political effectiveness of the mothers derived, first, from the fact that they were not intimidated by the threat of death. In the words of Hebe de Bonafini, when her children disappeared, she felt "tigers growing inside me."[31] Anger drove out fear. And, second, the abjection of women in Argentine society became a positive value because the government chose to dismiss them as *locas* (madwomen) rather than putting an end to their demonstrations. Nobody, the military believed, could possibly take seriously a group of old, tired, and obviously crazy women.

The women themselves underwent a process of conversion and change. No longer were they afraid to demonstrate publicly. They had been cast out of normal society so there was no need to act normally. But this ostracism also led them to breach the separation between public and private on which most political movements had been predicated. And they breached it most effectively by taking over public space—the Plaza de Mayo in Buenos Aires, which symbolized civil space. Marysa Navarro points out:

> Plaza de Mayo is in the heart of downtown Buenos Aires. In its center is a small pyramid erected to commemorate the beginnings of the independence movement on May 25, 1810. The large rectangular space is dominated by the Casa Rosada, the Pink House, Argentina's White House and seat of the Interior Ministry. Other buildings surrounding the Plaza are the Cabildo, the

cold colonial town meeting hall; the Cathedral where Argentina's Liberator, General José de San Martín lies; the National Bank and other government offices.[32]

The whole area is thus charged with references to independence and democracy. In Chile, women chained themselves to the closed Congress building.[33]

In thus going public women appropriated public space, though to do so they had to make a conscious effort to overcome fear and shame. De Bonafini described the determination she needed to go to the Plaza de Mayo every Thursday, especially after the disappearance of the movement's founder, Azucena Villaflor de Vicenti. These women had to struggle with fear as they smuggled the chains under their coats on the bus ride there.

Yet their courage brought personal transformation. De Bonafini states, "When one arrives at the Plaza, you feel big and strong because you feel that you are with your children. When there were just a few of us, in the beginning, we used to say, 'We don't feel so few, we feel that we are many because each of us is accompanied by the thousands of missing children.' "[34] And a Chilean woman describes her joy and satisfaction: "In the midst of it all, one feels happy to be doing something useful. I have never gone with any false illusions that this particular action will be the answer, since there has to be a process, some social change. But it is very significant that despite the undeniable fear, one feels that each comrade, man and woman, feels this sublime thing that we have to do."[35]

Whereas the male bonding of the death camps was based on well-established rites through which masculinity had traditionally been confirmed, women's solidarity had no such precedents because women's domestic experience was serialized—that is, it was not lived as a group experience. Solidarity had to be achieved by conscious effort, by overcoming fear not in the service of death but in the service of life and continuity. It also meant the adoption of a public self in the face of ridicule.

DISPLAYING PAIN

The Mothers of the Plaza de Mayo and the Families of the Disappeared in Chile have long-term influences beyond their immediate political effectiveness. Even though, as some critics have argued, the Mothers of the Plaza de Mayo lost some of their political strength with redemocratization, the movement has permanently affected the way we think of culture and politics. Michel de Certeau has described those tactics, which come out of everyday life; they are not great gestures made to posterity but nevertheless appropriate official language and public space, and deny exclusive legitimacy to the status quo.[36] To begin with, the mothers turned the intimidating function of the city under the police state into an alternative public sphere, transforming the Plaza de Mayo into a theater in which the entire population, whether actually present or not, became an audience and a witness to loss. The names of the disappeared were even written on peso notes that circulated throughout the city. The women did not shout slogans; they publicly displayed photographs of their children in eloquent silence. By refusing to accept that their children were terrorists, and hence outside society, the mothers of Argentina, Chile, and El Salvador were able to interrupt the dominant discourse.

The mothers also "remade" the world, restoring to individual lives a sense of significance and meaning. Their symbols were often drawn from life; the flowers used by Chilean women showed their faith in the germination of new life; the white scarves initially worn by the Mothers of the Plaza de Mayo for purposes of recognition were in sharp contrast to the black of mourning. But above all it was the photograph, the homely snapshot, that played a central role. Photographs are often placed on graves in Latin America, and this act prevents the conversion of death into an abstraction. The photographs carried by the Mothers of the Plaza de Mayo became proof of existence. Often taken on family outings, sometimes blurred and badly focused, they silently emphasized the fact that these people were not monsters but young men and women whose absence had to be accounted for. The military had tried to eliminate them from memory, but their images were turned into a commemoration; the public display was an eloquent reminder of an ethics based on collective memory and continuity.

In Chile, where the Families of the Disappeared was under the wing of the Catholic Church, religious ritual entered into the public demonstrations. It was also through the Church that women whose husbands had disappeared or had been imprisoned began to make *arpilleras*, scraps of cloth sewn to burlap sacks depicting scenes of everyday life. In some of the first *arpilleras* the women hid messages to the outside world. This traditional woman's work not only provided an income for families in need but it also transmitted eloquent political statements that reached an international public.[37]

The Argentine mothers' movement encouraged the formation of similar movements in other parts of the world—for instance, in El Salvador and among Palestinians. But its impact has also been important in literature and accounts for the feminization of the whole notion of resistance. Marta Traba's novel *Conversación al sur* was one of the first to include the Plaza de Mayo demonstrations as a central episode. Juan Gelman, a leading militant in the Montonero movement, composed an "oratorio" in 1985, *La junta luz,* inspired by the Mothers of the Plaza de Mayo. In Chile, Carlos Zurita's *Canto a su amor desaparecido* was also dedicated to *la paisa* (the feminized country), to the Mothers of the Plaza de Mayo, to the Agrupación de familiares de los que no aparecen (the Association of Relatives of the Disappeared), to the torture, to the doves of love, and to America and Chile.[38]

The foregoing description might lead us to conclude that women are not only different but better than men, and some feminist theories would seem to support this point. Nancy Hartsock, for example, asserts that the "female construction of self in relation to others leads . . . toward opposition to dualisms of any sort, valuation of concrete, everyday life, sense of a variety of connectednesses and continuities both with other persons and with the natural world."[39] However, such a valorization of feminine connectedness is in danger of simply inverting the Manichaean divisions of good/bad, strong/weak, active/passive. It is perhaps more useful to consider movements such as the Mothers of the Plaza de Mayo as strategies brought fourth in times when civil society scarcely exists.

Yet the women never acted simply as mothers in the traditional sense, for they subverted the boundaries between public and private and challenged the assumption that mothering belonged to only the private sphere. They exploited the traditional view that mothers were the vessels of reproduction, but they also went beyond any essentialist definition of *mother* and thus demonstrated that it was possible to transform protest into a broader ethical position, one based on life and survival. Along with a growing number of other nontraditional social movements— indigenist, ecological, squatters—the mothers' movement crossed traditional national and class boundaries to constitute an alternative public sphere. Finally, it also established new alliances between culture, as an affirmation of life and survival, and politics.

NOTES

1. Elaine Scarry, *The Body in Pain: The Making and Unmaking of the World* (New York: Oxford University Press, 1985), 35.

2. Ibid., 35.

3. Editorial in the *Washington Post,* reprinted in the *Manchester Guardian Weekly* (April 28, 1985). See also Peter Schrag, *Mind Control* (New York: Pantheon, 1978).

4. José M. R. Delgado, *Physical Control of the Mind: Toward a Psychocivilized Society* (New York: Harper & Row, 1969), 215–16.

5. Amnesty International, *Torture in the Eighties* (London: Amnesty International Publications, 1984); *Nunca más: Informe de la Comisión Nacional Sobre la Desaparición de Personas* (Buenos Aires: Editorial Universitaria, 1984); Archdiocese of São Paulo, *Torture in Brazil,* trans. Jaime Wright, ed. Joan Dassin (New York: Random House, Vintage Books, 1986).

6. Mauricio Rosencof, "Victoria y derrota son convenciones," *Jaque* (Montevideo) 6 June 1885, p. 16.

7. Hebe de Bonafini, *Historias de vida* (Buenos Aires: Fraterna, 1985), 100–101. See also Julio E. Nosiglia, *Botín de guerra* (Buenos Aires: Tierra Fértil, 1985), which relates the odyssey of the grandmothers in search of grandchildren put up for adoption by the military after the disappearance of the parents; Emilio Fermín Mignone, "Desapariciones forzadas: Elementos básicos de una política," *Punto final* supp. no. 194 (June 1981); and Matilde Herrera, *José* (Buenos Aires: Contrapunto, 1987).

8. Martín Tomás Grau, "Testimonio" (Comisión Argentina de Derechos Humanos, Buenos Aires, 1983, mimeographed).

9. Andrés Valenzuela, *Confesiones de un agente de seguridad* (Santiago: Comisión Nacional Sobre la Desaparición de Personas, 1984), pages not numbered.

10. Jacobo Timerman, *Prisoner without a Name, Cell without a Number,* trans. Tony Talbot (New York: Knopf, 1981), 39.

11. Interview given to *Familia cristiana* and quoted in *Clarín,* 13 May 1977.

12. "Deposición de Liliana Maria Antokoletz en el juzgado federal de primera instancia en lo criminal y correcional" (Centro de Estudios Legales y Sociales, Buenos Aires [n.d.]; mimeographed).

13. Valenzuela, *Confesiones.*

14. *Nunca más,* 65.

15. Griselda Gambaro, *El campo* (Buenos Aires: Insurrexit, 1967), does not specifically refer to any particular society, but the relations among the three principal characters in the camp are sadomasochistic, and many of the cruel jokes are reminiscent of death-camp situations. The author is interested in exploring institutional power. Elvira Orphée, *La última conquista de El Ángel* (Caracas: Monteavila, 1977) (written, according to the author, between 1967 and 1974) reminds us that the elements of the death-camp mentality were already in place in Argentina prior to 1976.

16. This subject has been widely explored in feminist criticism. For a recent discussion, see Jessica Benjamin, "Gender and Domination," in *Bonds of Love: Psychoanalysis, Feminism, and the Problem of Domination* (New York: Pantheon, 1988), 183–218.

17. Hernán Valdés, *Diary of a Chilean Concentration Camp,* trans. J. Labanyi (London: Victor Gollanz, 1975), 105, 121–31. In the same book, Valdés describes how one of the officers made Valdés crouch in a humiliating position

because he had no identity card on him and said, "Not having your identity card on you's like not having your balls on you" (79).

18. Ana María Araujo, *Tupamaras des femmes de l'Uruguay* (Paris: Editions des Femmes, 1980), 165–66.

19. Manuel Puig, *The Kiss of the Spider Woman,* trans. Thomas Colchie (New York: Random House, 1991).

20. Ernesto Guevara, *The Diary of Che in Bolivia, October 7–November 7, 1966* (Calcutta: National Book Agency, 1968).

21. Timerman, *Prisoner without a Name,* 91.

22. Alicia Partnoy, *The Little School: Tales of Disappearance and Survival in Argentina* (Pittsburgh: Cleis Press, 1986), 123–24.

23. Ibid., 88. The theme of seduction is dealt with in literature; see especially Luisa Valenzuela, *Cambio de armas (Other Weapons)* (Hanover, N.H.: Ediciones del Norte, 1982).

24. Omar Rivabella, *Requiem for a Woman's Soul* (London: Penguin, 1986), 82.

25. Isabel Allende, *The House of Spirits* (New York: Knopf, 1985).

26. Valdés, *Diary.*

27. Partnoy, *The Little School,* 46.

28. Ibid., 94–95.

29. Michael Taussig, *Shamanism, Colonialism, and the Wild Man: A Study in Terror and Healing* (Chicago: University of Chicago Press, 1987).

30. From an unpublished interview. See also Jean Franco, "Killing Priests, Nuns, Women, Children," in Marshall Blonsky, ed., *On Signs* (Baltimore: Johns Hopkins University Press, 1985), 414–20.

31. de Bonafini, *Historias de vida* (Buenos Aires: Fraterna, 1985), 100.

32. Marysa Navarro, "The Personal Is Political: Las Madres de Plaza de Mayo" (Dartmouth, N.H., 1985; mimeograph). See also Jean-Pierre Bousquet, *Las locas de Plaza de Mayo* (Buenos Aires: El Cid, 1983).

33. Hernán Vidal, *De la vida por la vida: La agrupación chilena de familiares de detenidos desaparecidos* (Minneapolis: Institute for the Study of Ideologies and Literature, University of Minnesota, 1982).

34. Quoted by Miguel Bonasso, *Proceso* (Mexico City), no. 441 (15 April 1985).

35. Sara Ruddick, "Maternal Peace Politics and Women's Resistance: The Examples of Argentina and Chile," *Barnard Occasional Papers* (Barnard Center for Research on Women, New York) 4, no. 1 (1989).

36. Michel de Certeau, *Heterologies: Discourse on the Other,* trans. Brian Massumi (Minneapolis: Minnesota University Press, 1986).

37. Marjorie Agosín, "Emerging from the Shadows: Women of Chile," *Barnard Occasional Papers* (Barnard Center for Research on Women, New York) 2, no. 3 (1987).

38. Traba, *Conversación al sur* (Mexico City: Siglo XXI, 1981).

39. Nancy Hartsock, "The Feminist Standpoint: Developing the Ground for a Specifically Feminist Historical Materialism," in Sandra Harding and Merrill B. Hintikka, eds., *Discovering Reality* (Dordrecht: Reidel, 1983), 283–310.

PART THREE

Resources, Strategies, and Constraints: Fighting Fear

SEVEN

Resistance to Fear in Chile

The Experience of the Vicaría de la Solidaridad

Hugo Fruhling

In September 1973, the Church of Santiago founded the Cooperative Committee for Peace in Chile (COPACHI). The committee and its successor, the Vicaría de la Solidaridad (the Vicary), were to function primarily as institutional responses to the use of terror as a state policy.[1] In the words of Corradi, terror, as a tool of government, is conditioned by the rulers' fear; the rulers, in turn, endeavor to spread fear among their adversaries.[2] The majority of the authoritarian Southern Cone regimes, however, implemented other forms of social control to coexist with and buttress terror. The strategic reason for official economic and social policies was to dismantle existing social movements and atomize society. Terror went hand in hand with state-run communications strategies that interpreted the meaning of social events and justified the existing power structure.[3] In contrast with other human-rights organizations that emerged in South America to respond to terror, COPACHI and the Vicaría were also responsible for inaugurating a broad spectrum of activities that constituted a partial response to the official strategy for social control. Although its founders did not consciously intend the Vicaría to be anything more than a human-rights office when it began in January 1976, the organization's social agenda came to dominate its activities.

Through repressive policies, the Chilean regime attempted to destroy the social and political organizations associated with the left and, to a lesser extent, with the center.[4] Merely destroying the power of the adversary, however, does not automatically ensure longevity. To secure long-

121

term power, an authoritarian regime must also act positively, success-fully convincing and persuading the populace to support its policies, building supporting coalitions, and institutionalizing itself.

Posing the problem in this way raises the question of whether the Vicaría and COPACHI succeeded in weakening the power of the Chilean authoritarian regime or at least in transforming the way it exercised power. The answer is a complex one and constitutes the central theme of this chapter. I hope to demonstrate that although the Vicaría was dis-tinctly able to harass an authoritarian regime that was attempting to consolidate its power base, Vicaría's range of action was limited. Not-withstanding, its work during those years was extremely important.

This chapter first describes the formation and institutionalization of COPACHI and the Vicaría. It moves on to analyze how these institutions contributed to the reproduction of resistance groups. Finally, it considers the impact of Vicaría and COPACHI on official social-control policies and on the way the regime constituted its power.

THE FOUNDING AND INSTITUTIONALIZATION OF COPACHI AND THE VICARÍA

COPACHI

The committee began as an emergency humanitarian response to a situation of extreme repression that knew no legal or moral limits. Cardinal and Archbishop of Santiago Raúl Silva Henríquez founded it, with the support of the Gran Rabino de Chile, and the Lutheran, Meth-odist, Pentecostal Methodist, and Orthodox churches. Its constitution bespoke a spirit of collaboration rather than one of conflict with the government, and its objectives were couched in vague and declarative terms.[5]

Between October 1973 and August 1974, the membership of COPACHI increased from the 5 original officers to 108 committee mem-bers, all of whom worked in Santiago.[6] By January 1975, there were COPACHI representatives in twenty-five different cities around the country. The internal structure of the organization had become complex and the number of programs increased daily.

COPACHI was institutionalized in three complementary stages. First, it had to establish relations with foreign organizations that would serve both as funding sources and as networks to channel information on the repression. Second, it had to clarify its own organization and construct a series of programs related to employment, legal aid, social assistance, and public information. These programs were to aid the material reconstitution of the social forces that had been destroyed and terrorized after the coup. Third, it had to establish communications with the social sectors affected by the repression and state policies.

COPACHI first established relations with the World Council of Churches, which provided the seed money for the organization and, through its international network, distributed the information COPACHI had compiled about the human-rights situation in Chile. Various Western European and U.S. religious and lay agencies then followed suit and contributed operational funds.[7] Foreign correspondents assigned to Chile used COPACHI as an information service, and their dispatches kept international concern focused on developments in Chile.

What began as a program to assist and advise the families of political prisoners expanded into a series of diverse programs that broadened the base of COPACHI's work. A Legal Aid Office was created to provide legal assistance to the victims of political repression; a Labor Law Department was organized to provide legal assistance to private or public employees dismissed for political reasons; a University Affairs Office counseled students who had been expelled from the universities and tried to obtain scholarships for some of them to study abroad. The Material Assistance and Health Department established the first children's dining rooms in November 1973, in select cases distributed direct aid to those affected by the repression, and helped the relatives of prisoners to travel to the concentration camps. COPACHI also provided technical and financial aid to unemployed workers looking for new jobs.[8] In other words, in an attempt to counter or at least offset the events that followed the installation of the authoritarian regime, COPACHI— originally a human-rights organization—intensified and broadened the scope of its activities. And, in fact, the programs made it possible for people affected by the repression to be in constant contact with an institution that took on the character of a sanctuary.

The question is how COPACHI managed to expand in a situation of generalized and unlimited terror. Objective factors, such as the ideological framework within which the Chilean authoritarian regime was originally instituted, conditioned relations between COPACHI and the regime. Although this framework did not proscribe the use of terror, it situated the regime within the group of countries that consider themselves civilized members of the Western, Christian world. Accordingly, the government would have been hard put to justify a direct attack on a nascent, ecumenically sponsored project. The regime was becoming increasingly sensitive to its image and to the fact that its human-rights record was causing its isolation from the world community. Because closing down COPACHI would have opened up a new area of tensions, this option was considered inadvisable.[9] Some members of the new government perhaps assumed at first that COPACHI would be merely a welfare organization, operating on a case-by-case basis; clearly they did not foresee that the committee's work would produce a network of opposition groups.

The initial official tolerance enabled COPACHI to expand its programs. Its achievement is a tribute to its members' enormous courage as well as to their ability to exploit the limitations of the regime for the sake of the organization's growth. The first members of COPACHI were affiliated with the political left and formerly held relatively insignificant positions in the Popular Unity government; their lack of political visibility provided them with a certain degree of immunity from the repression. Their political experience alerted them to the fact that COPACHI could play an important role if it were able to confront the human-rights violations through an integrated strategy of denunciation and organization of resistance to the abuses of power. It was no easy task.

Nor was the task of maintaining the support of its members. Because many of the bishops had considered the coup inevitable,[10] one of the first tasks of the COPACHI leadership was to convince them that the violations of basic rights committed by the security forces compromised the national social fabric as a whole. In addition, the support of some of the religious groups was strictly pro forma. It was necessary to prove to them that the projected work was basically humanitarian and not political.

Once the regime realized that COPACHI was a potential threat, it sought to weaken the committee's links with the churches that participated in its directorate. Officially instigated press campaigns accused COPACHI of fueling international attacks on the regime.[11] The government revoked the German Lutheran bishop's residence permit in September 1975 and pressured the Protestant churches to withdraw from COPACHI.[12] As 1975 drew to a close, the government began to crack down on the committee officers themselves, and on November 11 Pinochet ordered the cardinal to dissolve COPACHI, which was described as a threat to public order.[13] The cardinal complied but declared that the various churches would continue "the charitable and religious work performed to date by the committee."[14]

THE VICARÍA DE LA SOLIDARIDAD

Just over one month later, in January 1976, Henríquez founded the Vicaría de la Solidaridad. Conceiving it as an organization that would continue the work of COPACHI under the auspices of the Catholic Church, its founders hoped that the regime would be more tolerant of the Vicaría. Clearly, the creation of the Vicaría responded to a growing awareness within the church hierarchy that the survival of the regime was contingent on recourse to repression. COPACHI too had taken a critical role by creating a community of people affected by the repression who regularly visited the parish churches around Santiago to plead that the victims not be abandoned.

At first, the Vicaría had a more ecclesiastical character than COPACHI. However, because its members were mainly lay people whose politics covered a wide spectrum, it was a rather anomalous body within the Church. Notwithstanding the specific circumstances that led to the creation of the Vicaría, this character is clearly responsible for its broadened agenda and for the addition of new programs to those formerly run by COPACHI. The assistance work was expanded to include seminars focusing on study and reflection, human-rights work, and community and peasant leadership-training programs. Moreover, with the benefit of experience, the organization became increasingly professional and efficient. Vicaría attorneys followed up lawsuits and lodged appeals, in contrast with the former legal-aid work, which was conditioned by the emergency and was more testimonial and less effective.

The Vicaría's early development corresponded to the evolving relation between the Church and the authoritarian regime. Its work really got under way when the Church began to speak out, in 1976, against government policies. Statements issued by the hierarchy of the Church of Santiago and the Episcopal Permanent Committee provided the framework for explicit authorization of the Vicaría's work.[15] This direct relation between the Vicaría and Church policy was counterbalanced by the Church's relation with its parishioners. When those Catholics who supported the regime criticized the Vicaría, their criticism had repercussions within the Church, which in turn put pressure on the Vicaría. In 1981, just before he was due to retire, Henríquez introduced a series of changes in the Vicaría to ensure its viability under a new archbishop who might be more influenced than he by the criticisms of the sectors loyal to the military regime. His plan was to close the Peasant Office in 1983 and transfer the program directly to the peasant organizations themselves.

Likewise, the human-rights work and social-assistance programs in the shantytowns were decentralized and assigned to the various parishes of the Santiago Church. A small team in the Vicaría continued to coordinate these programs.

Analysis of the Vicaría's work reveals that the organization was able to provide a response to the social-control policies implemented by the authoritarian regime. Analysis also points to the Vicaría's effort to reconstitute the social forces that were effectively atomized and fragmented by the culture of fear that dominated various sectors of Chilean society to different degrees. We shall consider the following broad areas of the Vicaría's work: legal defense of life and liberty; denunciations and communications; outreach, assistance, and training.

Legal Defense of Life and Personal Freedom. A noticeable increase in the skill with which the legality of government actions was challenged followed the formation of the Vicaría.[16] Its lawyers systematized existing information on people who were imprisoned and who then disappeared, and they petitioned the Supreme Court to appoint ad hoc judges of the courts of appeals to conduct investigations of the cases compiled. In August 1976 the Vicaría filed a petition accompanied by an impressive collection of documented evidence pertaining to the different cases.[17] The legal assault on the problem of disappearance was intensified in 1976. Generally, once the appeal for habeas corpus in a case of disappearance was rejected because of official refusal to recognize the detention as such, the case was sent to criminal court to be investigated under the presumption that it was a common crime. From 1976 on, then, what had been simply denunciations became lawsuits brought by the families of victims and filed by Vicaría lawyers. The families thus became parties to direct penal action and were able to expedite the investigations. The lawsuits provided a framework for the systematization of the growing body of information about the repressive methods used by the regime.

As the legal-aid work developed, the number of cases and appeals brought on behalf of political prisoners increased; the Vicaría presented legal actions for people who had been tortured and provided legal assistance to exiles prohibited from returning to Chile for political reasons.[18] It is not my intention here to analyze whether the legal actions were successful in themselves. What must be stressed is the enormous importance of the product of the work. The Vicaría office compiled from its legal records an impressive amount of information about the conduct of the judiciary during those years. At regular intervals, the Vicaría presented documented evidence of judicial negligence vis-à-vis official human-rights violations to the Supreme Court. These denunciations may have been responsible for altering the attitudes of certain judges, and they certainly compromised the legitimacy the regime believed it had achieved by maintaining the formal independence of the judiciary. The legal action also provided objective information about how the repression fluctuated and how its methods were modified. Published reports that documented these patterns had indisputable national and international impact. Quantification of the repression revealed the true state of affairs underlying the public image of the authoritarian regime. Furthermore, reports published by the Vicaría focused on how the repression varied from year to year and documented qualitative changes in repressive methods.

Denunciations and Communications. From the beginning, the Vicaría produced a series of publications that supplied a public wary of the official press with information. When there was no alternative to the official media, this aspect of the Vicaría's work became important; from 1980 onward, opposition publications enjoyed some official tolerance, which increased after the beginning of political decompression in 1983.

The Vicaría published a bimonthly bulletin called *Solidarity,* which, over a period of three years, built up a circulation of about thirty thousand, primarily among the popular sectors.[19] Its central topics were the repression, the social movement, the working-class family, the student movement, and the Church both in Chile and abroad.[20] The Vicaría also published various booklets, such as *Donde están,* which described the presentations made by the different bishops to the Ministry of the Interior on the disappeared. Likewise *Estudios jurídicos* analyzed the repressive legal decisions handed down by the regime, as well as the existing jurisprudence on individual rights.

Popular Outreach, Aid, and Training. The Vicaría not only took up where COPACHI had left off but also intensified its predecessor's work of supporting the activities of the peasant organizations that lacked official backing, channeled social assistance into the slum areas, and helped groups searching for new forms of organization to meet their most pressing needs.

The independent peasant organizations were offered legal assistance and training programs. At first, legal assistance was provided to individual peasants who had been dismissed from their jobs and to small commercial peasant enterprises formed after the agrarian reform was terminated. In 1977, both central teams and networks of lawyers were established and assigned to the various union organizations affiliated with the Vicaría's peasant office.[21] In this way legal-aid work could be extended to the provinces. An evaluation of this work showed that, of the conflicts in which Vicaría's lawyers had intervened, 21.97 percent were civil cases, 9.2 percent were criminal, and 68.83 percent were labor-related.[22] Legal-aid work with the peasant sectors was combined with leadership training within the organizations themselves. In 1977, 410 peasant leaders participated in different training activities;[23] in 1980, 279 leaders did so.[24]

In the shantytown areas, the Vicaría developed social work and training for those suffering from unemployment, hunger, and health and housing problems. The first children's dining room had been built in the Herminda de la Victoria area in November 1973 by COPACHI, but the initiative never became popular, and it subsequently shed its purely charitable character. After the Vicaría was founded in 1976, the children's dining rooms were converted into working-class cafeterias, which functioned also as training and solidarity centers.[25] Interest in alternative solutions to the problems of hunger and unemployment gave rise to food warehouses and wholesale purchase-and-supply cooperatives. The importance and influence of these organizations varied in accordance with the prevailing political conditions. What is interesting at this point, however, is that these organizations fostered the participation of a population subjected to severe hardships. By the end of 1979, the cafeterias mobilized around 44,000 people to join in activities and campaigns.[26]

Other organizations concerned with the problems of hunger and unemployment were supported by the Vicaría during those years, either through training programs, infrastructural support, or supplying food. Among these were productive enterprises such as the *arpilleras* (women's embroidery cooperatives), which also spoke out on political issues, and the employment agencies, which denounced the causes of unemployment and organized subsistence workshops and housing organizations.

The variety of responsibilities assumed by the Vicaría throughout these years clearly indicates that it was more than simply an institution defending against authoritarian abuses of power. Although that was the reason it was founded, the organization evolved into one committed to strengthening the popular organizations and to searching for new ways to resist and denounce arbitrary abuses.

THE REPRODUCTION OF OPPOSITION GROUPS

Two principal elements lend themselves to a culture of fear: first, the sense of insecurity, which increases in direct proportion to the lack of available information about the exact objectives of state repression; second, the sense of powerlessness, of the impossibility of creating spaces within which to organize in the face of terror. I wish to consider this second element in particular in the context of the Vicaría's multifaceted effort to build up communication networks among those who sought to confront authoritarianism.

Of all the countries to have suffered under authoritarian regimes, only Chile had an organization to defend human rights that, almost from the start, encompassed a plethora of activities and programs. In Uruguay, these kinds of organizations did not begin to function until the regime had been installed for almost seven years. In Argentina, although the Permanent Assembly for Human Rights existed from the beginning, its programs were on a noticeably smaller scale than those of COPACHI and the Vicaría. In the Chilean case, the initial struggle to reorganize society was based on the defense of human rights. Therefore, and for a long time, political activity took place through social and humanitarian organizations.

THE EMERGENCE OF A HUMAN-RIGHTS FRONT

The existence of COPACHI and the Vicaría was important in itself for the emergence of other human-rights groups. Experience suggests that once a human-rights organization succeeds in establishing a space inside a society ruled by an authoritarian regime, a demonstration effect results. Human-rights organizations began to proliferate after 1978 for a number of reasons. Among these were, first, the conviction of the opposition parties that the defense of human rights was a symbolic element in the collective denunciation of the authoritarian regime and, second, the fact that the new organizations met the lengthening list of social needs that the Vicaría's programs were unable to meet.

Two basic effects occurred once the human-rights organizations expanded their agendas and became institutionalized. First, the struggle for human rights spread; organizational capacity increased, and committees were able to reach a wide variety of social sectors. The Chilean Human Rights Organization, founded in 1979, for example, improved contacts between the human-rights community and political parties. In addition, links were forged between human-rights activists and intellectual sectors of the opposition. This mutually beneficial communications network had a variety of expressions and had a particularly important role during the early years of the military regime. Social scientists affiliated with independent research centers carried out studies of the repression and its ideological justifications, and people affiliated with human-rights organizations attended seminars or activities at these centers. This informal network bypassed the barriers that would otherwise have separated people who carried out different professional activities.

Second, the methods used to defend and promote human rights were diversified. Starting in 1980, the Servicio Paz y Justicia (Peace and Justice Service) and COPACHI itself ran popular education programs in the shantytowns; they consisted of day-long reflection and discussion of the national political situation.

The growing diversification of human-rights organizations created spaces for public political activity that focused on the struggle for basic freedoms and included the political parties. Party organizations, particularly the left-wing parties that were forced to work underground, selected some of their members to work inside the human-rights organizations. Some of these party members became publicly known for their professional work in the field of legal defense or of psychological services for torture victims. Other party members saw that working through the Church or the human-rights organizations would enable them to meet more urgent social needs and to reach more people than would underground political work, which in the years immediately after the coup was limited to reconstructing the party organizations. Thus, the human-rights front that emerged from the work of the Church facilitated the reconstitution of a national opposition movement.

THE STRUGGLE AGAINST TERROR
AND ITS CONSEQUENCES

Implicit in first the COPACHI and then the Vicaría programs was the intention to offset the wave of terror sweeping through Chilean society. Despite the limited effectiveness of their strategies, these organizations assumed a critical role during periods of harsh repression. In 1978 the policy of disappearance was discontinued, but after 1982 repression was intensified to respond to increasing opposition to the regime and to the emergence of armed opposition groups.

A preliminary step in the struggle against terror was to open lines of communication with and begin to organize the sectors affected by the repression. The Vicaría's legal-aid programs allowed the families who had appealed to the Church for help in locating relatives who had disappeared or been taken prisoner to meet with one another and to organize. The families of the prisoners and the disappeared also became acquainted through their visits to Vicaría's lawyers. Beginning in 1977, the Association of Relatives of the Disappeared began to act publicly, staging symbolic protests to call attention to their situation.[27] Still other organizations of relatives of political prisoners and exiles presented new challenges to a regime whose principal weapon was social fragmentation and atomization.

The battle against terror could attract supporters as long as the opposition sectors felt that an institutional structure existed to provide them with assistance should they require it. The ongoing presentation of lawsuits on behalf of political prisoners and the international denunciation of human-rights abuses carried out this function. In every case the effects of the strategies were limited, but they did succeed in reassuring the political activists, or at least the student leaders and the Christian community members, that everything possible was being done to protect them.

During the years following the coup, not only did defense lawyers provide moral support for those detained by the authorities, but because of their right to argue before the military tribunals, they were also the only ones who could communicate the prisoners' situation to the outside world. Similarly, psychological care for torture victims allowed them to resume their lives and eventually return to political activity.

Paradoxically, terror feeds both on silence and on information, distorted information. Silence draws a curtain over human-rights violations, conferring on them a sense of the clandestine. The violence continues because society at large remains ignorant of the way violence is perpetuated. The majority feel that they know nothing, and the minority assume that, as individuals, denouncing the situation will lead nowhere because they will be able to present at most a collection of insignificant personal testimonies that will only put them in danger. And a culture of fear is as dependent on distorted official information about the nature of repressive activities as it is on silence. The official voice insists on depicting the problem as one of confrontations between the forces of order and isolated groups of terrorists who are alienated from the national community.

The Vicaría tenaciously fought both silence and distorted information via constant and documented denunciation of the repression. Its tools were legal actions, public denunciation, and detailed factual reports. Denunciations that initially reached only select circles began to be published in partial form by official newspapers, augmenting the political costs that the regime incurred by committing arbitrary and aberrant acts.

THE CONSTITUTION OF NEW OPPOSITION GROUPS

The Vicaría's demonstration effect helped to constitute a front of human-rights organizations, and their struggle against terror played a role in reconstituting the political forces most affected by the repression. And Vicaría's organizational activity extended still further. It was partially responsible for the emergence of international concern with human-rights violations and with the growth of other opposition groups.

Almost from the start, the authoritarian regime was politically isolated in the world community for a number of reasons. First, before the coup, whose aftermath was extremely repressive, Chile had enjoyed a long period of democratic stability. Second, the Chilean opposition parties had good contacts with their counterparts in other countries and with the democratic governments in Europe and the United States. To complete the picture, the Vicaría and the other Chilean human-rights organizations developed and maintained relations with similar foreign organizations and with the governments of the developed capitalist countries. The flow of reliable information about human-rights violations coming from these nonofficial sources within the country kept world public attention focused on the Chilean situation. The Vicaría became a privileged interlocutor with governments concerned about developments in Chile. Highly placed political representatives of Western governments who visited the country met with Vicaría officials once they held talks with government representatives. In brief, the Vicaría's work in this particular area hampered the unrestrained implementation of terror in a country extremely dependent on its foreign relations and sensitive to its international image.

The Vicaría also played an important role by keeping the hierarchy of the Catholic Church informed about human-rights violations. Nonetheless, the Vicaría cannot claim sole responsibility for the Church's position on government policy. The opposition of the Chilean Church to a regime that excluded the popular sectors is one that evolved over several years.[28] Moreover, during the dictatorship, the close relations between the Church and the Christian Democratic opposition party spurred the Church to defend the liberties threatened by the government. But the Vicaría took a critical role in sensitizing the Church to the factual details of the repression, in bringing it gradually to a position that was essentially protective of opposition activities, and in fact in establishing the Church itself as an opponent of the regime. Only cautiously at first, in 1977, and then openly later did the bishops declare themselves in favor of a return to democracy;[29] did they discuss the trauma of political exile;[30] did they support the families of the disappeared when they staged hunger strikes;[31] and did they speak out against the plight of rural and urban workers.[32] Although all these statements, in particular those referring to the exiles, the prisoners, and the disappeared legitimized the Vicaría's programs, they also amounted to a direct response by the Church to events that had been perpetuated for years under the cover of silence.

The tripartite relationship of the Vicaría, the Church, and the government was a complex one. The Vicaría was the focus of the discord between the ecclesiastical hierarchy and the Catholics who supported the regime. The more the regime institutionalized itself and consolidated the personal leadership of Pinochet, the more virulent the right-wing Catholic attacks on the Church became.[33] The contentious situation with the sectors holding power was a source of concern to the Church and created tensions with the Vatican. Although for institutional reasons the Church could not afford to perpetuate serious internal divisions, neither could it lose sight of the fact that the consolidation of the regime was a significant political reality in itself. As a result, especially after 1981, the Church was under considerable pressure from the Vatican to play down its role as an opposition political actor so that its voice might be heard as a conciliator, a proponent of dialogue between the opposition and the regime. These pressures led Archbishop Fresno to initiate a dialogue between the Democratic Alliance and Minister of the Interior Sergio Onofre Jarpa, at the end of 1983, and then to sponsor the National Accord in 1986, a political document agreed to by most of the opposition and some conservative political parties and rejected by the government. This clerical conciliatory approach encountered serious difficulties.

The Vicaría was also an invaluable support to the peasant movement, which was particularly hard hit by the new power relations that accompanied the installation of the authoritarian regime. Vicaría legal assistance allowed local organizations that had been severely weakened by the social changes introduced in the rural sector to survive. Legal aid also proved crucial for support of collective bargaining. It helped to mitigate falling membership in labor organizations and contributed to the main- tenance of those labor organizations most vulnerable to repression. Without this legal support, the peasant movement probably would have experienced greater fragmentation than it did.

The increase in opposition groups that resisted the terror and other forms of social control led the government selectively to repress human- rights activists—expelling lawyers from Chile, forcing the dissolution of the Committee for Peace in 1975, prohibiting Vicar of Solidarity Ignacio Gutierrez from entering Chile in December 1984, and arresting lawyer Gustavo Villalobos and physician Ramiro Olivares and charging them with violations of arms-control law in 1986.[34] Thus, although the gov- ernment paid a political cost for massive repression in the form of a steady proliferation of resistance groups, the culture of fear did not disappear, and official violence against dissidents did not diminish. The repression simply became more selective.

THE VICARÍA'S IMPACT ON THE INTERNAL FUNCTIONING OF THE AUTHORITARIAN REGIME

The work of defending and promoting human rights created certain difficulties for a regime intent on repressing its opponents, primarily by forcing the authorities to constantly modify their repressive policies. This work also hampered the attempts of the regime to consolidate its power and construct a new hegemony by combining repression with drastic changes in the Chilean socioeconomic structure. However, when the Vicaría tried to build structures that would prevent the new regime from consolidating its power, the Vicaría's weaknesses began to show. These weaknesses were not the result of its methods but were rooted in its position as an apolitical human-rights organization constrained from working with political parties.

THE IMPACT OF THE VICARÍA'S WORK ON REPRESSIVE POLICIES

The Vicaría's legal strategy of defending human rights had three funda- mental objectives: to contribute to the respect of human rights, to create public spaces where people could speak out against the situation, and to reveal the truth about repressive activities.[35] The Vicaría's use of the courts in each repressive situation was aimed at pressuring the judiciary both to become independent of the executive and to protect human rights. Although the overall results were not encouraging, in some cases a positive judicial attitude limited the excesses of the repressive apparatus. For instance, the courts proved unwilling to find against people who carried out public, nonviolent protests, contrary to the State Security Law; certain legal investigations found the police guilty of summary executions, although these were reversed on appeals; and habeas corpus appeals sometimes provoked representatives of the courts to make on-site investigations into places of detention.[36]

The judicial investigations that formed part of the legal strategy constituted a forum for the distribution of information about repression; the legal actions also provided evidence for the construction of sound hypotheses about the forms and tactics of repression used by the security apparatus. The basic effect of the legal strategy implemented by the Vicaría lawyers was to create a sense of uneasiness among the civilian sectors that supported the regime, prompting them to demand that the authorities limit and legalize the actions carried out against dissent.

In 1977, some sectors of the right began to speak out against certain repressive activities and increasingly called on the regime to control its security forces. This position contrasts with the total support lent by these sectors to the wave of terror unleashed after the coup and is connected to the pressure the right put on Pinochet to institutionalize the regime. These sectors continued to express concern over the more savage excesses, such as those that took place at the end of March 1985, when three leftist activists were kidnapped and later found with their throats cut. One of them worked with the Vicaría.

Although the regime was never afraid that these civilian sectors would go so far as to join the opposition, it nevertheless had to acknowledge their demands, and some of the changes in the repressive apparatus can be attributed to their influence. Between 1977 and 1981, the repression eased slightly, and the disappearances of persons ceased. When the economic crisis hit in 1982, the regime utilized alternative or parallel tactics to meet the growing popular discontent. At first, it tried to frighten the population and then to dismantle the political organizations. When these tactics failed, the regime closed the public spaces it had allowed to open in 1983 and implemented a state of siege. The changing perception of the authorities about the threat the opposition posed to political stability determined the extent to which the means of repression were modified. The fluctuations can also be attributed to the fact that the regime simply could not afford to alienate its narrowing base of support by unleashing a massive and permanent process of repression such as the one it imposed on the country after 1973. In 1987 the government enacted legislation allowing the organization of political parties, and a year later it held a plebiscite to ratify Pinochet as president for another eight years. On October 5, 1988, he was denied this ratification by popular vote.

Undoubtedly the Vicaría's legal strategy had important, albeit limited, effects on sectors that supported the regime. Growing sensitivity to the atmosphere of violence in the country, and the fact that this violence would only undermine the institutionalization of the regime, precipitated regular conflicts between the hardliners and the more flexible loyal sectors who would otherwise be expected to uphold the legality of authoritarianism. Because these sectors never sustained a broad opposition position, however, their potential for pressure was limited.

The Vicaría's social-assistance work and its promotion of opposition organizations helped those sectors affected by the repression and social spending cuts to reorganize themselves. This reorganization was related to the rise of a new popular culture, festivals, and reflection days. Between 1978 and 1979, the wave of alternative cultural and political expression reached its peak and then declined. Between 1975 and 1980, seventy different cultural organizations, more than half of which were from the popular sectors, were formed in Santiago.[37] Although the growth of a cultural movement formed mainly of artists, political parties, and students cannot be attributed solely to the Vicaría, it is impossible to imagine that such a movement would be able to flourish in the absence of the opposition activity and promotion for which the Church, via the Vicaría, was ultimately responsible.

The regime's capacity to modify its policies while retaining the loyalty of its power base—the armed forces and the large business sector—does not mean that these changes were insignificant. The growing influence of the opposition owed much to the poverty and insecurity that were social effects of the official economic policies; its influence derived also from the gradual opening up of spaces for intellectual, professional, and political activity. These changes had their fullest expression during the protests that began in 1983.

The Vicaría programs in support of the popular sector forced the regime to respond with a range of different policies. State-run children's feeding programs and so-called open centers of social work and assistance directed by Pinochet's wife and staffed by volunteers from the

upper stratum constituted the official counterpart to the popular cafeterias. When social discontent began to mount in 1982, the regime
responded by being more tolerant than formerly of the opposition view-
point; it restored the status of selected "reprobates" and allowed their
ideas limited expression in the government-controlled mass media. In
1987 the government permitted the distribution of two opposition newspapers.

It is striking that the dynamic expansion of resistance groups born of
the Church's work with the urban popular sectors caused the authorities
to adapt official discourse. The proliferation of resistance groups precipitated the establishment of a dialectic relation between the government
and the opposition. Under these circumstances, it was natural that sectors close to the regime should modify their position, possibly because
they had become sensitive to the social problems of the popular sectors,
especially once the 1982 economic crisis was under way. Clearly this
modification of their position concerned the military regime, which
initially had enjoyed a free rein and few challengers. Soon, though, it was
obvious that power had limits and that the state could not repress
everyone at the same time and with the same intensity. For the first time,
the government seemed to become aware of the relative complexity of
Chilean society. It responded just as it had to the legal challenge to state
terrorism, applying social control with increased flexibility. Although
costly, the combination of selective repression and attempts to control
the direction of the new cultural and popular movements had certain
advantages. The cost was that the state, in spite of itself, had to accept
realistic limits. The advantage, however, was that the regime could
project itself as relatively tolerant of a social reality whose existence it
could not deny.

Thus, the Vicaría's work seems to have had an impact on the repressive policies implemented by the regime in the following ways. First, it
created ongoing tension between the military and the civilian groups that
backed the regime. This tension noticeably undermined the initial legitimacy conferred by the civilian sectors on the repression. Second, it
created a dialectic relation between the government and the opposition
forces that enabled the opposition to pressure the authorities and force
them to diversify their tactics of social control in order to maintain the
stability of the regime. Finally, the discourse in favor of human rights
had an ideological impact inside the regime itself, a regime that initially
denied that it intended to return to traditional democracy. It is clear that
after 1987 the military began creating the conditions that would enable

Chile's return to democracy. Pinochet's defeat in the 1988 plebiscite opened the way for congressional and presidential elections in December 1989. After 1989, the visibility of the Vicaría significantly declined.

THE VICARÍA AS AN INSTRUMENT
OF REDEMOCRATIZATION

The task of defending and promoting human rights assumed by COPACHI and then by the Vicaría was at once defensive and creative work. In its programs and activities aimed at protecting the personal and social rights threatened by official policies, it was clearly defensive. In its conscious commitment to support the reconstitution of the social panorama of a country torn by fear and by drastic social transformation, it was creative. However, this creative aspect and its ability to contribute to the construction of democratic institutions at the social level ultimately depended on the political parties for political expression. Only they could replace the regime. It was never the intention of the Church, the Vicaría, or any of the other human-rights organizations to replace the regime. They lacked the necessary leadership; had they assumed this task, they would have risked losing the legitimacy conferred on them by their specific role.

The task of the human-rights organizations then was to do the groundwork—to prepare the social organizations to form a broad front together with the parties. This groundwork in fact paved the way to negotiations with those sectors within the Chilean regime that saw the need to initiate a political transition.

The inherent political limitations of the Church on the one hand and of the human rights organizations on the other were complicated still further by material limitations. Although the Church—through the different bishops or through the Vicaría itself—was responsible for a multitude of programs, the human and organizational resources it was able to mobilize cannot compare to those available to government or the business sector. For example, the ideological impact of the Vicaría publication *Solidarity* could not equal that of the official mass media, which controlled the television stations and most of the newspapers. Likewise, the popular cafeterias were unable to mobilize anything like the resources that the officially supported organizations could. Consequently, the social-development and promotion programs of the Church and the Vicaría remained small; they could provide only the seeds that would flourish within the broader social networks. They were in no position to replace the state organizations. Nor was it possible for the beneficiaries of the state social-development programs to withdraw from them.

The work done by the Vicaría, and the Church in particular, buttressed the struggle against terror and seriously hindered the authoritarian regime's effort to legitimize its rule. For the reasons outlined above, however, its capacity to erode the bases of official power was limited. One of the paradoxes of the conservative authoritarian regimes that ruled in the Southern Cone is this: the institutions and organizations in the forefront of the struggle against terror never had the wherewithal to put an end to them.

CONCLUSION: THE VICARÍA'S ROLE IN OVERCOMING FEAR

The Vicaría was unique among the organizations that emerged to defend the rights of persons threatened by Southern Cone authoritarian regimes. It was outstanding for the variety and number of the programs it developed in response to the repression, to the destruction of social organizations, and to the deterioration of the living conditions of the popular sectors. The Vicaría was able to respond to the social-control policies implemented by the authoritarian regime because as an ecclesial institution it was relatively immune from repression; because the regime was politically dependent on its foreign relations and sensitive about its international image; and, finally, because the military regime situated itself in an ideological paradigm that tied its own hands.

The expansion of the Vicaría's work allowed it to contribute decisively to the proliferation of groups active in resisting the military regime and its policies. The human-rights organizations that emerged directly from the Vicaría experience in turn facilitated the struggle against terror.

The Vicaría had a considerable impact within the authoritarian regime, shattering its monolithic image and undermining its legitimacy by showing it to be in constant violation of its own laws. By helping to reconstruct social and political organizations, the Vicaría and the Church in general inhibited the government's freedom of movement. Nevertheless, the Vicaría's success in paving the way to redemocratization was limited. These limitations were inherent in its position as church and as human-rights organization. Although the struggle for human rights is a particular form of politics, the process of democratization in

Chile could not be contingent on the success of that struggle alone. What the human-rights movements started was brought about, as it had to be, by the political process.

NOTES

1. For an analysis of the emergence of human-rights groups in Chile, see Hugo Fruhling, "Nonprofit Organizations as Opposition to Authoritarian Rule: The Case of Human Rights Organizations in Chile," in Estelle James, ed., *The Nonprofit Sector in International Perspective: Studies in Comparative Culture and Policy* (New York: Oxford University Press, 1989), 358–76.

2. Juan E. Corradi, "Towards a Sociology of Fear" (paper presented to the Eleventh Latin American Studies Association Conference, Mexico City, 1983), 2.

3. See José Joaquin Brunner, *La cultura autoritaria en Chile* (Santiago: FLACSO–Latin American Studies Program, University of Minnesota, 1981), 17.

4. For an analysis of repressive policies, see Hugo Fruhling, "Stages of Repression and Legal Strategy for the Defense of Human Rights in Chile: 1973–1980," *Human Rights Quarterly* 5, no. 4 (1983), 351–74.

5. "Comité para la paz en Chile. Crónica de sus dos años de labor solidaria" (Vicaría de la Solidaridad, Santiago, 1975, manuscript).

6. "El comité de cooperación para la paz en Chile: Una tarea que debe continuar" (Vicaría de la Solidaridad, Santiago, 1974, manuscript), 1.

7. Brian H. Smith, *Churches as Development Institutions: The Case of Chile 1973–1980,* Working Paper 50 (New Haven, Conn.: Program on Nonprofit Organizations, Yale University, 1982), 30–33.

8. For detailed descriptions of the work of COPACHI, see Corradi, "Towards a Sociology of Fear," and Brunner, *La cultura autoritaria en Chile.*

9. A complete analysis of Chile's international situation is in Heraldo Muñoz, *Las relaciones exteriores del gobierno militar chileno* (Santiago: Las Ediciones del Ornitorrinco, 1986).

10. Brian H. Smith, *The Church and Politics in Chile: Challenges to Modern Catholicism* (Princeton, N.J.: Princeton University Press, 1982), 210.

11. The campaign against COPACHI gathered strength when *Excelsiór,* a Mexican newspaper, published various parts of an internal COPACHI document that denounced violations of basic rights.

12. Humberto Lagos, *La libertad religiosa en Chile: Los evangélicos y el gobierno militar* (Santiago: Vicaría de la Solidaridad, 1978), 48 ff.

13. See "El comité de cooperación," app. 1.3.

14. Ibid., app. 1.4.

15. See notes 29–32.

16. See Hugo Fruhling, *Limitando la acción coercitiva del estado. La estrategía legal de defensa de los derechos humanos en Chile* (Santiago: FLACSO, 1982), 76.

17. *Informe sobre 415 casos de desaparecidos* (Santiago: Vicaría de la Solidaridad, 1976).

18. *Vicaría de la Solidaridad, Sexto año de labor, 1981* (Santiago: Vicaría de la Solidaridad, 1982), 107–11.

19. "La Vicaría de la Solidaridad. Una experiencia de educación para la justicía" (Vicaría de la Solidaridad, Santiago, 1979, manuscript), 14.

20. *Vicaría de la Solidaridad. Octavo año de labor, 1983* (Santiago: Vicaría de la Solidaridad, 1984), 62–69.

21. "Sistematización trabajo programa jurídico (Octubre 1977 a Octubre 1982)," (Departamento Campesino, Vicaría de la Solidaridad, Santiago, manuscript).

22. Ibid., 43.

23. *Vicaría de la Solidaridad. Tercer año de labor, 1978* (Santiago: Vicaría de la Solidaridad, 1979), 51 ff.

24. *Vicaría de la Solidaridad. Sexto año de labor,* 62.

25. *Informe programa comedores populares de la Vicaría de la Solidaridad,* pt. 2 (Vicaría de la Solidaridad, Santiago, 1982, manuscript), 51–53.

26. Ibid., 46.

27. See Hernán Vidal, *De la vida por la vida: La Agrupación chilena de familiares de detenidos desaparecidos* (Minneapolis: Institute for the Study of Ideologies and Literature, University of Minnesota, 1982). Patricia Verdugo and Claudio Orrego, *Detenidos-desaparecidos. Una herida abierta* (Santiago: Aconcagua, 1980).

28. For an analysis of this evolution in the position of the Chilean Catholic Church, see Smith, *Church and Politics in Chile.*

29. "Nuestra convivencia nacional," *Mensaje 26* (April 1977), 166–69.

30. "El sufrimiento del exilio," *Mensaje 27* (January–February 1978), 84.

31. "Los detenidos desaparecidos y sus familiares en huelga de hambre," *Mensaje 27* (July 1978), 428.

32. "Carta a los trabajadores cristianos del campo y la ciudad," *Mensaje 28,* (January–February 1979), 79–80.

33. See Jaime Ruiz-Tagle, "Iglesia, gobierno y pueblo," *Mensaje 29* (July 1980), 308–11. José Arteaga, "Iglesia y partidarios del gobierno," *Mensaje 30* (June 1981), 234–36.

34. "The Vicaría de la Solidaridad in Chile," *Americas Watch Report* (December 1987), 35–42.

35. See Fruhling, *Limitando la acción coercitiva del estado,* 109–10.

36. See "Vicaría de la Solidaridad in Chile," 20–24.

37. Anny Rivera, *Transformaciones culturales y movimiento artístico en el orden autoritario. Chile 1973–1982* (Santiago: CENECA, 1983), 124.

EIGHT

Fear of the State, Fear of Society

On the Opposition Protests in Chile

Javier Martínez

For Chilean politics 1983 and 1984 were watershed years. After a decade of military rule (1973–83), when the only defense against the government's continuing human-rights violations had been the Catholic Church, a period of civilian rebellion against the dictatorship was inaugurated, characterized by the "days of protest."

A call for a national strike against the policies of the regime, issued in April 1983 by the powerful Copper Miners Confederation (CTC) and later changed to an appeal that all sectors of society actively and non-violently express their opposition to the regime on May 11, sparked this unexpected protest movement. The appeal met with an overwhelming popular response, and on the appointed day thousands of people poured into the streets for impromptu gatherings; schools, high schools, and universities had unprecedented absentee rates; motorists joined the demonstration by noisily sounding their horns; and burning barricades put up during the night by groups of demonstrators snarled traffic all over the capital. The din of housewives banging spoons against empty pots— a decade earlier the symbol of middle- and upper-class resistance to the socialist government of President Salvador Allende—could be heard in every Santiago neighborhood; this was a popular way of expressing exasperation and protest against the regime, led by General Augusto Pinochet Ugarte, that had come to power under similar circumstances.

The scale of this expression of discontent and the near-riot conditions in some areas of the city despite violent police repression suggested that the population had lost its fear. From that day on, it was thought that means other than coercion would have to be employed to ensure that the civilian population remained obedient to the military government. Few people believed that anything other than coercion would, or could, effectively maintain this aberrant subordination.

Days of protest were held during the second week of every remaining month of 1983 and four more times during 1984. The political conflict intensified as the demonstrations gathered momentum, seriously threatening the stability of the Pinochet regime. Every month, hundreds of foreign correspondents were assigned to Santiago to cover the downfall of the dictatorship that had made tragic headlines in many parts of the world for nearly a decade. The growing civilian protest and the government's inability to control it seemed to many unmistakable signs that the end was in sight and that Chile would soon be caught up in the democratic tide that was sweeping over the rest of South America.

It did not happen like that, however. The year 1984 came to an end with Chile in a state of siege; the country had lived through eighteen months of intensive mobilization and repression that left 160 people dead and 500 injured. The opposition movement that remained was sizable, but confused, and it was rapidly losing touch with its social bases. To complicate matters still further, polls carried out during these months indicated that the majority of the population, although it continued to support an immediate change of government and a return to democracy, also supported the state of siege.

The subject of this chapter is how the civilian population overcame its fear of the military regime by means of the protests that took place in Chile during this period. But it is also essential to understand why this form of collective action progressively lost momentum and why only a handful of groups seriously considered it a valid response to the extreme situations created by official or para-official action.

There are two key questions. First, how can we explain the advent of such sudden, massive protests as those that took place from May 1983 on, when for an entire decade opposition to the military regime was weak and dispersed? Did the regime make a false move, which could not be predicted until the actual moment, or was the fact that the actors themselves had realigned and joined forces responsible? Second, why did the momentum of the protests build to a certain point and then drop off, instead of continuing, as many observers had hoped? Did a force inherent in the movement itself bring about the decline, or was a well-coordinated response by the opponent (the military dictatorship) sufficient to break it? And, as a corollary, what role did fear, in its many guises, play? Or conversely, what can a contradictory experience such as this teach us about how fear operates as a political factor?

The argument developed in this chapter is a simple one: although the protests transformed resistance into nonheroic action (as defined below), they failed to articulate a social alternative to the authoritarian order. Such an alternative would have allowed the challenge to state power to build progressively. Under static conditions, civil society is caught between fear of the state and fear of its own self-destructive tendencies. The depth of the national schism in the period leading up to the 1973 coup, the scarce appeal that the military government's project to modernize the economy had for important sectors of the population, the inadequacy of the project to temper the effects of the crisis, among other factors, tipped the balance in favor of inertia—fear of the state. Hindsight suggests that there were almost insurmountable obstacles to overcome before the protests could be transformed into mobilizations or before a new social-democratic consensus could be consolidated. But hindsight may be a poor guide to developments that could have had a different outcome.

THE PROTESTS AS A NONHEROIC FORM OF RESISTANCE

Few demonstrations of popular discontent took place during the first decade of military rule in Chile. The majority were staged by small, politically active groups that failed to attract much attention or public support. A group of clandestine organizations repeatedly appealed to the population to join forces against the new regime, and various sectors of civilian society called on the people to oppose the government. These sectors had survived the first stage of Pinochet's "consolidation process," a key policy of which was to dissolve the social and political organizations that supported the Allende government—including those organizations that had been too "lenient" toward it—and to deprive them of their leadership. Ten years is a long time, however, and the number of demonstrations did not increase significantly, nor were those that were held any more warmly received. How, then, can we explain the large-scale protest demonstrations of May 1983, which seemed to come out of nowhere?

Clearly, an economic analysis could be attempted, taking into account the drastic contraction the national economy had experienced since the second quarter of 1981, which followed on the heels of the impressive but illusory boom between the end of 1976 and 1980. The rapid succession of these two abrupt cycles (from a 9 percent growth of the gross national product to a sharp drop of −15 percent) lends credibility to the interpretation that massive frustration of the expectations built up during the boom years produced social rebellion.

Although this analysis might explain certain aspects of the phenomenon, it barely touches on the broader picture. Not every situation of massive frustration leads to the same conclusion, and, in fact, the economy went through a similar recession between 1974 and 1975 (following a period during which purchasing power had increased, workers had the experience of social and political participation, and leading indicators revealed sustained modernization during the 1964–73 period). The 1974–75 recession, however, did not provoke protests, as was the case a decade later. Two fundamental factors that were present in 1974–75 but not in 1983, neither of them economic, help to explain this difference: the historical proximity of a profound political schism in Chilean society and fear of repression. Sociopolitical, as well as economic, interpretation is called for if we are to clarify how generalized frustration is converted into protest or rebellion. Not only must the material conditions be right for the conversion to take place, but the relations among the actors themselves must undergo a transformation that can be described as the overcoming of the heroic syndrome in relation to power.

A kind of vicious circle of fear, or inertia, results when political activity is suppressed and the state, by reverting to police methods of control that extend beyond the public sphere into private lives or by routinely imposing punishments that are in no way proportionate to the behavior that is deemed reprehensible, overcomes the first line of resistance presented by the previously established social organization. From this moment on, fear reproduces itself and progressively isolates the most active individuals and groups engaged in resisting the authoritarian order. Machiavelli clearly described this cycle several centuries ago when formulating "How cities or principalities which lived under their own laws should be administered after being conquered."[1]

Our concern is whether the society is capable of breaking out of this vicious circle by itself, without the intervention of exceptional situations or events. If so, what are the principal preconditions for this process, and what are the most likely setbacks it will encounter?

As I suggested above, exit from the vicious circle depends on breaking down what I have called the heroic syndrome: the perception (which tends to become generalized under these circumstances) by those in the dominated group that they have a specific form of equality in relation to a central and superior power; the common condition is that of being equally defenseless in the face of power. They come to believe that, rather than rational, instrumental strategies, only expressive, exceptional action can affirm a set of superior ethical values and constitute resistance to power. Given that all members of society are denied access to the resources of power equally, expressions of protest follow the unequal distribution of courage among individuals. In this situation, the majority of the population plays the role of the dominated public, and an individual or small group plays the hero; heroism can be followed only by acts on a similar scale, which means that the gulf between the individual or small group and the majority is widened (by indifference, rejection, or sanctification).

Three specific elements: the social significance of those who convened the protest, the scale of the actions, and the ensuing collective reinforcement enabled the population to overcome the heroic syndrome during the Chilean protests of 1983. These elements must be borne in mind if we are to understand the consequent loss of momentum.

THE CONVENERS

The first National Protest, held on May 11, 1983, was called by the CTC. The people's belief in the strategic position of the convening group was largely responsible for the success of the protest. As mentioned, calls to protest, resist, stop work, and rebel were issued regularly during the first decade of military rule. This particular call met with a different response, however, because a considerable cross-section of society—having the benefit of historical experience—understood that copper mining was the primary national economic activity and that a strike in this industry would create economic chaos and force the government to negotiate.

In purely economic terms the Great Copper Mine accounted for approximately 11 percent of the national production-and-distribution infrastructure; in financial terms it was still more important, given that it was the largest single source of collateral for all the loans made to the public sector and, indirectly, for those made by foreign private banks. The political/labor alliance that struck the Allende regime in October 1972 and, in the words of former President Richard Nixon, squeezed the Chilean economy to make it scream, was staged by an alliance of economic sectors that together managed to paralyze substantial sectors of the economic infrastructure. Remembering this event, Chileans did not underestimate the importance of a call to strike issued by the CTC.

To understand the significance of the copper miners, it is necessary to go beyond the ideological interpretations of recent Chilean history that reduce the union movement to one that is homogeneous, politically radical, and class conscious, and to identify two important streams of organized labor that have gone their separate ways since the end of World War II. The first movement was based mainly in the large manufacturing industries and traditional mining enterprises that were protected by the state from foreign competition and were traditionally in the private sector. Given that this sector did not have much strategic importance in the national economy and that management was unable to withstand the demands of labor at the microeconomic level, this movement traditionally tended to express itself politically, combining a radically class-conscious rhetoric toward management with a preference for negotiation with the state. The struggle against the impact of inflation on real wages precipitated a long-term alliance between this sector and the associationist movement within the public and private bureaucracies. This alliance gave rise, in 1952, to the Worker's Central (CUT), an umbrella organization for all labor unions.

Another, more powerful, labor movement, whose agenda was always more labor-oriented than political and whose base was the large strategic state or multinational enterprises (copper, electricity, petroleum, shipping, steel), was developing at the same time. It only entered into partial alliances for specific struggles with its counterpart in the private sector; the two never merged into one bloc. Given its privileged strategic position and the economic power of its employers, this labor sector did not need to enter into broad alliances to lend weight to its demands; it negotiated directly with management.

A call issued by the copper workers, then, had the power to unite the two currents of the union movement at a time when traditional unionism was depleted. Its base had shrunk when the government removed protective tariffs on traditional industry and cut back the bureaucracy. In addition, this body of organized labor had been extremely compromised by its association with the Allende regime, a factor that reduced its capacity to attract new members. In contrast, the base of the union sector represented by the copper workers was not greatly affected by the economic policy of the previous decade, and its capacity to ally itself with the union organizations of the middle class was intact.

These economic and sociological factors translated, from the moment the strike was called, into the first break with the heroic syndrome that had shadowed antiauthoritarian resistance prior to 1983. Together these factors shattered the perception that individuals were equally impotent against the state and raised a strong protective barrier that provided the necessary security for expressions of support for the protest.

THE SCOPE OF THE ACTION

This protective barrier allowed individuals to overcome the second characteristic feature of the heroic syndrome: in a situation of equal powerlessness, the disequilibrium itself feeds an ethical need for expressive action, compelling individuals or small groups to act beyond their ordinary capabilities. The existence of a protective barrier thus allows them to act from whence they stand: as individuals or small groups whose capabilities are ordinary. A pawn in a chess game might be able to attack like a bishop, but it is taken like a pawn. A pawn protected by a bishop, however, by making the small movements permitted it, can act with great audacity and threaten a king from its own little square. Only with difficulty can others follow a heroic actor, not so a protected actor. The rationality of instrumental action displaces the expression of emotion.

The participants in the 1983–84 protests did nothing particularly heroic. The conveners asked the people only to keep their children home from school, to refrain from shopping or doing business on that day, to boycott public transportation, to stay home and beat on empty pots at a predetermined time or sound their horns at the same time if they were driving, and so forth. Some people did more than they were asked to do, to a certain extent. But this overperformance also followed the line of behavior particular to individuals and small groups with ordinary abilities.

The protest actions as a whole tended to push back the frontiers separating the everyday (private) spaces from the public spaces, making for progressive domestication of the public spaces. This shift has allowed the protests to be analyzed from a perspective of territory. According to Alfredo Rodríguez, for example:

> To a great extent, the territorially staged days of protest constituted social practices of reconstruction and reformulation of public life. The private space erupted into the public space through a series of actions which used the places where the residents of Santiago carry out their day-to-day lives—their houses, schools, and workplaces—as points of departure. The protest actions included massive marches and confrontations (with the police) through which the demonstrators attempted to occupy parts of the city.[2]

It is interesting to note, as Rodríguez does, that this occupation of public spaces was true for all the social sectors in the city, although the actual demonstrations that took place in each part of the city, corresponding to a particular social sector, were different.

The city center, the most important symbolic/ceremonial space (where in the past the mass rallies and marches were held and where the presidential palace, offices of the government junta, and main monuments are located), was gradually occupied by the demonstrators. This phase began on the morning of the first day, with university students rallying on the campuses near the city center. Although the rallies took place within a private space (the universities), they constituted a challenge to the university authorities imposed by the regime. The students then moved out into the environs of the university to occupy nearby streets and in doing so delineated the boundaries of a public space that was at once distinct from the private but near their refuge. They finally advanced on the public space (the city center) itself.

> At night, the demonstrations spread all along the Alameda [the main avenue of Santiago]. Motorists (the private circulating in public) blockaded . . . the avenue. The din of the drivers sounding their car horns and people banging on empty pots was deafening. . . . The nighttime occupation was very different from the daytime one; it was extensive, sustained, and simultaneous. The private occupied the public space: houses and offices supplied the noise, and cars blocked the streets.

The scale of the protests was more visible in the socially mixed neighborhoods. University students and people from the poor neighborhoods and the nearby middle-class residential areas participated in the protest together, and the level of conflict was extremely intense.

> It went from a very focused struggle to a mass protest that swept up people from the different social sectors, all of whom participated on their own territories. The public space bounded by the avenues became the common ground wherein the private territories of the students, shantytown residents, and [residents of] housing projects converged. In the case of the latter two, the high population density, social homogeneity, and proximity favored their participation. These factors were reinforced by the layout of the neighborhoods and housing projects, which allowed protesters to retreat to the interior of the blocks.

A particularly telling variation on the same theme tended to occur in the shantytowns. Rodríguez says:

> The protests reached their peak at night. Residents marked out their own territory by putting up barricades that marked the boundaries of the public

space within which their demonstrations and acts of protest could take place. Clashes with the police took place primarily on the outskirts of the occupied territory, at the points of entry to the shantytowns and on the nearby roads that had been cut. The police or the army could enter the "occupied territory" only by exercising extreme brutality. . . . Unlike [the protests] in the city center and mixed neighborhoods, . . . the protests in the shantytowns were spread out throughout the zone, in large areas. Within these zones, the size of the territory dictated the different forms of action; the protest and repression were not confined to specific locations or blocks.

The spatial expression of the protest in the upper- and middle-class neighborhoods was entirely different. The first two days of protest (in May and June 1983) were marked by caravans of automobiles moving slowly down the main streets and avenues of the sector in a showy demonstration that lent the activity considerable spatial continuity. Because it was not a densely populated zone, the demonstrations tended to focus on the apartment buildings and (when the automobile blockades were circumvented by the institution of the curfew) were easily isolated.

Rodríguez's excellent essay clearly shows that, from the territorial point of view, the protest comprised an infinite variety of actions that avoided the central space of the game board (which belongs to the spectacular or heroic action). They tended, rather, to advance on the center from the periphery, from the individuals' private and daily spaces. This tactic favored maximum dispersion of the forces of repression and diminished the imbalance between the defenseless individual or small group and the repressive forces. Even when demonstrators went beyond the passive forms of resistance proposed by the conveners, the heroic syndrome was overcome.

COLLECTIVE REINFORCEMENT

Exceptional (heroic) behaviors that overcome fear, although often idealizing "the people," tend to rest on metaphysical referents such as "God and History." In contrast, participants who overcome fear through ordinary behaviors need the collective reinforcement that springs from their assurance that many people are doing the same as they are or more. They, therefore, are not particularly culpable (or at least their personal conduct does not stand out among the more obviously punishable behaviors). For ordinary protest to take place, individual behaviors must merge with the behavior of the majority, must be confused and mingle with it, not stand out or be in any way different. If the reinforcement is to be effective, the majority must be reassured, first, that the protective barrier remains strong; second, that a group of people is doing more than the majority is being asked to do; and, third, that the majority is acting as it is expected to act.

In the 1983 and 1984 protests, the activities that took place on the days immediately before the protest were distinct from those on the day of the protest itself and in the following night. On the days immediately preceding the protest, the conveners reiterated the call to strike and emphasized the fact that new actors and important people now supported the action and would be consolidating the protective barrier. Successful "tests" confirmed the strength of the barrier: for example, although the courts found certain leaders guilty of inciting the repressive violence in the preceding protests, they set others free because there was no evidence linking them to the organization of the protest. The regime became slightly more tolerant of certain activity, and the Church came to the defense of those who had suffered repression. Media coverage was responsible for focusing public attention on these facts in the morass of contradictions.

On the day of the protest itself, the challenge to fear and the fear of the protest combined to produce the first visible results: children stayed away from school, people stayed off public transportation and did not participate in normal activities in the city, and the first shops closed. In the meantime, the social and political activity began: the students, intellectuals, and militants started to demonstrate in different parts of Santiago (particularly in the city center), indicating that this was no ordinary day and that the protest had begun. This demonstration included the performance of certain acts requiring more courage than the acts demanded of the majority. During the night, the noise of people banging empty pots and sounding car horns, the activity in the neighborhoods, and the news coming from different points in the city and the rest of the country reinforced the perception of the majority that what they were doing was not distinct from what others were doing.

Essential to this set of reinforcement mechanisms was an efficient communications network. For the reinforcement to be effective, people had to be kept up to date and to know what was happening where, given that most actions were developing in locations other than the central spaces. The opposition radios played an absolutely crucial role in this regard, and the government, predictably, consistently responded by banning their news bulletins.

GROWTH AND ROUTINIZATION
OF THE CHALLENGE

If collective victory over fear of the state depends first on overcoming the heroic syndrome, it must be followed by consistent and mounting challenges to power. The construction of a protective barrier displaces expressive emotionality and replaces it with a certain degree of rational instrumentality. The difference between the two is that rational instrumentality requires that the actions be proven efficient, that history be perceived not as a black hole but as a tunnel from which exit is eventually possible if a given course is followed. It is as important that the protesters remain optimistic about the future as that a protective barrier be constructed, and to the extent that the first steps in defiance of power have been taken, optimism grows and develops its own momentum.

The Chilean protests went through at least two phases in this regard. The initial one lasted from the first to the fourth protest, when the challenge to power seemed to be mounting even though there was no evidence of a parallel increase in the actual scope of the actions taken by the civilian population; the second began with the fifth protest (September 1983), by which time the demonstrations seemed almost routine, had decreased in size, and had increased in intensity.

GROWING CHALLENGE

It is odd to verify that, between May and August 1983, the scale of the actions carried out by the civilian population during the days of protest changed little; nevertheless, both local and foreign observers agreed that each event put the regime under more pressure and that the military government was rapidly losing control over the social and political situation. Although the movement grew significantly in the period between the first and second days of protest and incrementally, although less spectacularly, over the following two months, the perception that the regime was under intensified pressure can be attributed more to the behavior of the government itself than to the number of participants in the protest.

The military government's loss of control was, above all, a loss of control over its own responses. The police control over Santiago, which had functioned relatively efficiently during the day of the first protest, was stretched beyond its limit during the first night of protest, when the actions in the shantytowns both proliferated and became more aggressive. The uncertainty that this development produced in the police ranks caused the government to react with disproportionately repressive measures; these apparently left the military with few new resources to combat the protests that followed in the coming months. On the day after the first protest, while the opposition majority celebrated its newfound unity and the prospect of a broadly based opposition movement, the military cracked down. It ordered the radio stations closed, brought suit against the protest organizers, and conducted massive search-and-arrest sweeps through the poor neighborhoods. The perception that the government was responding disproportionately could have sprouted new fear, but fear could not take root in the sustained exhilaration of the first large demonstration of collective discontent in ten years. The collective security provided by the discovery that the people could be an active majority endorsed not fear but a different reading of the official response: "If the government is cracking down like this, it must be because we are on the right track."

There was more: the military's repressive response to the first protest was both ineffective and vacillating. Hoping that the massive sweeps through the poor neighborhoods would turn up something important such as weapons caches, urban guerrillas, or activists who had instigated the movement, it found nothing at all and had to set almost all the prisoners free. Because the news media, including the official stations, made such a story of this failure, the government had to lift the ban on opposition radio stations and allowed them to broadcast news bulletins. This disjointed series of responses, rather than making participants feel that it was dangerous to commit themselves to other demonstrations, reinforced their perception that the protests were a triumph.

The official policy of disproportionate but equivocal response was sustained for the three following protests, each of which was marked by a still larger demonstration: after the second one, the president of the CTC was violently arrested and indicted only days before the date set for the third protest (July 12). Several days before the fourth protest, the entire leadership of the Christian Democratic Party (including the president) was detained and held incommunicado. During the third and fourth protests, a strict afternoon curfew was enforced. For the fourth protest (August 11) the streets of the capital were occupied and patrolled by 18,000 armed soldiers. The number of prisoners and victims rose (particularly during the fourth protest). Even if the protest activities themselves remained exactly the same, therefore, the fact that official repression was intensifying so rapidly (becoming hysterical in August) sustained the perception that the challenge to state power was increasing.

This perception was augmented by the fact that the government made certain concessions in the direction of a political opening: for instance, it issued more permits enabling exiles to return to the country, lifted censorship on books, and gave new opposition media limited license to function. The protective barrier was afforded a degree of official protection (the courts unconditionally released the Christian Democratic leaders, stating that to call nonviolent protests was not a crime). The leaders of the National Trade Union movement were also released, as was Rodolfo Seguel, the president of the CTC. This series of events reaffirmed the popular perception that the government's repressive measures were desperate, inefficient, and uncoordinated, which boosted the still fragile collective confidence that the path chosen would lead to good results and that fear as a limiting factor was losing ground.

The growing solidity of the protective barrier, combined with the ineffective official responses, helped to dissolve fear and reinforce the perception of progress. The first protest was convened by the CTC. The second one was convened by the recently formed National Workers Command, which brought the remaining professional-association unions into the CTC fold. The line now boasted the Democratic Workers Union (which included dock workers and financial employees as well as unionists from the strategic sectors such as steel and petroleum), the Confederation of Private Employees (of well-known moderate tendencies), CUT, and radical workers through the National Union Coordinator and the United Workers Front.

The strike was also endorsed by organizations such as the Project for National Development, the professional associations, and the Superior Council of Land Transport (truckers' union), whose members included the older political and union leaders who had been in the front lines of the struggle against the Allende government. It was also supported by a former member of the military junta (Air Force General Gustavo Leigh). Various private associations, although they did not explicitly endorse the protest, lengthened their list of grievances and demands concerning the economic policy of the regime and showed their sympathy for the opposition movements. On the third day of protest, which went ahead with the CTC leader in jail, the organizers (union and professional groups) invited the political parties to endorse the protest. The recently formed

Democratic Manifesto (a multiparty organization that included Christian Democrats, Socialists, Radicals, Social Democrats, and rightist Republicans) was responsible for circulating the appeal, endorsed by the convening organizations of the earlier protests.

By June 1983, therefore, a new national sociopolitical majority had been constituted. For the first time in the ten years since the Popular Unity government had been overthrown, the schisms that had separated the parties on the left from those in the center, the unions of the great modern companies from those traditionally at the base, and these from the associations of small companies seemed to have been breached. The realignment of important forces finally overcame the paralyzing polarization of the early seventies. Perhaps at this point fear least influenced the behavior of the civilian population, strengthened as it was by the obvious failure of authoritarian control and the receding specter of chaos. This decrease in fear explains why the July 12 and August 11 and 12 demonstrations were the peak of the antiauthoritarian movement.

ROUTINIZATION AND DISENCHANTMENT

The two factors that combined to push back fear (the defeat of the heroic syndrome and the perception of progress) depended on circumstances that were, however, undergoing a series of modifications during the first months of antigovernment mobilization. The effects of this process began to be felt at the time of the turning point suggested by the August peak. Once maximum pressure had been reached, the political and social actors were faced with the decision of which piece to move to checkmate their opponent and begin the process of democratization. This was a strategic moment because the psychosocial factors that had heretofore limited collective action had been overcome.

The material factor—the organic force provided by the protective barrier against fear—was initially the danger of a general strike by the copper miners. The CTC had first called, in April 1983, for a national work stoppage, not a public protest. The decision to replace the stoppage with a protest was made only days before the date set for the strike, owing to the difficulties other unions were having in mobilizing their rank and file around such an extreme goal as a work stoppage. Nonetheless, the idea of a general strike was kept alive during the first two protests, which were seen almost as a test of strength with the view to possible reissue of the original strike appeal. However, the change from work stoppage to protest brought the most powerful section of labor together with the two largest and most dispersed social groups in the country: the middle classes and the marginal and excluded classes.

On May 29, 1983, the government ordered the arrest of Seguel. In accordance with an earlier decision to strike if reprisals were taken against its leaders, the CTC met to discuss whether this was a viable option. Seguel was quickly freed on bail, though, and the call was never issued. On July 12 he was arrested again, this time violently, and the CTC responded immediately by calling on its rank and file to strike the following day. In contrast with the procedure for public protests, the appeal was issued only to workers in the copper industry and was a test of the union's strength. Although workers in three of the five production zones responded positively to the call to strike, the administrative employees and workers in the other two zones were less responsive. The state-owned company CODELCO immediately dismissed 1,800 workers and began hiring to fill the vacancies, drawing long lines of unemployed workers. This action had a negative effect on the locals that had not yet voted to strike. Seven days later, after the strike was broken, the truck drivers' union called on its members to strike. This strike took effect on June 23 and 24 but did not have an impact on public opinion because news was censored. There was, as yet, no possibility of the two movements' joining forces, and the truck drivers returned to work on June 25, having negotiated successfully with the government.

From this moment on, the entropic tendency in the CTC, which in the past had kept it out of the mainstream of the larger union movement, began to gather momentum. The truck drivers' union was in similar straits. Although the inclusion of the political parties in the convocation of the July protest had reconstituted the national movement for democratization and kept the protective barrier intact, the movement's main material force had been damaged.

The political parties' strength lay in their capacity to convene the national population. This strength, however, was more symbolic than material, as was also the case for most of the union confederations (other than the CTC). The real failure of the military's modernization project (in contrast with that in other countries, Brazil in particular) was that new social groups were unable to find their way into strategic places in the national occupational structure. Instead, existing groups, already weakened, underwent a process of accelerated decomposition. The inorganic character of the employment structure undermined the ability of the actors to mobilize their forces in a disciplined way when called on:

between 1971 and 1982, the percentage of economically active wage workers fell from 53 percent to 38 percent; the formally unemployed accounted for 14 percent of the economically active population in 1971 and for 36 percent in 1982. Among youth, who constituted the principal base for mobilization of the protests, 70 percent were formally unemployed. In the middle-class professional associations, however, the withdrawal of the transport workers' organizations (which declared their support for the August protest) left the professionals and merchants isolated from a crucial ally.

The August peak could have been followed by one of several tactical moves by the protest leaders: incorporation of the movement into semi-institutional channels, routinization of the protests (in other words, additional mobilizations with no prospect of intensifying the challenge to power), or the chance that the urban masses might initiate an in-organic insurrectional movement. From September 1983 on, the size of the protests systematically decreased until new and brief cycles began in March/April and September/October 1984. Significant progress had been made, however, and there was no resurgence of fear of the state. Instead, disenchantment set in.

ENTROPIC TENDENCIES AND FEAR OF SOCIETY

The June 1983 realignment was short-lived. In fact, the conditions for its demise had been developing since its inception. During the first protest, observers noted that the nature and size of the mobilizations depended on whether they took place at night or during the day, and that this factor, in turn, varied among the different social sectors of the city. Growing social segmentation of the actions became increasingly evident between the second and fourth protests, as various forms of anomic violence erupted, mainly in the shantytowns. In these neighborhoods, confrontations with the police increased in intensity and were occasionally accompanied by looting and vandalism. The fact that the residents themselves perpetrated this violence in the interior of their own "liberated zones" was widely touted by the official press. As a result, it was much more difficult than in the past to distinguish the boundary between political protest and delinquent behavior, particularly among the youth. Both sprang from the same radical rejection of a social order that at once excluded and oppressed this sector. The violent behavior often went beyond the struggle with the police: stores were looted, buses were set on fire, and pedestrians and drivers were subjected to extortion. The protests provided a space of freedom that unleashed an undercurrent of energies and frustrations difficult to discipline by mere political logic.

However, it was increasingly clear that the repression was becoming socially differentiated, tending to intensify in the slums and diminish in the middle- and upper-class neighborhoods. This spiral of violence showed that the commonly accepted course of events was transposed: the mass of youths who lived in conditions of acute disintegration and anomie responded in a powerfully aggressive way to the excessive police brutality in the slum areas, not vice versa. Be that as it may, this factor tended to weaken the common identity of the protest movement and undermine the cross-class solidarity so painstakingly instilled in the civilian population by the democratic movement.

Added to this breakdown of solidarity was the paradoxical effect of the protective barrier. The barrier itself comprised actors who held relatively central positions in the political, social, and economic system. The centrality of the actors was often linked not only to their proximity to positions of power but to privilege and social "honor." Although these links might inspire confidence, they might also become the target of strong resentment. A country as politically polarized as Chile does not easily forget that the majority of the conveners and blocs in the protective barrier comprised the most militant core of the struggle against the Popular Unity government and President Allende, whose symbolic presence remained intact in the popular media despite the military government's systematic campaign to remove it. The paradoxical effect consists in the fact that the protective barrier also precipitated the struggle for identity by those sectors that had been longest and most terribly oppressed and humiliated. The depth of this demand for identity and autonomy can be better understood if it is borne in mind that the mechanisms used to convene the protest (banging on empty pots and honking car horns) were anti-Allende symbols and that people in the slum areas had always been exposed to much higher degrees of repression than those in other neighborhoods.

Conversely, the growing violence in the shantytowns, the demonstrators' increasing recourse to Allendista symbols, their open mistrust of the protest leaders and of the historic/political expressions of the middle-class groups brought back to the middle class a terror of polarization and of dictatorship of the masses that they had fought against only a decade earlier. The growing social fragmentation of the protests was converted into the mechanism that brought fear of the state back to one of its original sources: civilian society's fear of its own self-destructive tendencies.

The fate of the Chilean protest movement was sealed when, in August 1983, instead of trying to redirect the disintegrating tendency into a new political/social realignment such as that achieved in June, the leadership decided to represent the disintegration politically. The Democratic Alliance was formally constituted on August 7, 1983, four days before the largest projected demonstration against the authoritarian regime. Its affiliates were the parties that had signed the Democratic Manifesto. Their first act was to endorse the protest called for August 11 and 12. After the protest, on August 25, the majority of the parties in the alliance initiated a series of meetings with the government, represented by its new Minister of the Interior.

In protest, the Popular Democratic Movement was formally constituted on August 30; it comprised the Communist Party, the Leftist Revolutionary Movement (a fragment of the Socialist Party), and three small parties of the "new-left" movements of the 1960s. Their first public act was to categorically reject any form of dialogue with the government such as that sponsored by the Democratic Alliance. From then on, the semi-institutional opposition—committed to dialogue, demonstrations, authorized marches, legal process, acquisition of influence and control over social organizations—was explicitly differentiated from the semi-insurrectional opposition, which was committed to forming militias, terrorist tactics, and local strikes. Their only point of contact was the sporadic reiteration of routinized protests.

Fear of the state seemed to have been overcome despite the retreat and renewed state of siege at the end of 1984. In the context of the movement's disintegration and seeming frustration, the populace tended to become disenchanted and impatient with politics as a whole, first and foremost with the military government, but also with the direction being taken by the opposition. Politics had, in effect, returned to a state of war between armed camps and negotiations between elites. It could be said at this point that there was little likelihood that fear of society, or social chaos, would again translate into a middle-class demand for authoritarian rule, given that the people as a whole had grown tired of eleven years of dictatorship and of a regime that habitually went to extremes when confronted with a semi-insurrectional strategy.

The 1983 protests (not those that took place in 1984) must be analyzed as movements that could have succeeded in overcoming the 1973 social schisms but did not. The failure of the protests discredited the political process in the eyes of the majority of the population. The political approach would not be legitimized until the schisms were substantially breached. In the same way that the 1973 coup has often been identified as a textbook case of the Marxist theory of the state, which holds that the armed forces will always defend class interests, it can also be argued that the Chilean protests of 1983 and 1984 proved Hobbes's theory that the persistence of military dictatorship, rather than being the product of the relations between civilians and the military, can be traced to the nature of the relations within civilian sectors of society.

THE PROTESTS AS PRELUDE

In the end, the most important event in breaking the hold of the military dictatorship was a popular plebiscite, called by Pinochet himself, in which the Chilean people voted against the continuation of Pinochet's rule. Many analysts have sought explanations for the victory of the democratic forces in the differences between the strategy in 1988 and that in 1983–84. While the plebiscite is seen as an example of conformity to the rules of the system, the protests are characterized as defiant confrontations with these rules.

I believe this analysis is in large part wrong because it takes the apparent for the real. In fact, the continuity between the protests and the electoral strategies explains the victories in the 1988 plebiscite and the 1990 elections. Not only did the protests make way for the plebiscite, but without the protests, the Chilean political groups would not have known how to fight against their main enemy: fear.

There is an almost perfect homology between the 1988 "NO" campaign and the first five protests in 1983. Both were major mobilizations against fear; their success depended on confronting the heroic syndrome and overcoming civil and political schisms. Both collective actions could be described using the same categories. The 1988 success resulted from one important element: a preestablished date for a national decision. This difference made a desired result obtainable.

NOTES

1. Chapter 5 title of Niccolò Machiavelli, *The Prince* (London: Penguin, [1514] 1961).

2. Alfredo Rodríguez, *Por una ciudad democrática* (Santiago: Ediciones SUR, 1983) is the source for this and subsequent quoted material in the chapter.

NINE

Testimonial Literature and the Armed Struggle in Brazil

Joan Dassin

A rich body of testimonial literature published during the *abertura*—the period of "opening" from 1979 to 1984, which preceded the 1985 changeover to civilian rule—yields many insights into the "culture of fear" under the Brazilian military regime (1964–85).[1] Written largely by former guerrillas or their sympathizers, the works re-create the universe of those who opted to join the armed struggle against the dictatorship. The history of the Brazilian guerrilla movement, which reached its height from 1969 to 1973, is one of deep ideological rifts and fragmentation among numerous splinter organizations.[2] Nonetheless, the testimonies touch on common themes of enforced clandestinity, torture, imprisonment, exile, banishment, and other manifestations of state terror. Hence they reveal much about the "authoritarian culture and experience."[3]

Admittedly, the guerrilla experience is quite atypical of Brazilian society as a whole. At its height, the armed struggle involved approximately 6,000 individuals out of a total population at the time of some one hundred million. In addition, it was concentrated largely in the major cities, particularly Rio de Janeiro and São Paulo. There were only two important rural guerrilla training camps, one in São Paulo State and the other in the Araguaia region in northern Brazil. And by 1973, largely because the repression was so relentless and the guerrilla groups so small and unprepared, the armed movements had been largely decimated.[4]

The testimonial literature is also fragmentary. Paradoxically, only the repressive forces in Brazil may have access to enough of the unpublished details of these individual histories to reconstruct the complete history of the period. Fernando Gabeira, undoubtedly the author-guerrilla whose works have been most widely read, observed: "Only one source could trace that history [of the guerrilla movement] with precision: the security organs of the government, which have under their control the most formidable library about the period, not counting the innumerable testimonies and letters that fell into their hands."[5]

Despite the isolation of the Brazilian armed struggle and the incomplete state of the available texts, study of the guerrillas' testimonies still provides insights into the culture of fear in Brazil. Written in a variety of reportorial and fictional modes and often, but not exclusively, by the protagonists themselves, the works were published largely between 1979 and 1984—in greatest numbers from 1979 to 1982. They thus appeared in Brazil when the "exit from fear" was the major item on the national agenda.[6] Their content, however, covers the earlier period of repression—1969–73—and records the effect of fear on the opposition to the regime.

This chapter is organized around these two historical moments. The first part categorizes the texts, and the second part examines the relation between the testimonies and the politics of *abertura*—in particular, questions of human rights and free expression. The final part analyzes selected works on the basis of three principal questions: What processes led some resisters to conquer fear and join the armed struggle? What kinds of fears did that choice in turn engender, and what were the guerrillas' "recipes for coping"?[7] How did the guerrillas themselves assess the objectives, successes, and failures of the armed struggle?

CATEGORIZATION OF WORKS

The testimonies, dubbed "literatura de exílio e poesia na prisão" by culture critic Heloísa Buarque de Hollanda, were the cultural fruit of the 1979 amnesty.[8] The measure allowed most exiles to return to Brazil, resulted in the release of the few remaining political prisoners, and became a symbol of the *abertura*. And as part of the *abertura*, particularly during the first few years, the reading public eagerly sought to learn more about the armed resistance movements and the torture, imprisonment, and exile that had characterized the previous repressive period.

The works were popular because they restored to Brazilian readers parts of the historical record that were lost to censorship of news about dissent and social conflict as well as to the military's well-publicized propaganda about its own policies. Censorship and propaganda had worked in tandem to create a false image of a harmonious society uniformly committed to security and development. But with *abertura* and the gradual lifting of censorship, the Brazilian press broke news about human-rights abuses, corruption, and other scandals of the regime.

These stories dominated domestic news in 1977 and 1978, just prior to the declaration of the amnesty, the restoration of habeas corpus, and the reestablishment of the multiparty system in 1979. Indeed, the press coverage provided considerable ammunition for the opposition's campaign for the return to the rule of law that eventually resulted in the end of the military regime.

The political memoirs were part of the same collective opposition effort to set the historical record straight. In some cases, such as Alex Polari's *Inventário de cicatrizes,* the texts themselves were circulated as documentation of the regime's repressive excesses.[9]

In general, the testimonies examine forms of political militance and the effects of official repression on activists, sympathizers, and ordinary citizens, all of whom were subject to systematic intimidation by civil and military police after 1968. Stylistically, they are characterized by a mixture of journalistic and fictional elements. For example, fictional narrative modes such as dialogue and scenic description are liberally employed, but the accounts are presented as "true" events witnessed personally or reconstructed from firsthand evidence. Historical analyses, political commentaries, photographs, replicas of newspaper articles, letters, and revolutionary communiqués augment the impression of authenticity.

Probably the one author most associated with the testimonies is former journalist and militant Fernando Gabeira. His 1979 work, *O que è isso, companheiro?* topped best-seller lists for weeks and was published in multiple editions. As of October 1984, more than 200,000 copies had been sold.[10] Although Gabeira hardly established the genre, he certainly popularized it. Some notable works in this line were published earlier: among the most important are Frei Betto's *Cartas da prisão* and *Das catacumbas,* and Augusto Boal's *Milagre no Brasil.*[11] The Boal work was published in Brazil in 1979 but had appeared previously in Portugal.

A particularly rich collection of individual testimonies appeared in a work entitled *Memòrias do exilio: Brasil 1964–19??.*[12] Published in Portugal in 1976, the volume is the first systematic attempt to collect the testimonies of exiled Brazilian militants. It is methodologically self-conscious and explicitly poses the sociological questions inherent in collecting personal testimony. In 1980, a companion volume entitled *Memòrias das mulheres do exílio* was published in Brazil.[13] The two collections are more straightforward and less dramatized than the more popular works published by Gabeira and his successors.

After *O que è isso, companheiro?*, Gabeira published two other autobiographical works in quick succession: *O crepùsculo do macho* and *Entradas e bandeiras.*[14] Other, younger writers also published autobiographical accounts of their political adventures. Among the most interesting are Alfredo Syrkis's *Os carbonàrios,* Alvaro Caldas's *Tirando o capuz,* and Herbert Daniel's *Passagem para o pròximo sonho.*[15]

Typically, these works trace the history of the period from the perspective of middle-class students or young professionals who joined the armed struggle. On the whole, they unfold chronologically, recounting the origins of the armed guerrilla struggle in the student protests and mass demonstrations of 1968; the organization of the armed guerrilla groups; guerrilla actions, including bank robberies and other thefts to finance various operations, largely abortive efforts at popular mobilization, and, most spectacularly, the kidnapping of foreign diplomats—in Gabeira's case, American ambassador Charles Elbrick in 1969; the risks and features of clandestinity; the fear and reality of capture and imprisonment; and the techniques of torture and the victims' relationship with the torturers. Some also recount the years of exile and the protagonists' return to Brazil.

In addition to the primarily autobiographical accounts, other works of personalized reportage highlight different aspects of the late 1960s and early 1970s. Among the most notable are Clovis Moura's presentation of the *Diário da guerrilha da Araguaia,* an anonymous account of the small rural guerrilla band whose activities precipitated the most ferocious counterinsurgency campaign of the entire repressive period, Emiliano José and Oldack Miranda's *Lamarca, o capitão da guerrilha,* a virtual hagiography of Carlos Lamarca, one of the most important guerrilla leaders, and Boal's *Batismo de sangue,* which recounts the involvement of the Dominicans in the capture and murder by the police of Carlos Marighella, also an important guerrilla leader.[16] *Batismo de sangue* includes a special dossier of documents about Frei Tito, a young Dominican whose savage torture at the hands of São Paulo special investigator Sérgio Fleury and subsequent suicide in France became a cause célèbre in both Europe and Brazil.

A number of journalistic works exposing the repressive apparatus were published in this period as well, initiating a much more aggressive style of investigative journalism than had been possible during the period of strict censorship (1968–76). These include Antonio Carlos Fon's *Tortura: A història da repressão política no Brasil;* Fernando Portela's collected articles on Araguaia, *Guerra de guerrilhas no Brasil;* and Paulo Marconi's *A censura política na imprensa brasileira, 1968–1978.*[17] These and other similar texts are based on empirical evidence and in some cases firsthand knowledge of the events described but are not focused principally on the authors' personal experiences.

Although not the subject of this study, many explicitly fictional works published in the 1970s also examine state terror and resistance movements. Antonio Callado's novels, for example, are the touchstone for a whole subsequent generation of political fiction. Other important works are Renato Pompeu's *Quatro-olhos* (1976); Renato Tapajòs's *Em camara lenta* (1977); Ivan Angelo's *A festa* (1976) and *A casa de vidro* (1979); Rodolfo Konder's short stories and fiction, *Tempo de ameaça* (1978), *Cadeia para os mortos* (1977), and *Comando das trevas* (1980); and Artur Jose Poerner's *Nas profundas do inferno* (1979). Selected novels by Márcio de Souza, Sinval Medina, Sèrgio Sant'Anna, and Carlinhos Oliveira also deal with repression, the costs of political actions, the crisis of the Brazilian left, and the failure of the armed struggle. This fiction is rich, in part because literature was generally less subject to censorship in the 1968–78 period than were other forms, such as journalism or film, that reached a wider audience.

The 1979–84 political testimonies, in particular, marked an important phase of the Brazilian transition. They appeared during a politically propitious moment, when the opposition forces had secured at least a partial restoration of civil and political liberties—victories that would be deepened after the actual changeover to civilian rule. In cultural terms, the works filled in the details of the recent past for many Brazilian readers, bringing the state's repressive excesses to light and thereby opening the way for a more democratic order. Gabeira sums it up. "What people wanted," he said in a press interview, "was history as seen by the vanquished, because they already knew the victors' version."[18]

TESTIMONIAL LITERATURE AND
THE POLITICS OF *ABERTURA*

How, specifically, are these works—particularly the autobiographical accounts of Gabeira, Syrkis, Caldas, and Daniel, which focus on the authors' personal involvement in the armed struggle—linked to the process of the Brazilian *abertura?* Manuel Antonio Garretón's notion of the *efecto demonstración,* the making public of opposition to the regime, is particularly useful in considering this question.[19]

For Garretón, the *efecto demonstración* is one of three interrelated processes in the loss of fear, which is in turn a key stage in the evolution of resistance. Phenomena that have this *efecto demonstración* include controversial art works, humor or critical jokes, underground or alternative publications, and public testimonies by personalities. In Brazil, the so-called midget press played a key role in keeping opposition attitudes visible throughout the 1968–78 period. From 1969 on, for example, numerous articles satirizing the Brazilian military government appeared in the irreverent weekly *Pasquim.* Serious criticisms of major policy issues, such as foreign investment and the social cost of the regime's economic policies, appeared in the weekly review *Opinião* from 1972 to 1975, and in its offshoot, *Movimento,* from 1975 to 1978.

Even during the cultural vacuum created by the harsh repression of the Médici era, from 1969 to 1974, journalists and artists attempted to break though official propaganda. They sought to contest the slick image of "Brasil Grande," which dominated the controlled media and was promoted through government publicity campaigns. The alternative press, and also theater, popular music, film, and literature, took on political questions when the Congress, the courts, labor unions, and political parties were reduced to rubber-stamping official positions, and when the universities, professional associations, and major media were also purged and censored.[20] The Brazilian Church played a similar surrogate role in the political debate.[21]

The political memoirs of the repression had an evident *efecto demonstración.* Although they appeared in the late 1970s and early 1980s, when the *abertura* was already well under way, the political memoirs portrayed the period of repression that had begun some ten years earlier. In harking back to that time, they challenged in particular two features of the political process then unfolding: the amnesty and the government's concession of press freedom. The reciprocal amnesty was designed to benefit both those who were legally sanctioned for national security crimes and those who committed human-rights abuses in political investigations. The measure was deliberately intended to discourage public vindictiveness against the security forces. Although the dirty war conducted against internal subversion was on a proportionally lesser scale in Brazil than in the other Southern Cone countries, torture of and

other brutality against political prisoners as well as against the population at large were systematically employed. Moreover, the traditional
rules of the political game were violated when severe repression, including torture, was directed at the children of the Brazilian middle class.

Nonetheless, both the outgoing military and the incoming civilians
largely agreed to let bygones be bygones. Fears of "Argentinization"—
polarization and heightened social conflict—were invoked both by regime supporters and the opposition to brake the liberalization process
throughout the Figueiredo period; this invocation of Argentinization
came to the fore during the 1984 presidential campaign. In agreeing
largely to avoid the issue of human-rights abuses committed by the
security forces, the military sought to avoid prosecution; the opposition,
to avoid jeopardizing the *abertura*.

In view of this semitacit accord, the testimonial literature, like the
many news stories and opinion pieces about human-rights abuses published in the Brazilian press, was an important arena where the painful
question of human-rights abuses could be explored and blame assigned.
The recollections by former guerrillas and exiles, in particular, were
individual attempts to close the accounts of the repressive period because
no definitive legal action had been taken in this regard. This closing of
accounts implied not only taking responsibility for the military and
political failures of the resistance movements but also identifying, often
by name and in photographs, those who were responsible for the torture
and intimidation of political prisoners and suspected subversives.

The public fascination with these testimonies must be at least in part
explained by this function. Although they eventually lost popularity,
such works metaphorically served in lieu of official sanctions against
torturers, who were never held to account for their actions. Symbolically, the works are a form of justice and compensation for victims of the
repressive forces, and they provide information about the repressive
apparatus. The romantic self-presentation by author-protagonists in the
autobiographical works and the primarily personal and psychological
focus do not mitigate their political significance.

The publication of the testimonies also tested the limits of free expression during the *abertura*. Grudgingly granted during the Geisel administration (1974–79) to shore up the regime's fading legitimacy, relative
freedom allowed the press to become the watchdog of other basic freedoms in Brazil. Press denunciations of human-rights abuses, for example, helped to maintain public pressure on the regime to restore habeas
corpus for political crimes. As noted, the press played a vanguard role in

the events of 1977 and 1978, devoting extensive coverage to government negotiations with opposition leaders, which ultimately set the stage for the rise of civil society.

In 1978, in particular, the amnesty campaign dominated press coverage of the national political scene. Political prisoners previously stigmatized as terrorists became increasingly familiar to newspaper readers. Details of exile were published for the first time. Although major press organs were virtually unanimous in their support of João Batista Figueiredo's 1978 presidential bid, they also published prominent stories about the security apparatus, torture, police violence, corruption, and the collaboration of Southern Cone security forces.[22]

Both this press coverage and the political memoirs made public those stories that had been most censored by the regime. And once the information was in the public domain, it was difficult for the regime to censor similar topics even when they were presented in forms with potentially large audiences, such as film.

As the *abertura* progressed, political debate figured more prominently in the national press. Arbitrary censorship, particularly of the electronic media, did persist after 1979. Nonetheless, from the moment in 1984 when TV Globo, the major Brazilian network, resolved to cover the mass campaign for direct presidential elections, television became a key factor in the transition to civilian rule. Before that occurred, however, the testimonial literature and the press coverage of the late 1970s and early 1980s tested the regime's concession of relative free expression by revealing some of the state's more closely guarded secrets.

POLITICAL TESTIMONY
AND THE CULTURE OF FEAR

THE CHOICE

When Garretón poses the general question of how fear affects opposition movements, he notes that one component problem is the impact of fear on political organizations, which may be weakened or strengthened by fear.[23] Political militants themselves also react to fear in a variety of ways, ranging from solitary withdrawal to clandestine heroics. What do these testimonies tell us about the relationship between activism and fear, on both an organizational and an individual level? Specifically, how do they portray the climate of fear in Brazil and the choice, notwithstanding, of so many young middle-class students to take up arms against the regime?

Some historical background makes clear how the state created a climate of fear in an exaggerated response to the supposed guerrilla threat.[24] The strategy of armed rebellion against the national security state had been debated among opposition groups since the early 1960s. But only in 1967, when Marighella, a member of the executive committee of the Brazilian Communist Party, publicly split with the party by advocating urban guerrilla warfare, did the movement for armed resistance gain political importance. Even more militants adopted the tactic after the passage of Institutional Act 5 (AI5) in December 1968.

AI5 was a crucial turning point because the measure granted virtually unlimited emergency powers to the state and initiated a cycle of repression that lasted from 1969 to 1974. Unlike the repressive cycle immediately following the 1964 coup, which specifically targeted political figures associated with the ousted government of João Goulart, as well as workers and peasants, or the second repressive cycle from 1965 to 1966, which removed opposition office holders from all levels of government, the cycle of repression initiated by AI5 was intended to crack down on the whole of civil society.

Drawing on its newly expanded powers, the regime conducted extensive purges of political organizations, universities, informational networks, and the state bureaucracy. Special executive decrees allowed the state to circumscribe the political activities of university professors and students and limit even further the political activities of individuals whose political rights had already been suspended. Decrees also curbed the power of Congress, closing it entirely from December 1968 through October 1969. In this manner, the regime institutionalized controls in the so-called psychosocial area, particularly in the press, the universities, and the political organizations, and also established a "legal" framework for its economic policies.

In addition, ostensibly in response to intensified and sometimes violent protests against the regime, the repressive apparatus unleashed by AI5 directed indiscriminate violence against all social classes, even the previously unharmed middle sectors. Nationwide searches and arrests created a general climate of intimidation that strongly deterred both political action and social organization. Eventually, the repressive apparatus became a semiautonomous power, which at times contested even the national security state itself. The 1968 crackdown was a victory for those sectors within the military that justified all measures to maintain internal security, including extensive campaigns of terror against the population at large.

Caught between the demobilization of civil society on the one hand and the entrenchment of the repressive apparatus on the other, many political militants felt that the only way to express dissent was to take up arms against the state. Not even the threat of capture, torture, imprisonment, or reprisals was enough to dissuade them from this course of action. On the contrary, the escalated violence of the state, powerfully symbolized by AI5, was the final argument that convinced many middle-class people to join clandestine party organizations engaged in the armed struggle. Not until after the defeat of the guerrillas, in 1973, did the opposition reassess its strategies. The post-1973 *abertura,* for example, was negotiated by social forces specifically not connected to groups involved in the armed struggle.

It is precisely this dynamic relationship between the evolution of the armed struggle and the increasingly repressive state that the political memoirs depict. Participation in the student movement, especially, led naturally to more extreme actions. An illustration of this escalating involvement is found in *Tirando o capuz,* by the journalist Alvaro Caldas.[25]

In his memoir, Caldas isolates the moment when the relatively open political struggle of the 1966–68 period shifted to a phase marked by clandestinity and urban guerrilla actions. He re-creates the scene with nostalgia. In March 1976, Caldas participates in a slogan-painting episode. Accompanied by a professor and two student friends, he paints the Rio walls with slogans like "The Dictatorship Continues" and "Only a Change of Dictators" to protest the fact that another military man, Marechal Costa e Silva, was to succeed Marechal Castelo Branco as president of Brazil.

At 2:00 A.M., their mission successfully completed, the group cannot resist a final paint job. Naturally, the military police come upon the culprits, and they are arrested. They all end up in the hands of the political police but still have time to invent an alibi before the questioning begins. They agree to say that they were at the movies, went to a bar, and suddenly discovered a bag of paints and supplies on the floor by their table. After that, they would claim, everything happened fast: the idea of the protest; the slogan painting; and their arrest. Although the alibi is pathetically unconvincing, the group is released the following day.

Caldas comments that the incident became a symbol for him. After 1967, as the society closed down, he and his slogan-painting companions devoted themselves to other concerns: the internal struggle within the left; the formation and consolidation of clandestine organizations;

tactical and strategic discussions. The times changed too. Caldas reflects that up to the moment of his first arrest, politics were "romantic," infused with poetry. After that time, Caldas writes, "poetry died and discipline and the preoccupation with security began to stretch tight a bureaucratic web." Slogan-painting was superseded by planned violence.

Former guerrilla Polari's personal testimony paints a similar picture. In an interview he granted while awaiting release from prison after serving nearly ten years, Polari recalls that in 1964 the dictatorship had tried to stop a social process begun in the early 1960s.[26] Following a two-year hiatus caused by the implantation of the regime, protests surfaced anew, principally in the student movement. Like Caldas, Polari remembers the 1966–68 period as a time of political initiation. For him, it was when he began his "useful political-genital existence, went surfing, listened to the Beatles." Political participation was a widely shared value for his generation, and political militancy, a "seductive alternative." At the same time, however, the space for such activities narrowed as the regime closed down, so that a moderate course became increasingly difficult to follow.

By 1969, the choice was completely polarized: drugs or the armed struggle; drop out to arrange "any old Nirvana for refuge" or "risk one's life." The possibilities for reform were nil because opting for a middle course was synonymous with "total integration, corruption . . . mediocrity." Moreover, the left was where the action was. Polari recalls that he joined the guerrilla movement during what seemed to be a period of great effervescence. It was in fact a moment of great internal fragmentation among the clandestine groups.

Polari's personal history with the guerrilla groups demonstrates much of the fervor, confusion, and self-deception that occurred. For example, Polari first belonged to the National Liberation Commandos (COLINA). When he opted for the armed struggle, in 1969, the Armed Revolutionary Vanguard Palmares (VAR-Palmares) was his group of choice. However, VAR-Palmares split, resulting in the formation of a new version of a previously existing group called the Popular Revolutionary Vanguard (VPR). Interestingly, Polari does not explain how each group differed or interpreted revolutionary theory. He simply says he opted for the VPR because it was "more to the left."

This rather offhand reasoning is a reminder that Polari's generation of guerrillas was neither militarily nor theoretically prepared for the course they chose. The testimonies agree on this point. Despite the endless discussions based on a handful of works—Régis Debray's *Revolution within the Revolution,* Lenin's *What Is to be Done?,* the handbooks of Mao Tse-tung, Trotsky's trilogy, and a few other random classics on history and revolution—the young militants' intellectual preparation for the struggle was at best haphazard.

As Polari notes, symbols and legends were much more concrete inspirations: Che Guevara, whose murder in Bolivia was a symbol of sacrifice for the coming revolution, never an indication of defeat; the Venezuelan guerrilla leader Douglas Bravo; Camilo Torres in Colombia. The Uruguayan Raul Sendic and the Tupamaros in general were the ideal urban guerrillas to the young Brazilians. Inspired by Cuba, radicalized by Vietnam, and influenced by the Latin American romance with continental revolution, the young Brazilian guerrillas were prepared to battle the dictatorship for their own revolution.

Potential perplexities such as how to justify the 1968 Soviet invasion of Czechoslovakia and the reduction of Cuban support for the Latin American guerrilla movements were sidelined or ignored in light of the urgency of events in Brazil in the 1966–68 period. The revolutionary spirit grew as the student guerrillas rode a wave of middle-class protests against the regime that reached their height in 1968 with the murder of the student Edson Luis and the so-called march of the hundred thousand. One protest led to another, and when the military crackdown began, many youths were already committed to armed action.

For Polari, this period was a golden age, a time unlikely to be repeated that each person is entitled to only once. That description suggests a connection between the intensity of political involvement for the first time and a sexual and emotional coming of age. Indeed, Polari makes the connection explicitly:

> The vision of armed struggle fit our needs like a glove, even more, perhaps, than it described the reality we hoped to transform. It was a moment when we were discovering the World. . . . We turned onto politics at the same time we learned about making love, about sexuality. . . . All our fantasies and our socialist ideas harmonized perfectly.

Quite apart from historical and political explanations of the factors that led student militants into the armed struggle, this generational analysis also bears weight. Gabeira, who came of age in the 1950s, notes that while his generation confronted their families in the struggle for self-definition, the generation of 1968 in Brazil slammed smack into a conflict with the repressive regime. This view is supported by the testimonies. Hence the texts provide ample evidence of a generation that thought primarily about political questions, often to the exclusion of personal ones. The language of the day, captured in these accounts, is a humorous indication of the politicization. Personal problems were immediately labeled "ideological," and any lack of resolve or a cautious second thought was evidence of a "petit-bourgeois upbringing."

But the politicized vocabulary could not disguise the fact that even irremediable decisions were often made on purely personal and individualistic grounds. Again, Polari's testimony is very much to the point. Why in the end did he join the armed struggle? The following anecdote is his response:

> One day, when I was wandering around on the Voluntàrios da Patria [a street in Rio] and I couldn't put off certain decisions any longer, an idea came into my head: either I'd drop out and learn to play the recorder, put together a renaissance music group, or I'd join the guerrillas. I joined the guerrillas. At the time, I thought that was what I had to do. I still think so.

FEAR AND THE ARMED STRUGGLE

On the other side of this intensity and romantic political involvement were the doubts, fears, and questioning that accompanied the young guerrillas' exuberant acts. Not that any of the accounts implies that the struggle was not worth pursuing. On the contrary, despite all the errors that later became evident, the idea that they had gained in stature, courage, and maturity for having fought the good fight underlies all the testimony. The author-protagonists are defeated guerrillas but heroic narrators. Nonetheless, the accounts also dwell at length on what Patricia Fagen calls the techniques of fear-mongering: arbitrary arrests and punishments; torture; disappearances; the removal of political crimes from normal judicial procedures; the denial of or limitation of such rights as freedom of movement and association; and censorship and the manipulation of information.[27]

The descriptions of the responses to torture, in particular, demonstrate the complex relationship between activism and fear. The mechanisms that insulated actors from fear, what Corradi called "recipes for coping,"[28] are laid bare. And there was no doubt that the recipes were necessary. According to the International Commission of Jurists, for example, there were at least 12,000 political prisoners in Brazil from 1969 to 1974.[29] But regardless of the exact number of persons who passed through the prisons and torture chambers of the regime, it is well known that massive search-and-arrest campaigns in the cities as well as large-scale military and police operations in the countryside resulted in a high turnover of prisoners.

It was also well known that torture was routinely used with political prisoners and detainees, both to break their will and to obtain information that could lead to other arrests and to the infiltration and dismantling of resistance groups. Torture was usually most intense during the first hours or days after an arrest because under the National Security Law suspects could be held incommunicado and without charges. Torture was also used during the initial period because the authorities often had no formal charges to file against those who were detained, and preventive arrests could legally be extended for up to only twenty days.[30]

The legalities aside, arrest and torture were indissolubly linked in the public mind. As Maria Helena Moreira Alves observes, because almost any political activity could be considered a crime against national security under the broad scope of the National Security Law, the fear of political arrest was intense. The serious risk of torture thus served, at least in the short run, as a deterrent to political participation. The use of torture was never publicly admitted by the Brazilian regime, but it was without question an important policy tool in the post-1964 period.[31]

The testimonies provide explicit descriptions of these psychological ploys. In *Passagem para o pròximo sonho,* for example, Herbert Daniel recounts a recurrent nightmare.[32] In the dream, he is taken prisoner and placed nude in a room in front of a table piled high with official-looking papers. At times, Daniel is alone; at others, another figure—perhaps himself—who has already been prisoner for some time and so knows what to expect, is also present. Later on in the dream, the other figure— at that point definitely a waking version of himself—explains to his dreaming self that the important thing is to be patient, to wait for the torture to begin. At the same time, policemen enter and leave the room but take no note of him. When he asks when he will be interrogated, no one hears, except for one particularly repellent torturer who laughingly tells him his turn is near.

The moment never arrives. Daniel tries to prepare himself for the inevitable by keeping up his morale and repeating the formulas of the day: that pain should stimulate hatred, not panic; that he should forget everything and enter totally into the moment of terror as if only that instant existed; that he should anticipate nothing. Yet these strategies are futile. He is disconcerted by the impossibility of anticipating nothing because he also has to wait for the moment of torture to begin. He hears the torture of others clearly; a victim is thrown at his feet. He rises to confront his fate; but the door of the torture chamber is closed, and he awakes.

Daniel's commentary on this dream, which he had often during his clandestine phase, is particularly significant.

> Maybe it was because of this recurring nightmare that I detested hearing about torture, particularly relatively detailed stories about what happened to the victims. It always seemed disagreeable but necessary to know that torture existed and to know something about the techniques. But to know the victims' names and the fine points of the case was always terrifying.

Daniel then describes his mental preparation for torture. For years, he lived with the certainty that sooner or later he will be arrested and tortured. As in the dream, he is condemned to waiting. In suspense, the best he can do is not imagine what will happen. "It was important not to make real pain worse with my imagination." Nonetheless, he concludes, there are too many things to do, and it is impossible to think constantly of the danger. Later on, when the danger becomes intolerable, he reenters legal existence with a false identity. He and his companions become "model citizens, like everyone in the same shitty situation."

In *Os carbonàrios,* Alfredo Syrkis reveals similar attitudes.[33] One scene from the book makes them clear. The time is New Year's Eve 1970; the setting, Ipanema beach in Rio de Janeiro. The narrator meets a friend who insists that the 1970s will be Latin America's "decade of revolution." That desperate affirmation stimulates the narrator's fantasy: gun in hand, black beret with five-pointed star à la Guevara, olive-drab uniform, he envisions himself surrounded by "fervent and determined peasants," crossing the mountains toward yet another armed encounter. The ironic tone is intentional, for he is really worried at that moment by macabre thoughts about death and torture. Marighella had been murdered by the military in São Paulo that November, and just a few days before Syrkis had received the first denunciation of torture smuggled out from the Linhares prison by members of the COLINA. In the document, dozens of torture cases from Minas and Rio are described in detail, revealing both the sadism and the scientific methods of the torturers. The document also reveals that torture "classes" are held with live victims. Torture is effective, the narrator notes; most arrests are made on the basis of torture-induced confessions.

Curiously, the line of reasoning ends there. In the next sentence of the passage, the narrator switches abruptly to the attitudes guerrillas were supposed to adopt regarding torture—when they thought about it: "The issue was taboo; the attitude *macho*. Whoever talks is a weak, petit-bourgeois traitor. Real revolutionaries don't squeal." When militants did reveal information under torture, the question of how to judge them, how to balance comprehension of their plight with the certainty that if information were revealed the guerrilla organizations would be defeated and the torturers would triumph, was "the worst thing about militancy." The passage concludes with a recitation of clichés that recall the phrases of Daniel. Thus the perfect guerrilla should "have faith in the Revolution and hate the oppressors. Whoever hates enough won't squeal."

The sequence of the narration makes clear how remote that ideal was. With an abrupt cut, the reader and the narrator arrive on the main avenue in front of Ipanema beach. The narrator reflects that nothing bad will happen to him; he believes in his lucky star. He tries to outrun his dark thoughts and jumps onto the soft beach sand. Taking off his shoes, he surrenders to the strong physical sensations of the setting. He hears the spiritualist faithful singing to the goddess Iemanjà. He asks an old black woman for a flower, the traditional New Year's offering to Iemanjà, and wades into the surf watching his flower float out to sea. The relief from fear is like a sexual release: "I left the water feeling spent and sated, as you do after an orgasm. . . . Fear and anguish had been banished to a remote corner of my mind."

When the testimonies deal with torture directly, they often take a cool analytical stance. The effort to identify, classify, and describe the inner anguish of the victim and the nuances of his relationship with the torturer in itself becomes a mechanism for reducing fear. This strategy is evident in Caldas's *Tirando o capuz*.[34] Although Caldas uses fictional re-creation of scenes and events in his account, the dispassionate, straightforward tone impresses the reader with the narrator's self-control and survival capacity. In the telling, at least, the narrator evinces no fear, although he describes it in detail.

One scene from the book provides an illustration. At a certain moment in the interrogation, one of Caldas's torturers nearly strangles him. When his father sees the bruises still visible on his son's neck in their first encounter sixty days after the arrest, he is horrified. Like most individuals who had not actually been imprisoned, Caldas's father is reluctant to believe that torture is routine. Even for political militants who know about torture, the reality is much more brutal than any fantasies they could invent.

It is precisely the contact with that unimaginable world, however, that allows Caldas and his companions to survive. Knowledge about the torture experience aids the victim in squaring his psychological accounts. The simple analysis of why it is difficult to be rational under torture is a demystification of both a totally heroic posture and a collaborationist attitude. While being tortured, Caldas finds he is to a certain degree detached from the outcome but also imbued with a hatred that compels him not to give in but to react and to resist. Living, he concludes, is his primary concern.

In the torture sessions, Caldas also learns about the competitive relationship between the torturer and the victim. He theorizes that the torturer fears the guerrilla, who after all has put his life on the line. Like his victim, the torturer is clandestine because his behavior is subject to moral condemnation even though it has been legitimized and institutionalized by the dictatorship. Thus handicapped, the torturer can seek to dominate the guerrilla only in the actual moment of torture, when he must be more manly, overcome all resistance, and humiliate and attack his victim in all possible ways, including sexually. The torture sessions begin with the prisoner nude and specifically target the most sensitive parts of the body, particularly the sexual organs.

Valid or not, this theorizing about the psychology of the torturer is a useful survival strategy. It may even be argued that the experience of having passed through torture—provided one survived, of course—was in most cases the beginning of the loss of fear. Alves makes a similar point about Brazilian society in general.[35] She notes that the regular use of torture by the national security state eventually limited its effectiveness as a means of political control. Indeed, the fact that so many people experienced torture but survived drained the experience of some of its terror. In interviews conducted in 1981, Alves concluded that militants viewed torture with less panic than they had in 1964 or even in 1969, precisely because they had outlived the pain. One urban leader had been arrested and tortured thirty-two times since 1964, yet reported that his fear diminished with each subsequent arrest.

Overall, the recording of these strategies for coping with both the anxiety of anticipation and the reality of torture is part of the loss of fear, because the authors are obviously survivors. At the time the events occurred, moreover, these "recipes for coping" at least in some measure helped militants run the risks of political participation. The question logically follows of what, overall, was the nature of their resistance. How do the narrators of these testimonies assess the objectives, successes, and failures of the Brazilian armed struggle?

POLITICAL ASSESSMENT AND SELF-CRITIQUE

One approach to the question of assessment is to note significant lacunae in the testimonies. They are most revealing on a personal and psychological level. As social analysis, they provide insights into the polarized choices faced by the generation of 1968, into the relations among the guerrillas and their perceptions and behavior toward others who appear in their increasingly limited sphere of operations. A parade of shallow characters—the occasional sympathizer; bewildered parents; faceless, suspicious, or even compassionate landladies who rent the guerrillas rooms for hideouts and apartments and houses for clandestine meetings; inquisitive neighbors; and now and then slum dwellers or factory workers whom they hope will join the revolution—march through the testimonies, indicating the progressive alienation and distancing of the guerrillas from the very people for whom they were supposedly preparing the revolution.

Curiously, however, the works present virtually no profile of Brazilian society and little systematic analysis of the Brazilian political situation. They do not take on even the most pertinent question of what the armed struggle meant in general for the Brazilian political process or what its dimensions were. On the contrary, the general assessment of the movement is couched as self-criticism that at its most collective is a criticism of certain illusions shared by the guerrillas. Mentioned most often is the romantic deception that the armed guerrilla groups were in fact the vanguard of a popular revolution. But the criticisms are presented with profound ambivalence. Although the authors regret their own naiveté and general lack of preparedness, their underlying conviction that the struggle was worth waging and was probably the high point of their youth precludes too extensive an analysis.

The analysis would have been revealing. As noted, no more than 6,000 guerrillas participated in the armed struggle throughout the entire period. Nor was there much popular support for the guerrilla organizations, despite public sympathy awakened by urban maneuvers such as bank robberies and kidnapping of diplomats. Indeed, popular adherence was discouraged by the real risks run by the guerrillas, amply publicized in widely reported police and military ambushes and captures of "terrorist" troublemakers.

In the countryside, the severity of the repression made popular adherence to the guerrilla groups even less likely. The repression of the few attempts to establish rural centers amounted to pacification campaigns against the local inhabitants. Ten thousand soldiers participated in the encirclement operation conducted against Lamarca and his band of nine rural guerrillas in the Vale da Ribeira. Lamarca escaped but was later killed in the backlands of Bahia. In Araguaia, a region of great strategic and economic importance, 20,000 men were employed in three separate military campaigns between 1972 and 1974 to liquidate sixty-nine militants. Their subversive activities included building a school, providing health care, and giving agronomy lessons to the local population while training in the jungle by night. The local population was apparently unaware of the clandestine training. In both cases, the unarmed population was subjected to arbitrary arrest, imprisonment, and violence.[36]

A pattern emerges of spectacular but uncoordinated actions by splintered and ideologically fragmented groups, undertaken in the increasingly fragile hope that the country and the rest of the world would notice the armed struggle against the Brazilian dictatorship. The actual struggle involved actions that were more defensive than offensive, such as the kidnapping of foreign diplomats in exchange for the liberation of captured members of the underground organizations or the robbing of banks and theft of automobiles to pay expenses and provide transportation. And over a relatively short period even these defensive actions were forced to a halt as the repressive apparatus thinned the ranks of the underground organizations. Substitution of imprisoned members became impossible as the repression closed in. And the testimonies often comment on the impossibility of recruiting new cadres for the guerrilla organizations.

But the guerrillas' defeat is not in the foreground of these works; it serves rather as the backdrop for individual acts of courage, daring, and good-humored risktaking. Gabeira's dramatic re-creation of the kidnapping of Elbrick in *O que è isso, companheiro?* is an example.[37] Gabeira is at his playful best in this description of events that in fact captured the imagination of countless Brazilians, catching the military by surprise and striking directly at North American imperialism—for the guerrillas, the real enemy.

The scene is worth describing in some detail. Gabeira starts slowly, teasing the reader with small detours before settling down to the story at hand. He claims he does not quite remember what kind of day it was when the events occurred. All he remembers with certainty, in fact, is a sentence that Richard Nixon may *not* have uttered to his then-Secretary of State William Rogers upon learning of the kidnapping: "Rogers, what the shit is this?" Like Proust's bit of cake and cup of tea, this Nixonesque phrase sets off Gabeira's memory, "opening the way for a thousand and one details."

The details of the kidnapping follow, recounted with wit and irony. The reader learns how the plot was hatched and planned, what manifesto the guerrillas intended to write, and what demands would have to be met for the ambassador to be set free. Gabeira weaves the texts of these manifestos and Elbrick's letters to his wife in the narrative, adding to the aura of authenticity. He describes his conversations with Elbrick in detail, indicating the ambassador's thoughts about Vietnam and his surprise at the brutality of the Brazilian regime.

Toward the end of the chapter, the level of suspense and anxiety increases. The house where the ambassador is being held is watched by the police. Both Elbrick and his kidnappers fear an absurd accident that will kill them all. The final scene recounts the tension as the police try to intercept the militants who are releasing Elbrick after the safe departure of the prisoners for whom he is exchanged. Elbrick safe, the repression closes in swiftly, and many of Gabeira's companions are captured. Many who were merely implicated in the kidnapping are also arrested and tortured. Gabeira makes a final accounting of what happened to the participants themselves. Two die under torture; some are taken prisoner and released after serving time; others are exchanged for diplomats in subsequent kidnappings and live in exile; some flee; one goes mad in the streets of Paris. As for Gabeira, he survives and thinks it "interesting" to tell the story.

With that understatement, Gabeira goes on to tell how the repression closes in on him. Forced after the kidnapping into the deepest clandestinity, he moves to São Paulo but is arrested soon afterward. He is wounded during capture, tortured, passed from prison to prison, and finally released in exchange for another kidnapped diplomat. The narration is suspenseful, moving, and replete with detail about the necessity of bargaining with one's torturers in order to survive. Comments on prison conditions and the social relations among the prisoners are also woven into the text.

The self-criticism and political errors are those most frequently noted in all these accounts: authoritarianism or macho attitudes within the guerrilla organizations; the romanticization of torture; and the lack of objectivity about the isolation and alienation of the armed organizations. Nowhere, however, is there any mention of the arguably most serious consequence of the armed struggle—namely, the way in which the national security state used the pretext of civil war waged by guerrillas to unleash violent and extended state repression.

Had Gabeira been interested in pursuing this analysis, it certainly would fit logically into his book after the account of the Elbrick kidnapping. That episode, in fact, deeply impressed the military junta then in power and confirmed the theories of internal security with the general doctrine of national security. After bowing to the pressure of the U.S. government and meeting all the guerrilla's conditions for Elbrick's release, the Brazilian regime passed two Institutional Acts, the National Security Law of 1969 and the Constitution of 1969—all within two months of the kidnapping. These measures, particularly the National Security Law, strengthened the legal framework of the repressive apparatus and further incorporated the precepts of the national security doctrine into the practice of the Brazilian state.[38]

Hence the testimonies provide relatively little analysis of the nature of the armed struggle and of how it contributed to the movement's overall objectives, successes, or failures. This lack of analysis is a consequence of the works' personal focus and underlying romanticism. Even the recognition by the authors considered here that their organizations suffered from "an incorrect political vision" resulting from their "lack of organic ties with the masses" does not override their apparent assumption that, in Polari's words, "politically speaking, our experience of the armed struggle represented, in spite of all the failures, errors, etc., an important step for the Brazilian left, a step that has still not been duly evaluated."[39]

Only further historical analysis will shed light on the significance of the armed struggle for the Brazilian left and for the military period in general.[40] In the meantime, the testimonial literature of the *abertura* period—precisely because of its personal and confessional nature—should be culled for the rich insights it provides into the dynamics of fear in Brazil.

NOTES

1. For the purposes of this chapter, the 1964–85 Brazilian military regime is divided into the following periods: 1964–68, period of regime consolidation; 1969–74, period of most severe repression; 1974–79, period of *distensão*, or controlled "decompression"; 1979–84, period of *abertura*, or opening, which was a prelude to the 1985 transition to civilian rule.

2. See Maria Helena Moreira Alves, *State and Opposition in Military Brazil*

(Austin: University of Texas Press, 1985), especially ch. 6, "Armed Struggle and the National Security State," 119.

3. Juan Corradi, "The Culture of Fear in Civil Society" (Report submitted to the Social Science Research Council, New York, 1983), 4.

4. Alves, *State and Opposition,* 119–37.

5. Fernando Gabeira, *O que è isso, companheiro?* (Rio de Janeiro: Editora Codecri, 1979), 44–45.

6. Manuel Antonio Garretón, "Respuesta al miedo y efectos de éste en la transición" (Report presented to the Social Science Research Council, New York, 1983), 2.

7. Corradi, "Culture of Fear in Civil Society," 23.

8. Heloísa Buarque de Hollanda, "A luta dos sufocados e o prazer dos retornados," *Jornal do Brasil* (13 December 1982), 10.

9. Alex Polari, *Inventário de cicatrizes* (Rio de Janeiro: Comite Brasileiro pela Anistia, 1978).

10. Elizabeth Orsini, "Exílio, sexo, política, corpo. O grito dos jovens ao contar a pròpria vida," *Jornal do Brasil* (23 October 1984), 8.

11. Frei Betto, *Cartas de prisão,* 4th ed. (Rio de Janeiro: Civilização Brasileira, 1978); Frei Betto, *Das catacumbas* (Rio de Janeiro: Civilização Brasileira, 1978); Augusto Boal, *Milagre no Brasil* (Rio de Janeiro: Civilização Brasileira, 1979).

12. Pedro Celso Uchoa Cavalcanti and Jovelino Ramos, *Memòrias do exílio: Brasil 1964–19??,* vol. 1, *De muitos caminhos* (Lisbon: Editora Arcadia, 1976).

13. Albertina de Oliveira Costa, Maria Teresa Porciuncula Moraes, Norma Marzola, and Valentina da Roche Lima, *Memòrias das mulheres do exílio,* vol. 2 (Rio de Janeiro: Editora Paz e Terra, 1980).

14. Fernando Gabeira, *O crepùsculo do macho* (Rio de Janeiro: Editora Nova Fronteira, 1980); Fernando Gabeira, *Entradas e bandeiras* (Rio de Janeiro: Editora Codecri, 1981).

15. Alfredo Syrkis, *Os carbonàrios: Memòrias da guerrilha perdida,* 7th ed. (São Paulo: Global Editora e Distribuidora, 1980); Alvaro Caldas, *Tirando o capuz,* 3rd ed. (Rio de Janeiro: Editora Codecri, 1981); Herbert Daniel, *Passagem para o pròximo sonho* (Rio de Janeiro: Editora Codecri, 1982).

16. Clovis Moura, *Diário da guerrilha do Araguaia* (São Paulo: Editora Alfa-Omega, 1979); Emiliano José and Oldack Miranda, *Lamarca, o capitão da guerrilha* (São Paulo: Global Editora e Distribuidora, 1980); Augusto Boal, *Batismo de sangue. Os dominicanos e a morte de Carlos Marighella,* 3d ed. (Rio de Janeiro: Civilização Brasileira, 1982).

17. Antonio Carlos Fon, *Tortura. A história da repressão política no Brasil* (São Paulo: Global Editora e Distribuidora; Comite Brasileiro pela Anistia, 1979); Fernando Portela, *Guerra da guerrilhas no Brasil* (São Paulo: Global Editora e Distribuidora, 1979); Paulo Marconi, *A censura política na imprensa brasileira, 1968–1978* (São Paulo: Global Editora e Distribuidora, 1980).

18. Orsini, "Exílio, sexo, política, corpo," 10.

19. Garretón, "Respuesta al miedo," 3.

20. See Joan Dassin, "Press Censorship and the Military State in Brazil," in Jane L. Curry and Joan Dassin, eds., *Press Control around the World* (New York:

Praeger, 1982), 149–86, and Joan Dassin, "The Brazilian Press and the Politics of *Abertura*," *Journal of Interamerican Studies and World Affairs* 26, no. 3 (August 1984), 385–414.

21. Ralph della Cava, "The Church and the Abertura in Brazil 1974–1985: Notes for a History" (Paper presented at a conference, Popular Culture and Democratization in Brazil, University of Florida at Gainesville, 1–2 April 1985).

22. Dassin, "Brazilian Press and the Politics of *Abertura*," 394–96.

23. Garretón, "Respuesta al miedo," 2.

24. Alves, *State and Opposition,* 103–37.

25. Caldas, *Tirando o capuz,* 102–7.

26. "Alex Polari," in Carlos Alberto Messeder Pereira and Heloísa Buarque de Hollanda, *Patrulhas ideològicas: Arte e engajamento em debate* (São Paulo: Brasiliense, 1980), 234–51.

27. Patricia Fagen, "Summary of Discussions on the Role of the Agents of Fear" (Report presented to the Social Science Research Council, New York, 1983), 12–14.

28. Corradi, "Culture of Fear in Civil Society," 23.

29. Alves, *State and Opposition,* 123.

30. Ibid., 125.

31. See Archdiocese of São Paulo, *Brasil: Nunca mais* (Petrópolis: Vozes, 1985), for documentary evidence of torture in Brazil from 1964 to 1979, and Joan Dassin, "Introduction to the English-Language Edition," in Joan Dassin, ed., *Torture in Brazil,* trans. Jaime Wright (New York: Random House, Vintage Books, 1986), ix–xxvii, for a discussion of torture and the Brazilian repressive apparatus.

32. Daniel, *Passagem para o pròximo sonho,* 39–42.

33. Syrkis, *Os carbonàrios,* 127–30.

34. Caldas, *Tirando o capuz,* 62–66.

35. Alves, *State and Opposition,* 127.

36. Ibid., 119–23.

37. Gabeira, *O que è isso, companheiro?,* 107–30.

38. Alves, *State and Opposition,* 117–19.

39. "Alex Polari," 240.

40. For political documents of clandestine organizations, 1961–71, see Daniel Aarão Reis Filho and Jair Ferreira de Sà, *Imagens da Revolução* (Rio de Janeiro: Marco Zero, 1985).

TEN

Cultures of Fear, Cultures of Resistance

The New Labor Movement in Brazil

Maria Helena Moreira Alves

CREATING A CULTURE OF FEAR

THE ORGANIZATION OF TRADE UNIONS AS INSTITUTIONS FOR SOCIAL CONTROL

In analyzing recent Brazilian history one is struck by the juxtaposition of old and new mechanisms of social control. The corporatist regulations that limit the freedom of labor to organize were established in the Brazilian Labor Code of 1944 (Consolidação das Leis do Trabalho, henceforth referred to simply as CLT). Based on Mussolini's Carta del Lavoro, they persisted through the democratic governments (1944 to 1964) and the subsequent authoritarian rule. Thus, the labor movement in Brazil has been shaped by regulations that both limit the representation of workers and provide the background for its current militancy. Section V of the CLT carefully regulates the organizational structure of trade unions in Brazil. It is worthwhile to devote some attention to the most pertinent mechanisms of social control embedded in it.[1]

In the CLT trade unions are defined as organizations for the mediation of social conflict. Their primary purpose, under the law, is to facilitate the resolution of conflicts between labor and capital through tripartite negotiations that involve the active participation of the state. Their secondary purpose is to provide social benefits. The organizational framework is corporative, forming a pyramidal structure that encompasses associations of blue-collar workers, of white-collar professionals, and of employers (*patronais*). The pinnacle of the pyramid is the Ministry of Labor.

Workers (or employers) who wish to form a trade union must apply to the Ministry of Labor for formal recognition. All unions must be formed in accordance with a predetermined organizational charter (*Estatuto Unico*), which places all administrative power in the board of directors. The regulations are intended to establish control by the Ministry of Labor, which not only has the power to withhold formal recognition of a trade union considered too radical but can also subdivide a specific union into several different sectors.[2] Electoral regulations concentrate power in the hands of incumbents by facilitating manipulation of votes. As a result, one of the most frequent complaints of opposition trade unionists (apart from lack of access to voters) is of open fraud and violation of the secrecy of the ballot.[3] In addition, the Ministry of Labor has the power to annul elections at all levels of trade-union organization or to cancel the right of certain candidates to run for office. Thus, even if opposition candidates win elections, another battle is often necessary in order to begin to carry out the mandate.[4]

The corporative nature of the trade unions is also ensured by voting procedures at the federation and confederation levels. Each local trade union in Brazil has the legal right to two representatives (but only one vote) at the federation level. Hence, a trade union with 100,000 members has the same representational voice as a trade union with 100 members. Furthermore, each federation has only one vote for the election of members of the boards of directors of confederations. Through such procedures the Ministry of Labor maintains its almost absolute control of elections for the higher levels of trade-union representation. Because the Ministry of Labor has the power to recognize trade unions, it often actively seeks to create unions with few members (known in Brazil as "ghost unions") so as to ensure a countervailing electoral weight to more active and representative unions with large numbers of members. For this reason it is difficult indeed to find representative opposition trade-union leaders on the boards of directors of federations and confederations.

Another important mechanism for the control of trade-union representation is financial ties to the Ministry of Labor. Most trade-union funds come from a compulsory tax levied on all Brazilian workers (whether or not they are members of unions). This tax (*contribuição sindical*) is automatically deducted from paychecks and collected by the Ministry of Labor, which also has the sole power to redistribute the funds to confederations, federations, and local trade unions. All funds must be deposited in a state bank and may be frozen by the government.

The CLT carefully establishes the portion of funds for welfare services. The CLT prohibits the utilization of tax funds for political campaigns, for the purpose of trade-union organization in the workplace, and for financing strikes. These controls are legally justified because the funds come from federal taxes and are considered public money to be administered by the state.[5]

The Ministry of Labor also has the power to directly intervene in trade unions, federations, and confederations. By a simple decree, therefore, the government can cancel the electoral mandate of one official or of the entire board of directors. In such cases the Ministry of Labor appoints new administrators to run the union until new elections are organized.[6] According to the CLT, trade-union officials who have lost their post through governmental interventions (*cassados*) become permanently ineligible and are prevented from participating in elections at any level of trade-union organization.[7]

THE IMPOSITION OF NEW CONTROLS

When the military took over state power in 1964, the mechanisms of control included in the CLT were strictly enforced. But the military also drafted new legislation. Only a few months after the takeover, comprehensive antistrike legislation was passed.[8] Public employees were denied the right to strike, as were workers in "essential services," a category that included health workers, workers in the pharmaceutical industries, transport workers, and bank workers. The law also prohibited all strikes that were defined as "social, political or religious in nature" or that were called in solidarity with other strikers. Strikes for better working conditions or salary raises were allowed in principle. However, the regulations for calling a legal strike were so stringent that it was nearly impossible for trade unions to fulfill all requirements. According to Kenneth S. Mericle, the law made illegal most strikes except those called to replace lost salary when employers failed to pay workers for more than three months.[9] Kenneth Erickson, in turn, states that the rigorous implementation of the antistrike law, when considered in conjunction with the norms of the CLT, did succeed in eliminating most strikes for a number of years. In 1963 there were 302 legal strikes in Brazil. This total fell to 25 in 1965, 15 in 1966, 12 in 1970, and none in 1971.[10] Between 1973 and 1977, there were only 34 strikes or slowdown operations.[11] As we shall see, this law became the focus of opposition by the new trade-union movement after 1977.

Another important measure for the control of workers was introduced with the reform of job-security legislation in 1966. The previous legislation established tenure for all workers employed by a company for more than ten years. The reforms introduced in 1966 canceled previous rights to job security and established a special fund for the payment of compensation to fired workers.[12] The cancellation of job security allowed firms to rotate the labor force, often firing trade-union activists and replacing them with nonunionized laborers. The regulations established a flexible system of trade-union control in the workplace, making it difficult for members of the opposition to organize in the factories.

Finally, the military governments enacted a series of laws to control wages. Collective bargaining over wages between workers and employers was prohibited. A system of wage indexing was introduced whereby the government, once a year, decreed the percentage raise in salary for all workers (whether or not they were unionized). This policy removed trade unions from any major role in the negotiation of salaries and reinforced their position as merely social-benefit distributors. The increases in salary were always below the real rate of inflation and had the effect of decreasing purchasing power.[13] The indexing of salaries neutralized collective organizational efforts and greatly benefited corporations by regulating industrial relations for long-term planning. The major purpose of the legislation, therefore, was both to decrease salaries and to attract foreign investment by ensuring a "safe climate" vis-à-vis labor.

AN IDEOLOGY FOR FEAR-MONGERING

The civil/military coalition developed a cohesive ideology that placed Brazil in a geopolitical context of superpower confrontation and clearly defined the limits of opposition. The Doctrine of National Security and Development (from 1964 to 1980) had three components: a geopolitical analysis of global warfare in the nuclear age; a theory of the "internal enemy"; and a model of economic development combined with security (segurança e desenvolvimento).[14]

In the world-view of the Doctrine of National Security and Development Brazil belongs within the influence area of the United States as an important country. Its mineral and human resources, coupled with its geographical position in the South Atlantic, make it a key nation for the defense of the West.[15] Within the overall geopolitical context of the doctrine, military strategists developed the theory of the internal enemy.

According to this view, in a nuclear age, traditional concepts of warfare no longer applied. The Soviet Union would avoid direct confrontation by supporting groups inside each country to overthrow pro-Western governments. Thus, the main danger would come from an internal enemy rather than from direct foreign aggression. The third component of the doctrine is its model of development. To stimulate the rapid accumulation of capital, the civil/military coalition in power designed a developmentalist model based on foreign, national, and state capital. Multinational corporations were seen as efficient and beneficial investors in the country. The model required large state infrastructural investments, a system of fiscal incentives for private investment in key sectors of the economy, the concentration of income to ensure a market for durable goods, and, finally, a disciplined labor market to facilitate planning and assure "safe" investment.

Because the benefits granted to multinational corporations were often at the expense of national firms, the model met with continued opposition from labor and national entrepreneurial sectors. In turn, the activities of various opposition groups were carefully followed by state intelligence services and catalogued according to their degree of organization. Surveillance followed guidelines developed at the Superior War College and the intelligence schools. According to these guidelines, it was necessary to determine the exact degree of "nonconformity" of an activity before taking coercive action. The state sought to determine whether an activity was simply "opposition," or "pressure," or a "contesting action." The *Manual básico da Escola Superior de Guerra*, for example, provides guidelines for the assessment of the level of dissent:

> (1) The [size] of nonconformist groups or nuclei. (2) The intensity of their political or social activity. (3) The quality and quantity of the people who belong to these nuclei. (4) The emotional repercussion that their activity manages to provoke among the population. (5) The . . . number of nuclei that are a direct, organized challenge in relation to the less-organized nuclei of opposition. (6) The proportion of voters who are members of the government's party and of the parties of the opposition. (7) The . . . number of votes that were obtained by the government's party and by the opposition parties. (8) The quantity, quality, and degree of actual influence of opposition ideas in public opinion.[16]

The greater the potential impact of the opposition on public opinion, the graver the threat to the state. At higher levels of organization the opposition was no longer considered simply an "obstacle" to national security policies but became defined as "antagonistic," in which case it required greater coercion.

In order to carry out such policies it became necessary to take full control of state power, to centralize this power as much as possible in the executive branch, and to place those closest to the information network and programming of internal security policy in key government positions. In practice, therefore, the theory of the internal enemy in the doctrine led to the establishment of a vast network of information and the implantation of a repressive apparatus capable of guaranteeing the elimination of the enemies hidden within the nation. The rigorous implementation of security policy, with time, tended to create a climate of suspicion, fear, and mutual denunciation among the population.

Several policies were implemented to control the population. First, military and intelligence operations were expanded. The role of the armed forces was modified to include among its primary responsibilities the maintenance of internal security. The military police, a paramilitary force that was traditionally responsible for crime prevention and answerable to the governors of the various states, were put under the direct command of the army and turned into an auxiliary branch of the armed forces. The military police became a major tool in the direct repression of opposition. To provide for intelligence and information gathering, the military government created the National Information Service (SNI), a widespread intelligence agency answerable only to the executive's National Security Council, with a partly secret budget and the legal right to transfer military and civilian public employees to its service. By 1978, the repressive apparatus comprised an estimated 562,750 people (277,750 men in the army, navy, and air force; 185,000 military police; and approximately 100,000 members of the various agencies of the intelligence community), with an official budget of two billion dollars.[17]

The second policy involved the constant organization of surprise road blockades to check documentation (in Brazil it became a criminal offense to fail to carry identification documents). The frequent "blitzes" organized by the army and the military police were patterned after the methods of political control used by German occupying forces during World War II. Finally, the military, particularly in the rural areas, organized programs that transferred parts of the population to controlled areas and involved permanent utilization of large numbers of troops.[18]

One must also note the importance of two other state-encouraged policies for the development of a culture of fear: first, the widespread use of torture, beatings, and police violence against the population; second, the unofficial encouragement of paramilitary organizations such as the death squadron and the *mão branca* (white hand) that operated with impunity after 1968.[19]

In Brazil during the period of military governments, control was attained not only through physical coercion but also through psychological repression. The aim was to make individual citizens feel uninformed, separate, fragmented, and powerless. The atomization of citizens creates a feeling of helplessness and hopelessness, which sharpens the underlying fear of participation in political or social opposition activities. Uncertainty was also encouraged. The various legal Institutional Acts enacted by military governments for the purpose of political control, as well as the National Security Law, provided only vague definitions of criminal acts of opposition.[20] Legislation was therefore open to different interpretations, with the result that each specific act of opposition was potentially punishable. Whether a particular activity could be subject to indictment depended more on its place in the categories of the theory of the internal enemy than on a strict definition of the law. This element of uncertainty was crucial in creating, in every citizen, a fear that his or her act of opposition could result in indictment, legal sanctions, or even imprisonment and torture.

Legal recourse was also limited through the utilization of special military tribunals to judge crimes against national security, the withdrawal for many years of the right to habeas corpus and other individual guarantees, and the limitations imposed on civilian judges so as to control their actions. During the worst years of repression lawyers who defended political prisoners were also threatened, and consequently the availability of legal counsel was limited.

The underlying fear was enhanced by the lack of information. Official censorship played an important role here. Stories of imprisonment, indictment, and torture abounded, but often it was difficult to be truly informed, with any certainty, of what was going on. Because so many citizens had personally experienced political repression or witnessed a public demonstration of physical force in the repression of demonstrations, assemblies, strikes, document searches, or blitzes, people did not hesitate to believe the stories of pain and torture. Censorship reinforced fear because the truth of such stories could not be determined, and they tended perhaps even to be augmented through popular communication. In addition, censorship limited the opportunities to influence public opinion, to demand justice, or to impose constraints on power. Therefore, censorship increased the citizens' feeling of being fragmented and separate from the community and rendered them powerless, helpless, and hopeless in the face of state coercion.

The development of a culture of fear was a consequence of a combination of elements: vagueness of legal definitions for criminal activity; limitations on legal and individual rights; lack of access to information and difficulty in communication; fragmentation of community and collective efforts (particularly through impediments to social organizations such as trade unions, political parties, and community grass-roots groups); and, finally, open utilization of physical coercion combined with semiclandestine activities such as torture and illegal executions.

BREAKING THE CULTURE OF FEAR: STRATEGIES OF RESISTANCE IN THE LABOR MOVEMENT

FIRST STAGE: WINNING BACK ORGANIZATIONAL POWER

The debate over the best strategy for obtaining autonomous organization of trade unions in Brazil is as old as the corporative regulations of the CLT. During the period of democratic and populist governments prior to 1964, the controls of the labor code were not severely enforced. Governments sought the support of trade unions and, increasingly, forged an alliance with labor leaders based on issues of national concern. Because, on the one hand, the mechanisms of control were not severely enforced and, on the other hand, labor leaders believed that the union tax and the system of *sindicato unico* (which guaranteed trade unions single representation for each branch of industry) were beneficial to the organization of labor, there was little incentive to organize outside the official trade-union structure. The major attempts to break the ties with the Ministry of Labor were, therefore, limited mainly to the parallel organization of a trade-union central—the Central Geral dos Trabalhadores.[21]

Circumstances changed, however, with the military coup of 1964. Because so many labor unions became directly controlled by government-appointed officials, it was important for workers to debate alternative strategies of organization. The debate revolved around two courses of action: to work within the "official" trade unions to pressure for more representative leadership, or to concentrate on the parallel organization of independent but illegal trade unions.

Given the repressive conditions, most trade unionists supported efforts to fight within the "official" trade unions to wrest control from government-appointed officials (known in Brazil as *interventores*). In mounting resistance to the military governments, workers eventually organized a widespread grass-roots movement of union opposition (*oposição sindical*). Members of opposition groups connected to various underground political parties or to the progressive sectors of the popular Catholic Church began slowly to organize pressure groups in both the urban and the rural areas. The major aim was to organize workers in factories and in agricultural areas. Once set up, these groups could collectively pressure the government for elections in particular trade unions and then challenge the incumbent boards of directors. Because the *oposição sindical* gave strong emphasis to the organization of workers in the factories, these workers gained experience in grass-roots, democratic forms of organization. It was also argued that once an opposition board of directors took office, the controls could work to the benefit of workers by ensuring strength to the new incumbency, guaranteeing *sindicato unico,* and placing in the hands of the opposition a large machinery with sufficient assets to ensure continuity. Of course, the government could combat this strategy through the use of its right to annul elections, to cancel the candidacy of certain activists, or simply to intervene in the union by decree.

In spite of such possibilities, most trade-union activists still supported the alternative of union opposition. Illegal opposition seemed too costly. Leaders who attempted to organize underground were ruthlessly persecuted, arrested, tried, and sometimes even killed or forced into exile. The most dramatic example was the effort of workers to set up factory committees to support illegal strikes in Contagem (Minas Gerais) and Osasco (São Paulo) in 1968. Particularly in the case of Osasco, the violence of the repression used to end the strike and break up the factory committees was remembered long afterward. The memory of this experience led workers to believe that industrial action could be successful only if carried out on a massive scale and with careful preparation.[22]

The years between 1968 and 1977, the most repressive phase in the history of the Brazilian labor movement, were largely characterized by the abandonment of efforts to organize parallel structures of union organization and by the increased activity of opposition groups within the official trade unions. The movement of *oposição sindical* was more successful in gaining legal office in local urban unions during this period than in gaining control of urban federations and confederations. The movement had even greater success in the rural sector. Activists of the union opposition—particularly in those groups that organized together with the Catholic movement in the countryside—were elected to the boards of directors of many federations of agricultural laborers. This position enabled them to gain control of the Confederation of Agricultural Workers in 1968 and to acquire representative leadership in all subsequent elections. This success may be explained by the fact that rural labor unions tend to have fewer members than their urban counterparts, so that ghost unions do not have as great an impact as they do in urban areas, where large unions are common.

SECOND STAGE: LEGITIMIZING CIVIL DISOBEDIENCE

One of the remarkable results of the process of development in Brazil since the late 1950s has been the concentration of industrial production in São Paulo. By 1976 São Paulo had the largest industrial park in the Third World. The most important industries were located in the metropolitan region known as the ABCD.[23] Multinational corporations in the automobile industry, responding to tax incentives and cheap labor, installed major production units in the region. A few giant factories congregated a high percentage of the labor in the area. This concentration of production allowed the formation of a modern urban proletariat comprising an estimated 210,000 workers in the metalworking industries of the area.[24]

The automobile companies encouraged a rapid turnover of the workforce, regularly firing thousands of workers just before the official date for wage increases. The turnover policy was organized by the major automobile corporations so that workers fired, say, by Volkswagen, would be hired by Ford to do the same job but with a lower starting salary. Management, therefore, utilized the Time-in-Service-Guarantee Fund to increase exploitation.[25] Ironically, this turnover may, in reality, have aided in the organization of metalworkers of the ABCD industrial region. The mobility of labor allowed leaders to move from factory to factory, carrying with them their organizational experience. This turnover also contributed to the development of a strong sense of collectivity and community. Although the corporations benefited from the elimination of job-security guarantees, they also cut one of the last bonds that tied a large number of workers to their employers.[26] Therefore, one of the major mechanisms of control of labor—fear of unemployment—did not work well with a labor force accustomed to high rates of turnover and frequent dismissals. In fact, though job-security guarantees would be one of the main demands of the labor movement in future years, it was not as prevalent a component of the culture of fear as the threat of physical repression.

I shall concentrate on the metalworking industry in the ABCD region for several reasons. First, the automobile and related industries are the most important and dynamic sectors of the Brazilian economy. Second, in this region one can best understand the process of the formation of an urban proletariat and the development of organizational skills capable of overcoming the initial paralysis of fear. Finally, although, as I have already pointed out, the rural social movements of trade unions and squatter/settler organizations (*posseiros*) are extremely well developed, the dispersion of the many groups in the vast interior wastelands of Brazil makes it difficult to achieve consistent structural strength sufficient to counter the culture of fear. Study of the ABCD region helps explain a process by which fear is dispelled, community ties are strengthened, and a new dynamic relationship develops.

The Metalworkers Union of São Bernardo do Campo and Diadema is the only legal representative of the metalworkers in both São Bernardo and Diadema, where most of the largest factories are located. The two other metalworking unions represent workers in São Gaetano and Santo Andre. For the metalworkers of the ABCD the system of *sindicato unico* would prove to be an enormous advantage, for it concentrated power in a few local unions. Furthermore, the accumulation of so many thousands of workers in a few plants facilitated the organizational efforts of trade-union militants. Metalworkers of the ABCD developed a clear consciousness of the power implicit in their numbers and in their strategic position in production. If they could stop the giants of the automobile industry, most of the industrial complex of Brazil would grind to a halt.

In the union elections of 1976 a new and militant group of union leaders was elected. It was headed by Luis Inacio da Silva (known by the nickname of "Lula"), a toolmaker at Villares and a union activist. The new board of directors began to organize groups of workers in each plant. Meetings were held to discuss trade-union legislation, the anti-strike law, regulations for salary increases, job safety, employment security, and other labor issues. Past strategies of organization in the plants were analyzed carefully so as to draw appropriate lessons from the experiences of many years. In addition, the union leaders asked opposition economists, sociologists, and lawyers to make presentations and to aid in the educational process of trade-union members. It was important to study strike legislation and to understand legal controls so as to develop proper strategies of industrial action. Any action taken would have to be carefully planned in order to prevent repression or intervention by the government. It was also important to understand the production and investment plans of the transnational corporations so as to pinpoint the best moment to take action.

For two years the small groups met, discussed alternatives, and learned to understand their legal, political, and economic environment. These meetings were crucial for the formation of new leadership capable of understanding the overall organization of production in the automobile industry and the specific limitations of the labor legislation. By 1977 the organization of workers in the major plants was already well advanced. The next step was the holding of meetings, by factory, to discuss issues of concern to workers in each corporation and to tighten the organization inside the plants. Each group became the core of trade-union representation in the factories, the link between the union and the workers.

Through this process of discussion and analysis an overall strategy was developed. It was necessary to dispel the workers' fear and show them that if they acted together, in large numbers, the government would hesitate in repression. It was also necessary to find a way to gain time for success to build so that negotiations could begin directly with management, thus overcoming the impediments to collective bargaining. One small victory would be crucial, for it would allow other workers to hope, to gain courage from collectivity, and to act in defense of their interests. With the aid of lawyers, workers determined that according to the terms of the antistrike legislation, a strike was defined as "not going to work." Careful examination of production and investment plans also showed that the best moment for industrial action was when export quotas had to be met by multinational corporations and smooth production was most important. The strategy relied on tight organization inside the factories, careful utilization of legal loopholes, and nonviolent action to eliminate possible justification for repression.

At 7:00 A.M. on Friday, May 12, 1978, 2,500 workers of the Saab Scania plant in São Bernardo do Campo came to work, punched in their cards, and sat in front of their machines with their arms crossed. Soon workers coming in for different shifts in twenty-three other major corporations began to act in the same way. By the second week the movement had spread to Santo Andre, São Caetano, and Diadema, with a total of 77,950 workers on strike. When asked, workers denied they were on strike, claiming that they were in fact coming in to work and punching in their cards as specified in the law. The major demand was for collective bargaining by the union and the employers. The military government was taken by surprise. Management of the large automobile corporations worried about the increasing disruption of production. If the strike continued, they would be unable to meet shipment deadlines for vehicles already sold abroad. On May 31 the Metalworkers Union signed an agreement with the auto companies to provide salary raises above the government's official index.

It was an important victory. The government's rigid legislation for the control of salaries had been overturned, and the principle of collective bargaining had been accepted by management. In addition, workers had shown that it was possible to override antistrike legislation through coordinated action. The government had been forced to accept the negotiations and had been unable to repress the strikers directly. It had been important to act within the letter of the law. The effect in this case was to cause a momentary confusion and allow time for more workers to lose their fear and join the strike. It was also important to keep demands flexible and small. Management, fearful of huge losses, entered into negotiations to reach a quick agreement. Surprise, confusion as to interpretations of the law, coordinated action by thousands of workers, and minimal demands were elements that, when combined with the huge daily losses from disrupted production, led management to urge the government not to interfere in the negotiations.

The fear had been overcome by a new kind of strike action, one without visible leaders, without pickets, and virtually without scabs. Within ten days the strike had spread to ninety metalworking firms. From May 12 to June 13, 1978, 245,935 metalworkers were on strike in São Bernardo, São Caetano, Santo Andre, Osasco, Jandira, Taboao da Serra, Cotia, and Campinas. Over 400 factories were affected, and the movement spread to eighteen different towns in the state of São Paulo. Other workers, in different trades, were quick to follow the example of São Bernardo do Campo. The heart of Brazil's industrial park had come to a halt. Throughout 1978 there were mass strikes among metalworkers and workers in the ports, in urban transport, and in the tobacco, glass, ceramic, textile, chemical, and pharmaceutical industries. They were joined by white-collar and professional workers: schoolteachers, university professors, doctors. By the end of 1978, 539,037 workers had been on strike.[27]

A vast and peacefully organized social movement of civil disobedience developed over the next years. The military government charged that the strikes were illegal and threatened the security of the nation. Trade-union leaders, echoed by prestigious lawyers and by the hierarchy of the Catholic Church, considered the decree laws of the military government illegitimate:

> Therefore, we affirm that there is a *legitimate juridical order* and an *illegitimate juridical order*. Legislation that has been imposed by an act of force constitutes an illegitimate juridical order. It is illegitimate because, above all, its origin is illegitimate. The only legitimate juridical order is the one composed of legislation rooted in the sovereignty of a people, born from the legitimate and elected representative system.[28]

Basically, the civil-disobedience movement challenged the decree laws, Institutional Acts, and complementary legislation that had been elaborated by the executive without the approval of, or even consideration by, a freely elected national Congress. The civil-disobedience movement derived its legitimacy from the struggle to undermine an imposed juridical system and to pave the way for a constitutional assembly capable of restructuring the juridical order on a foundation of democratic legitimacy.

In 1979 and 1980 the civil-disobedience movement continued to be spearheaded by the metalworkers of São Bernardo do Campo and Diadema. The first confrontation with the military authorities exploded the day before President João Batista Figueiredo took office. An estimated 185,000 metalworkers in the ABCD industrial region went out on strike. Although the strike had been carefully prepared by the trade unions, the corporations this time were ready to resist. Factories were locked so that workers could not take refuge inside the buildings. Workers were forced onto the streets in mass picket lines. With thousands of workers assembling in front of the gates of the major plants, violent incidents happened, traffic was disrupted, and the military police had to break up meetings to maintain public order. Unable to meet in the factories, too numerous to meet in the trade-union headquarters, metalworkers took over the Estadio Vila Euclides, the largest football stadium in the region. There they assembled by the thousands every day to discuss the continuation of the strike. A new kind of decision-making process developed in which all matters of importance were discussed in small groups and put to vote at the mass meetings. In 1979, therefore, the trade unions were able to connect grass-roots organization with mass decision by direct vote.

The corporations refused to negotiate unless the workers went back to work. A mass meeting of close to 100,000 metalworkers in the Estadio Vila Euclides rejected the proposal. The next day the military government ordered intervention in all the trade unions involved in the strike. Having lost their unions, the workers appealed for community support. The Catholic Church, for the first time, moved directly to provide open support to striking workers. Not only did the *comunidades de base*, the Church's grass-roots organizations in the neighborhoods, provide material support, but all the churches of the region were opened to the workers. From then on strike assemblies were held in the Cathedral of São Bernardo do Campo.

The metalworkers now faced difficult circumstances: the union was under intervention, there was widespread and violent repression of workers in picket lines, and, in spite of generous donations to the strike fund, the situation of workers and their families soon became grave. Part of the preparations had involved attempts to save enough to survive a period of strike. However, inflation rates of over 90 percent made this goal impossible for most families to meet. When the corporations offered a 63 percent raise (the original demand had been for a 78.1 percent raise so as to recover at least most of the purchasing power lost to inflation), Lula called another mass assembly in the Vila Euclides and urged workers to accept the agreement. For the first time Lula used his personal influence to swing the opinion of large numbers of workers. Once they had reluctantly returned to work, the military government canceled the intervention. The move was calculated to undermine Lula's influence by spreading doubt as to his motives in deciding to end the strike. But it backfired: in order to demonstrate support for their leaders, 150,000 workers held a massive rally on May 1, 1979. The rally had the support of all opposition parties and cemented an alliance that was to prove important for the further organization of the movement.

The year 1979 is a landmark in the social and political history of Brazil. The strike movement now spread to most important industrial, service, and white-collar sectors,[29] and to almost all states of the country.[30] In all, more than 3,207,994 workers were on strike throughout 1979.[31] The civil-disobedience movement succeeded in legitimizing strike actions in such a way that, although still technically illegal, strikes became an accepted and integral part of industrial relations in Brazil.

During 1979 members of the Metalworkers Union of São Bernardo do Campo and Diadema met frequently with their leadership to discuss aspects of their organizational framework. The experiences of the past two years were carefully analyzed so as to develop alternative strategies.

The first conclusion was that although it was important to avoid governmental intervention in the union, this should not be a primary goal.[32]

The second conclusion was that the organization was too dependent on the top leadership. In order to limit the influence of top leaders, to increase the participation of the rank and file in decision making and in the implementation of strategies, as well as to protect the movement from being immobilized by the arrest of its leaders, the internal structure of the union was modified. Assemblies were held by the production sector of each major corporation to elect representatives to an informal factory committee. These committees together—an estimated 20,000 to 30,000 metalworkers—formed the intermediate levels of leadership. Next, general assemblies of all workers were held, inside the plants, to form a committee of 450 members. The Committee of 450, elected with representation from each factory, would be responsible for the coordination of the movement. Open assemblies, in the union itself, elected the members of the two higher levels of organization: the Committee of Salary and Mobilization—composed of sixteen members—and the rank-and-file-board of directors (*diretoria de base*)—which had thirteen members who became de facto shop stewards. The regular board of directors of the union (twenty members) was responsible mainly for overall coordination and for the legal representation of the metalworkers in the negotiations to be carried out with the corporations and the government.

Finally, it was concluded that mass pickets were a dangerous mistake, to be avoided at all possible cost. Experiences in most strikes, in all trade categories, indicated that the military government used the pickets as an excuse for overt, violent repression. Hence, it was decided that the strike actions of 1980 would have to be tightly organized inside the factories so as to enable the continuity of the movement even in the face of lockouts, repression, intervention in the union, or arrest of the top leadership.

When the metalworkers of the ABCD region decided to go out on strike again, in April 1980, the new organizational strategy was implemented. The strike action was organized by production sectors in each plant. The intermediary leadership at the rank-and-file level was responsible for the continuity of the movement and for the overall network of internal communication. The Committee of 450 and the Committee for Salary and Mobilization coordinated the strike and implemented major decisions made by vote in the huge daily assemblies held in the Estadio Vila Euclides. The *diretoria de base* acted as an alternative to the legal board of directors, who were almost immediately placed under arrest.

This time, to avoid the repression of pickets, all workers stayed home. At the end of the first assembly, which voted to begin the strike, Lula simply told workers: "OK. It has been decided. You all know what to do." Thousands filed peacefully out of the soccer stadium either to go home or to aid in the organization of the strike fund.

The metalworkers of the ABCD, who, with their families, numbered close to one million, received decisive support from community grass-roots organizations throughout the country. A strike fund was organized by members of the opposition and funneled through the Catholic Church. Every week, metalworkers formed long lines around the cathedral to pick up packages containing food. Some 480,000 tons of foodstuffs were delivered to the strikers, and churches became focal points for collecting donations and organizing distribution. In addition, the strike fund was able to collect the equivalent of $3.4 million dollars throughout the country.[33]

This time the military government decided that the metalworkers had to be crushed. The corporations were ordered not to negotiate. The Minister of Labor ordered immediate intervention into the trade unions, arrested the board of directors of the Metalworkers Union of São Bernardo do Campo and Diadema, and occupied the union building with troops armed with machine guns. Nineteen days after the strike began, 10,000 soldiers occupied all the cities affected by the strike. Blitzes were launched, neighborhoods were surrounded, and leaders were taken from their homes, from meetings, even from inside the churches, at gunpoint.

The very force of the repression, however, cemented an alliance between the metalworkers and opposition political parties, Church leaders, and the Brazilian Bar Association. The evidence of state violence against a strictly nonviolent movement shocked the public and delegitimized the government.

The physical repression also mobilized the women in support of the striking workers. Women's support groups mushroomed across the country. The wives, mothers, and daughters of strikers organized resistance to the violent intervention of the army. A mass meeting of 40,000 women affirmed support for the strike but added a further demand: the release of all those arrested. The rally ended with a march through the city that gathered support from other women so that by the end of the demonstration police estimated the crowd at over 100,000. The women were accompanied by their children and carried armfuls of roses. At a certain point, the demonstrators were met by army troops. After a tense period, the soldiers refused to shoot and allowed the march to proceed peacefully. For the first time since 1964 members of the military openly showed their opposition to repressive orders. The march of the women marked a turning point in the history of the labor movement: side by side with fear, a culture of resistance to oppression gained increasing force. A new feeling of confidence developed in the people of São Bernardo do Campo—confidence in themselves, in their collective power, in their insertion into the community. Joy, hope, and positive aspirations began to replace feelings of isolation, powerlessness, and dread.

THE "REPUBLIC OF SÃO BERNARDO DO CAMPO"

The strike of 1980 ended in defeat. None of the original demands was granted. The workers lost their union, and leaders of the rank and file in the plants were summarily dismissed without compensation. The management policy of labor turnover now specifically targeted those who had been most important to the continuity of the movement. The intelligence services, including the powerful SNI, compiled long lists of leaders and worked closely with the corporation managers to eliminate them from the factories. The blacklist came to be a predominant criterion for the hiring and firing of workers in all major plants. This policy was so thorough that, to take a single example, Volkswagen fired 13,621 workers in 1981.[34] In addition, many of the national members of the opposition who had previously supported the strike movement now openly criticized the leadership as "irresponsible."

And yet, in São Bernardo do Campo itself there was a strong feeling of victory. Public debates were organized almost every night, in the churches or in headquarters of neighborhood organizations. People participated in analyzing the movement. The military police were still everywhere, but the fear had disappeared. There was a new sense of dignity, of self-respect, of independence in relation to the coercive power of the state. Visitors coming from other areas of the country or from abroad often expressed surprise at encountering such hope and joy. After all, they commented, the strike had been defeated and the workers not only had been forced to return to work but had actually lost many of the benefits that they had so painfully struggled to gain. What could account for this new confidence?[35]

The strikes of 1978, 1979, and 1980 had all been fundamentally organized around a specific and limited list of demands. But even though wage raises were undoubtedly significant in the mobilization of workers, it was the process of organization itself that proved to be the key element in producing the emancipatory effects of the strikes. The forms the struggle took—with the decision-making process through the mass assemblies coupled with increasing levels of immediate participation in groups organized by sector inside the factories—allowed the development of confidence and dignity. The process of organization, which concerned the democratization of power, enabled workers to feel that each person could be both a member of the collectivity and a significant individual actor in the overall movement. Hence, the emancipatory effect of the strikes was that workers created a new way of exercising political power, a new manner of finding community solutions.

After 1981 residents of the area began to talk about the "Republic of São Bernardo." The concept expressed their collective awareness that something profoundly liberating had happened—a chain of fear had been broken with their resistance. To their previous keen awareness of their privileged place in the system of industrial production, from which they derived their power to act, was now added a sense of history. In the endless discussions in the local clubs, squares, and bars, people often referred to themselves as active participants in history. After 1981 the social and political movement in the area can perhaps best be described as a developing "culture of confidence."

Union members were now entering a phase of construction, of deepening the organizational structures that had allowed them to live and to experience the joys of democratic participation in major decisions. Shopfloor representation was still illegal. The regulations of the CLT prevented the recognition of shop stewards, of union delegates in the workplace, and of factory commissions. Yet workers were increasingly aware of the importance of improving and broadening their organizations inside the factories while maintaining institutionalized connections to their union. Hence, the next years were devoted to industrial actions aimed at forcing a de facto, or even de jure, recognition of their representative structures. The overall strategy aimed at achieving structural transformations through the establishment, by stages, of a series of faits accomplis. The first step, which gained general acceptance of strikes and collective bargaining, had been accomplished with the massive strikes of 1978, 1979, and 1980. The next step was to force management to recognize freely elected representation inside the plants—both of shop stewards and of factory commissions. Eventually, efforts would be made to win back the union and to challenge the provisions of the CLT that prevented former union directors from running for office in any elections.

The management of some multinationals in the area attempted to neutralize the growing organization in the plants through the creation of "company representative committees." This was particularly an objective of Mercedes-Benz and Volkswagen. However, workers protested the managerial interference and openly rejected the initiatives of the corporations.[36] Instead, workers organized informal provisional commissions and enforced their recognition through the pressure of strikes.

The process by which workers in São Bernardo do Campo gained legal recognition for their factory commissions is perhaps best exemplified by events at Ford Motor Company. A careful analysis of Ford's investment plans showed that the best time to act was just before the multinational company began production of its World Car model, which was to be produced largely in São Bernardo do Campo and exported. The members of the informal provisional commission of Ford wrote, and then widely distributed, a note that stated their position:

> The government says that this country is in crisis. Meanwhile, the large multinationals are making even higher profits and program the expansion of their factories. Volkswagen says that it is in crisis, but, at the same time, it buys huge extensions of land in the state of Para, invests to develop control of the production of motorcycles and trucks, and announces the development of new automobile models. However, it fires 8,000 workers. Mercedes-Benz programmed, and is already implementing, a very large expansion of its production, opening even a whole new plant in Campinas. However, rumors have it that it will also dismiss a large number of workers. And Ford do Brasil, in 1980, had a raise in profits of 412.5 percent, and its capital investment was increased by 65.1 percent. The factories of Ford are being enlarged to be able to produce the World Car. The workers in its tractor factory are also now under a continuing program of enforced extra hours. We all know that the value of labor in the overall final cost of production is only around 5 percent. Even so, it is always the workers who pay the price of a crisis: right now, 450 are being thrown into the streets. In our country, this is the way things are. So that the corporations can have high profits the government does not care if thousands of unemployed workers and their families die of hunger.... This is why we are fighting. We, the workers of Ford, have begun today a decisive struggle to gain representation, so we can best organize to stop this situation. If we do not, all of us workers, react now, tomorrow will be too late. This is why, even though we are employed, we are on strike. We have stopped work, are running all risks, because we believe that the working class supports us and no longer accepts the injustice and exploitation that weigh so heavily on the poor.[37]

A strike began to protest the policy of mass firings, but it also aimed at establishing a permanent, and legally recognized, factory commission.[38] The occupation lasted forty-six hours; management finally signed an agreement that provided for the establishment of a civil association, with a legal charter and juridical recognition. The members of the Ford factory commission were to be directly elected by secret ballot of all Ford employees over eighteen years of age and with more than three months in the firm. They would have a two-year mandate. The first clause of the charter established the major objectives of the commission:

> I. To establish an effective communication channel between the corporation, the employees, and their representatives as well as to improve the relationship between the corporation and the union. II. To ensure a just and impartial treatment of employees based on strict application of labor rights contracted in a negotiated settlement. III. To improve the relationship between employees and their supervisors, based on mutual cooperation and respect. IV. To aid the development of a harmonious relationship of work in the factory and to be a channel to deal with tensions, misunderstandings, and confrontations. V. To solve conflicts with management through the establishment of direct negotiations.[39]

Finally, Ford also agreed to rehire the fired workers and not to dismiss any workers without prior consultation with both the union and the factory commission.

The first elected board of directors of the Ford factory commission took office on March 1, 1982. Although later analysis of the specifics of the legal statutes led workers to point out many flaws, nonetheless they became the basis for all further negotiations with corporations and for the establishment of other factory commissions.

The experience of democratic organization in the plants enabled workers of São Bernardo do Campo to gain increasing confidence. The establishment of factory commissions led to the formation of interfactory councils, coordinating different levels of organization. Their increased confidence, in turn, allowed them to challenge other institutionalized forms of state control, such as its continuing intervention in the union. In 1981 pressure by workers became so severe that the Ministry of Labor acquiesced in holding new elections in the Metalworkers Union of São Bernardo do Campo and Diadema. Although Lula and other members of his board of directors were prevented from being candidates, nothing could keep them from actively campaigning in support of other leaders who had been important organizers of the strikes of 1978, 1979, and 1980.[40] As a result, the slate supported by Lula received

97 percent of the vote. The new board of directors, headed by Jair Meneguelli, took office in July 1981. The intervention by the Ministry of Labor could not be maintained for more than a year.

In July 1983 Meneguelli and the Metalworkers Union of São Bernardo do Campo spearheaded a general strike called to oppose the federal government's agreements with the International Monetary Fund. In retaliation, the Ministry of Labor once more ordered intervention in the union. This was the third direct military intervention within four years. These recurrent interventions, however, increased the sense of unity, solidarity, and determination among workers in São Bernardo do Campo. They clearly demonstrated, furthermore, the need to challenge the entire edifice of control embedded in the CLT. As they had done before, workers began to meet to discuss alternatives capable of undermining the legality of the CLT.

Study groups analyzed different aspects of the CLT to decide which elements were beneficial to the organization of workers and which should be eliminated. They proposed to draft a legal document to be introduced in Congress by the Partido dos Trabalhadores (Workers' Party). In addition, they devised a strategy to challenge in court the constitutionality of some electoral impediments included in the CLT. A new wave of strikes, public rallies, marches, and assemblies mobilized the population of São Bernardo do Campo to demand new elections in the union. The Ministry of Labor came under pressure from the multinational corporations in the area, who were beginning to see some advantages in having a representative board of directors in the union.[41] Finally, a new date for elections in the union was set for July 1984.

The metalworkers had a further surprise: the only slate to register for the elections included five former union officers, among them both former presidents, Lula and Meneguelli. None of them, according to the CLT, could participate in union elections. The Ministry of Labor acted swiftly to annul their registration. This annulment allowed the metalworkers of São Bernardo do Campo and Diadema to enter a suit in the civil courts arguing for the maintenance of the five candidacies and questioning the constitutionality of the cancellation by the Ministry of Labor. The case went to the Supreme Court, which, in a historic decision, allowed these leaders to run for office. Because this time the government could not even find sufficient candidates to fill its own union slate, the opposition received 100 percent of the votes and took office, legally, in September 1984.

The steps taken to force de jure recognition of representative rights corroded the structural mechanisms of control built by the national security state. The metalworkers successfully carried out a strategy of change through pressure from the bottom. To use their own imagery, they were like thousands of little termites who go largely unnoticed until they have eaten away at the very foundations of a house. And, they hasten to add, in the "Republic of São Bernardo do Campo" they are not even waiting for the house to fall down; they are already busily constructing the new building.

CONCLUSION

Solidarity overcomes fear; in unity there is strength. The experience of the new Brazilian labor movement, particularly as exemplified by the metalworkers of the ABCD region of São Paulo, offers confirmation of these rather banal truths. Yet it also shows that such concepts need to be sharpened and qualified so we may grasp how it is that powerless, exploited, intimidated people can escape from a culture of fear and begin to build a new culture of confident resistance.

Central to the Brazilian experience, first, was the recognition that solidarity breeds strength only if it is a solidarity of participation. The resourcefulness, the resilience, the political acuity of workers of the ABCD were rooted, in large part, in the strength of their commitment to democratic forms of decision making. Organization was always constructed from the base up; leaders were expected to continually consult with and be directed by those whom they led. Leadership itself was systematically underplayed. This feature of the movement was misunderstood not only by the military government but by the "elite opposition" as well. Moreover, the general assumption that workers could not possibly act save at the direction of a vanguard cadre of troublemakers provided an enormous advantage to the movement. Thus, preparations for the 1978 strike were made virtually under the noses of management and the repressive apparatus of the state. Yet, because these preparations were carried out quietly, openly, and in small community and factory groups at the base of society, they went largely unnoticed. On the morning when 2,500 workers crossed their arms and refused to work, virtually the whole of the "elite"—the government, the security agencies, the press, the academic community—was astounded. "Where did this movement come from?" "How did they ever get so organized?"

Second, we have seen that under conditions of superexploitation, the circumstances that might otherwise obstruct the creation of solidarity (fear of unemployment, fear of arrest, fear of being branded part of the internal enemy and therefore brutalized by torture) may actually diminish. We noted the ironic consequence of the policy of job rotation in the automobile firms of the ABCD, and we observed how once community organizations (such as those sponsored by the Church) began to allow people to communicate with one another about their experiences and their fears, some of the effects of intimidation began to wear off. Even direct repression and torture have limits. The force of the repression pressed thousands of women to organize effective support and resistance. And as workers would readily point out, the pain of watching one's children go hungry every day far outweighs whatever pain results even from torture.

This does not mean that those at the bottom of the heap, those who have, so to speak, nothing to lose, are in the best position to turn the logic of a culture of fear around. The most forceful movement did not come from the constantly unemployed and underemployed, from the millions who, in Brazilian society, have to fight to survive from day to day. The automobile workers formed, to a considerable degree, an aristocracy of labor, and they were acutely aware of the privileges this position afforded them. But they were also aware, and surely it was the experience of base-level democratic politics that helped to make them so aware, of the responsibilities that accompanied that privilege. By virtue of their importance to the industry, by virtue of their numbers and their skills, by virtue of their concentration in a relatively small geographical location, they could challenge structures of labor control and labor repression that affected not just themselves but the entire workforce of the country. They were acutely conscious of this historical mission, and from it they derived both confidence and strength.

NOTES

1. For analysis of the legislation and its various mechanisms for state control over trade unions, see Maria Helena Moreira Alves, *Estado e oposição no Brasil (1964–1984)* (Rio de Janeiro: Vozes, 1984); Jose Rodrigues Albertino, *Sindicato e desenvolvimento no Brasil* (São Paulo: Simbolo S. A. Industrias Graficas, 1979); H. J. Fuchtner, *Os sindicatos brasileiros de trabalhadores: Organização e função política* (Rio de Janeiro: Edições Graal, 1980); R. A. Silva, *Estrutura sindical e perspectivas de mudança,* Document 3 (São Paulo: CEDEC, 1983). For sources in English, see Maria Helena Moreira Alves, *State and Opposition in Military Brazil* (Austin: Texas University Press, 1985); K. P. Erickson, *The Brazilian Corporative State and Working Class Politics* (Los Angeles: University

of California Press, 1977); Kenneth S. Mericle, "Conflict Regulation and the Brazilian Industrial Relations System" (Ph.D. diss., University of Wisconsin, 1974); and R. Munck, "State and Capital in Dependent Social Formations: The Case of Brazil," *Capital and Class*, no. 10 (1980), 125–54.

2. In the state of São Paulo alone, from 1980 to 1985 there were examples of both forms of control. The association of subway workers had to wait more than five years for recognition by the Ministry of Labor that allowed it to register as an official trade union. And the Ministry of Labor repeatedly attempted to break the organizational power of the Metalworkers Union of São Bernardo do Campo and Diadema by subdividing it into separate unions of automobile workers, auto-part workers, and electrical workers in the car industry. However, because of the level of militancy that workers in these sectors had reached, the government's immediate strategy failed. Nonetheless, the experiences demonstrate the nature of the controls embedded in the CLT.

3. In the elections of 1981 and 1984 in the powerful Metalworkers Union of São Paulo, which represented 400,000 metalworkers, the opposition accused the board of directors of manufacturing voting boxes with false bottoms and counting more votes than there were registered voters. Such complaints rarely lead to legal victories because of the difficulty entailed in providing evidence; the opposition lacks access to both lists of voters and the polling stations themselves.

4. Here again, an example can shed light on the workings of the electoral controls. The Bank Workers Union of Rio de Janeiro held three different elections in 1978 and 1979 before the opposition trade-union leaders, who were elected by a large majority, were finally allowed to take office. This is not an uncommon occurrence; often the Ministry of Labor gives in to pressure only after a number of electoral victories by opposition candidates.

5. It is interesting to note that although a large percentage of trade-union officials recognize that the trade-union tax is a significant mechanism of control by the state, they are divided in their opinions about whether the tax should be abolished. An important survey of trade-union leaders found that most officials believe that unions could not survive financially if the tax were abolished. Most, however, would like to see reform of the CLT so that administration of the tax funds is transferred to trade unions. For a detailed report of the findings of this research on a state-by-state basis, see *Sindicatos em uma epoca de crise* (Rio de Janeiro: CEDEC/Vozes, 1984).

6. The elections may be postponed, sometimes for a number of years, and the union remains under official intervention. The Bank Workers Union of Rio de Janeiro, for example, remained under intervention for eight years before the government finally gave in to pressure and allowed elections.

7. The military governments after 1964 relied heavily on this mechanism of control to eliminate from unions members of the opposition. Between 1964 and 1979 the Ministry of Labor intervened to cancel the electoral mandates of the entire boards of directors of 1,202 unions. In all cases the interventions were in either professional or blue-collar organizations. In no case did the military intervene in employers' associations. For a detailed account of trade-union interventions after 1964, see Alves, *Estado e oposição no Brasil*, in particular Table 8.3, p. 244.

8. I refer here to Law 4,330, of June 1, 1964, published in *Diario oficial da união,* 102, no. 104, of June 3, 1964.

9. See Mericle, "Conflict Regulation," 130–31.

10. Erickson, *Brazilian Corporative State,* 159.

11. *Cadernos do CEAS* (São Paulo, 1977), 34–36.

12. I refer here to the Time-in-Service Guarantee Fund (Fundo de Garantia por Tempo de Serviço), a program meant to provide readily available funds for compensation. For details on the workings of this program, see Alves, *Estado e oposição no Brasil,* 97–99, and Vera Lucia B. Ferrante, *FGTS: Ideologia e repressão* (São Paulo: Editora Atica, 1978).

13. For an analytical history of all the different salary-control legislation since the policy was first introduced by the military government in June 19, 1964, see "Dez anos de politica salarial," in *Departamento Intersindical de Estudos Estatisticos e Socio-Economicos—DIEESE,* Publication 3 (São Paulo, August 1975). The indexing formula of one raise per year was changed to raises every six months after the major wave of protest strikes in 1979, which involved over three million workers. Subsequent changes in salary legislation were imposed by the International Monetary Fund after the agreements with the Brazilian government in 1983. An account of the changes in 1983 may be found in Alves, *Estado e oposição no Brasil,* 289–314.

14. In Alves, *Estado e oposição no Brasil,* I analyze in detail the Doctrine of National Security and Development and follow its implications for Brazilian society over the years. Here I shall merely summarize the specific components of the Doctrine that are relevant to the development of the "culture of fear" in Brazil.

15. One of the most important theoreticians of the Brazilian Doctrine of National Security and Development was General Golbery do Couto e Silva. His best-known work on the subject is *Geopolítica do Brasil,* first published in the 1950s and released in a new edition that includes speeches and other writings on the subject of political control and military strategy. See do Couto e Silva, *Conjuntura política nacional, o poder executivo & geopolítica do Brasil* (Rio de Janeiro: Livraría Jose Olympio, 1981).

16. Estado Maior das Forças Armadas–Escola Superior de Guerra, Departamento de Estudos, *Manual básico da Escola Superior de Guerra* (Rio de Janeiro, 1976), 319–20.

17. For detailed information on the repressive apparatus and the mechanisms of political control and of censorship, see Maria Helena Moreira Alves, "Mechanisms of Social Control of the Military Governments of Brazil (1964–1980)," in David H. Pollock and A. R. M. Ritter, eds., *Latin American Prospects for the Eighties: What Kinds of Development?* (New York: Praeger, 1983), 240–303.

18. These programs were modeled on the American military strategy of pacification developed during the Vietnam War. One such pacification program was carried out in the conflicted region of Araguaia (in mineral-rich areas of the Amazon basin) and involved the use of an estimated 20,000 troops. For an account of this episode, see Alves, *State and Opposition in Military Brazil,* ch. 6, "Armed Struggle and the National Security State."

19. There is a great deal of documentation on torture and on the activities of underground organizations. For a detailed list of sources and a bibliography, see Maria Helena Moreira Alves, "The Formation of the National Security State: The State and the Opposition in Military Brazil" (Ph.D. diss., Massachusetts Institute of Technology, 1982), 546–49. In addition, see my article on the activities of the death squadron: Maria Helena Moreira Alves, "Organizações paramilitares: Assassinos de aluguel," *Retrato do Brasil*, no. 22 (January 1985), 258–60.

20. I refer here especially to Institutional Acts 1, 2, and 5, and their complementary acts.

21. For information on the history of trade unions in Brazil during the pre-1964 period, see Leoncio Martins Rodrigues, *Trabalhadores, sindicatos e industrialização* (São Paulo: Editora Brasiliense, 1974); Albertino, *Sindicato e desenvolvimento;* Francisco Weffort, "Partidos, sindicatos e democracia: Algumas questões para a historia do periodo 1945–1964" (Master's thesis, University of São Paulo, 1973); Boris Fausto, *Trabalho urbano e conflito social (1880–1920)* (Rio de Janeiro: Difel/Fifusao, 1977); Paulo Sergio Pinheiro, *Politica e trabalho no Brasil* (Rio de Janeiro: Editora Paz e Terra, 1975); Heloisa Martins, *O estado e a burocratizacão do sindicato no Brasil* (São Paulo: Hucitec, 1979); and Luiz Werneck Vianna, *Liberalismo e sindicato no Brasil* (Rio de Janeiro: Editora Paz e Terra, 1978).

22. For an excellent historical analysis of the events in Contagem and Osasco in 1968, see Francisco Weffort, "Participação e conflito industrial: Contagem e Osasco, 1968," *Cadernos do CEBRPA*, no. 5 (1972).

23. An acronym derived from the initials of the most important industrial towns of Brazil: Santo Andre, São Bernardo do Campo, São Caetano, and Diadema.

24. For an interesting analysis of the strikes of this period, see Bernardo Kucinski, *Brazil, State and Struggle,* published in 1982 by the Latin America Bureau, 1 Amwell Street, London EC1R 1UL; see also *Brazil: The New Militancy, Trade Unions and Transnational Corporations,* Transnationals Information Exchange Report 17 (1978). These reports are published by Transnationals Information Exchange: TIE Europe, Paulus Potterstraat 20, 1071 DA, Amsterdam, The Netherlands.

25. See *Brazil*, 30.

26. Kucinski, *Brazil, State and Struggle,* 68.

27. For details on the strikes, including demands, results, and government reaction, see Alves, *Estado e oposição no Brasil,* 249–66.

28. Goffredo Carlos da Silva Telles, Jr., *Carta aos brasileiros: Em homenagem ao sesquicentenario dos cusos jurídicos no Brasil* (São Paulo: Brazilian Bar Association, August 11, 1977), in *Revista da Faculdade de Direito da Universidade de São Paulo*, vol. 72 (1977), 411–23.

29. Metalworkers, urban transport workers, civil construction workers, wheat and mill workers, textile workers, bakers, workers in the food industry, workers in clubs and service industries, workers in ceramics, gravediggers, workers in gasoline refining and distribution, natural gas workers, paper and pulp workers, garbage collectors, miners, electrical workers, commercial and

shop workers, health workers, bank workers, teachers (all levels), public employees (all sectors), doctors, journalists, and rural agricultural workers.

30. Rio de Janeiro, São Paulo, Bahia, Pernambuco, Paraiba, Espirito Santo, Parana, Santa Catarina, Minas Gerais, Goias, Mato Grosso, Ceara, Rio Grande do Norte, Rio Grande do Sul, and Brasilia (federal district).

31. See details in Alves, *State and Opposition in Military Brazil.*

32. See *Brazil,* 48.

33. See Kucinski, *Brazil, State and Struggle,* 85–86.

34. See the table in *Brazil,* 30.

35. Although I refer mainly to São Bernardo do Campo, the analytical points are pertinent to all the towns of the ABCD area. The analysis that follows is based on participant observation and innumerable conversations with leaders, union members, and regular residents of the ABCD area. I frequently visited the ABCD region during 1978, 1979, and 1980, participated in most assemblies in the Vila Euclides and in the union, and was active in the organization of support for the strike. In 1982 and 1983 I lived in the area and could, therefore, closely participate in and observe the developing process of self-liberation that deeply transformed those who had felt oppressed and afraid.

36. At Volkswagen, management created a company committee and tried to legitimize it through holding elections in the plants. The workers of Volkswagen used the opportunity to organize a vast educational campaign on the importance of unity, of collectivity, and, more important, of autonomy. The elections turned into an impromptu plebiscite that rejected, by a margin of over 90 percent, the proposal for a factory commission tied to the company.

37. Note of the Comissão Provisoria de Trabalhadores da Ford, cited in Jose Carlos Aguiar Brito, *A tomada da Ford: O nascimento de un sindicato livre* (Rio de Janeiro: Vozes, 1982), 46–47. Aguiar Brito is one of the union organizers at Ford. The book is a detailed account of the process by which they gained the factory commission. It is based on taped interviews with workers.

38. See Aguiar Brito, *A tomada da Ford,* 21–23, 63. This description comes from a collective account by members of the Ford factory commission.

39. "Estatutos da Comissão de Fabrica dos Operarios da Ford," in Aguiar Brito, *A tomada da Ford,* 120.

40. The regulations of the CLT established that members of a board of directors who had been removed from office by official intervention could not run for any union post for the rest of their lives.

41. Strikes in São Bernardo do Campo had become so frequent, and production so disrupted, that management, in despair, often drafted agreements signed by both Lula and Meneguelli (who, of course, had no legal authority) and then themselves convinced the union *interventores* to sign under the names of the recognized leaders. They found that workers refused to go back to work unless agreements were signed by people they considered to be their legitimate leaders.

ELEVEN

Youth, Politics, and Dictatorship in Uruguay

Carina Perelli

Between 1968 and 1972 Uruguayan society experienced increasing agitation and violence. During those years, several emergency acts were successively enforced: the "prompt security measures," the "suspension of individual guarantees," the decree whereby the armed forces assumed command of the antisubversive struggle, the State of Internal War, and, finally, the State Security Law. These measures became the legal instruments that shaped a truly cybernetic hierarchy of control (which could involve physical repression or not) whose different stages fueled the successive one.

Caught between insurgent and counterinsurgent violence, the Uruguayan state and society were tested to their limits. Norms were undermined, limits stretched, taboos violated, and defects exposed. To many Uruguayans, the only mode of adaptation was violence to oneself, translated as vitriolic mockery and silence. This violence was exerted by society on itself in order not to have to change or at least in order not to have to modify its representation of itself.

Uruguayan society was wounded in the confrontation with its own mirrors and its refusal to open a discussion about events in the present. On the one hand, a permanent movement of foquist activism (guerrilla activity in one spot intended to trigger a general insurrection throughout the country) was aimed at opening society to change and, on the other hand, the barrier of tradition validated the rhetoric about an idealized past and happy future. These two utopias—the tomorrow-as-yesterday and the yesterday-as-tomorrow—did not generate a new one capable of mobilizing the citizenry for real change.

Finding the very essence of its peculiar vision of the world threatened, Uruguayan society recognized its impotence. Well before the military coup of 1973, discussions ceased to center on the problem of finding an alternative way out and focused instead on the survival of a society that was haunted by the ghosts of its collective representations. Uruguayans sought this survival by means of at least one of three mechanisms: magnification, silence, and displacement.

Identities and representations often turned into parodies of themselves. The legal system is a case in point. During the entire period preceding the coup and under the authoritarian regime, the notion of legality not only persisted but was magnified, despite the fact that law ceased to be inspired by principles of justice. During the authoritarian period, the rules of due process were scrupulously respected, and new criminal forms were created so that everything, even dissidence, would fall under the purview of the law. The formal features of law were accentuated to such an extent that even political denunciations had to be signed.[1] In fact, new rules that had little or nothing to do with consensually accepted concepts of justice were being continually created and re-created. The regime related to law, in effect, as a ritual practice.

Criminal justice evolved into a dual system. Common criminals were assured a minimum of guarantees because they did not threaten the system but were, rather, negatively integrated into it. Political criminals, however, were subjected to a form of justice that consisted of only ritualistic guarantees, entirely lacking in substance. In this dual system, the functions of courts were also perverted, as the legal process became part of police procedures.[2] The courts no longer upheld the suspects' legal rights but instead supported new forms of investigation and police actions.

These changes were due not to distortions of procedure but rather to the new concept of legality that underlay its application. Citizens ceased to be equal under the law, not because they ceased to be citizens but rather, as George Orwell commented in *Animal Farm,* because "pigs are more equal," and one could qualify as a "pig" provided one did not threaten the foundations of the new "farm."[3]

INXILE

In this context of perversion through displacement of forms, citizens could survive only by means of hyperreal representations, punctiliousness, and formal obedience to the imposed norms. Inxile[4] was an internal exile, a new way of relating to an order that was external but was nonetheless legitimized by the very fact that it was being obeyed. The basic mechanism through which inxile operated was dissociation between self and world, between behavior and self.

Inxile was more than the privatization of activities that were previously regarded as being in the public sphere. It was part of a mystique of fear that the subjects internalized: fear not only about the potential threat of establishing significant relations with others, but also of simply coming into contact with them. This vision went beyond a perception of the environment as dangerous. It involved recognition of the incriminatory potential—even if unintentionally—of association with others, including all significant others. It reached its climax in the discovery of an accusatory potential in the self in its relation to others. It was a perverse reflection, and a sophisticated panoptical construction of the world, through which the victim became an instrument of the oppressor. In this way, the victim participated in the inevitable dialectic between the human capacity to produce power and the tendency of power to acquire the appearance of a superhuman entity, alienated from its producer.[5] Thus fear was based on a perverse complicity of victims and victimizers.

Inxile also involved an identity that dissociated from itself in order not to fall apart. A "real" identity refused and feared to fit in with the identification provided from the outside. This identity could adopt multiple and varied forms depending on the context and the situation. These forms, however, had a distinct common feature: they were attempts to subvert the axiom whereby no self-identification is possible without reference to others' definitions.

As we have seen, the mystique of fear was represented by the tendency to regard power as superhuman and omnipresent. The reaction to this mystique was magnified by the urgent and often unconscious necessity of the subject to justify his or her dissolution. The result was a daily exercise of violence on the self in the public sphere in order not to yield to the violence that preserved order.

This reaction involved the denial of time-as-becoming. A private time plurally constructed, a plural time that was ignored as such, the time of inxile was the amalgam of isolation, distrust, abdication, dissociation, and embarrassment. It was a time whose future had been severed and whose present was bracketed by dreadful obedience: a time of intemporality. As a result, the past was revitalized and became more present than the present. Hope, proscribed for a future that no longer existed, was directed to the reconstruction of the past, in whose ghostly myths one's own existence acquired meaning. Inxile was a world of private hallucinations.

In this chapter I will examine the formation, the construction, and the consolidation of the identities of some of the actors who belonged to the so-called middle classes. The group under study was located in the traditional breeding ground (*semillero*) of the Uruguayan elites: the secondary schools. (These are high schools, run mostly by the state, that educate an overwhelmingly middle-class group of students between the ages of twelve and seventeen.) The analysis will also focus on how students related to their significant others and to their respective symbolic universes. The assertions made here will be limited to the secondary school population of Montevideo because in a typically urban country like Uruguay the countryside is not representative. Likewise, although the effects of the macroprocesses of socialization were general, this chapter refers to an elite among the elites—the militants. The broader theme of the political socialization of Uruguayan children under the dictatorship remains to be explored.

HOW DO WE KNOW?

How can we reliably reconstruct the events and especially the subjective realities of the period of repression? How is it possible to avoid or at least to control the defensive heroic recollections of those who did not resist? How do we avoid the trap of those reports that tend to fabricate the rosy legend of a proud people in order to forget the embarrassment of fear and submission? How do we prevent fear, the defensive mechanisms against fear, and the later recovery of self-esteem from affecting the quality of the information? These are some of the methodological problems that one faces when undertaking research of this kind. In addition to the problems of an ex post facto study, there are also the difficulties of establishing intellectual distance, given the proximity of the events being examined and the fact that the identities of the actors are so closely bound up in the issues.

The information for this study was collected at the moment of the "exit," when there was a sudden proliferation of accounts of the events of the "infamous decade."[6] The first problem the research team had was not so much to gather the reports as to select those reports that were both relevant and pertinent to the topic of study. At a time when the political parties were fabricating the official version of the legend in which the people were the central factor in the fall of the military government, it was easy to find those who had "resisted." It was difficult, however, to persuade those who had opposed the regime to rescind the vow of silence about their own activities and the activities of their organizations. In order to select our sample, we applied the methodology developed by Maravall for Spain, taking each person—and especially those with a high rank within the organizations—as an interviewee in the strict sense (who supplies answers to a predetermined set of questions) and, at the same time, as a qualified informer (who is asked to provide an analysis of the situation because of his or her strategic position).[7] This procedure was also advantageous to us as a "letter of introduction" to the grass-roots militants as well as a means of access to the sources of information within the organizations.

The second problem was the validity of the information in the reports. This was a problem not because we assumed bad faith but, rather, because of the emotional coloring of the topic itself, which sometimes led to a distorted reconstruction of events as a defensive way of preserving self-esteem, especially in individual cases. We faced a different type of possible distortion with the political and union organizations: the magnification of the role that each group played during the resistance.

As far as possible, every report was checked against complementary sources of documentation (pamphlets, records, training material). This task was not as difficult as might be assumed; Montevideo is the literary city par excellence. In addition, we used reports that overlapped one another, a procedure that enabled us to establish a certain amount of control over the information. We also took into account indirect evidence recorded during the dictatorial period, such as the reports given by primary school teachers about their pupils' indiscretions on political matters (which revealed a "discordant" socialization in their homes).

We looked into the contradictions that emerged from the reports not so much for the sake of neopositivist rules but rather as a way of making the analysis fruitful. We assumed that the contradictions might indicate different perspectives and approaches to reality, which would imply counterposed, or at least dissimilar, world visions—and, therefore, identities.

At all times our action and reflection were guided by the notion that the "how do we know?" cannot be separated from the "what is to be known?" or the "why do we want to know?" We understood ourselves to be responsible for triggering an evaluation of a painful experience and a taking stock of the past—that is, an interpretation of "what we are" as a means of starting the discussion about "where we are going." We were constantly aware that the construction of the object of study is conditioned by the way in which the problem is approached, and in the Uruguayan context this approach was not merely academic. Despite all necessary precautions, we are aware that our research is not value free and that the final results lack the "objectivity" so dear to neopositivists. However, we do not believe that these drawbacks invalidate the goals of the study. Our purpose is to rescue a part of the collective memory. We have attempted to show how memory, as a part of the intertextual tissue of society, is tied to the social construction and reconstruction of reality and the production of collective identities.

In this respect, the distortions that have been introduced by the actors in their recollections, and even the "imaginary accounts" of the subjects about their own performances during the period, are important data in themselves. What the subjects think their behavior could have been or should have been in a limited situation of control and repression is as relevant to the reconstruction of reality and collective memory as their objective behavior is.

EDUCATION AND REPRESSION

In most contemporary societies the educational system is perceived to generate radicalism. It may even be said that the university is intended to ghettoize protest and, at the highest levels of the system, to serve as the field of experimentation for ideological innovations. Such functions are usually tolerated—and even promoted—by the rest of the society because they are controllable and, therefore, low-cost forms of dealing with deviance. Furthermore, in countries like Uruguay these forms were regarded as endowed with a positive formative value, to the extent that the university was considered as the natural environment in which "young birds could try their wings" without a great deal of danger. In this way, students could best prepare themselves to assume the responsibilities of adult life.

This attitude began to change as Uruguay's identity crisis became pronounced. The educational system, the state, and civil society, which once marched together, began to take divergent courses. With the slogan "the university is the country," the educational system grew more autonomous.[8] This process implied the generation of a counterideology that spread down readily to the lower levels of the system, especially to secondary education. At the same time, the increasing violence of Uruguayan society changed the process of ideological reproduction. The relative autonomy of the educational system was less tolerated and the educational system itself was less tolerant.

The Law of General Education (LGE), passed in 1972, crystallized this new tendency to integrate the educational system with society under the aegis of a totalizing state.[9] In this sense, the LGE and the ensuing ordinances, regulations, and protocols that made it effective were yet another mechanism by means of which the totalizing state prevented social deviation and dysfunctions.

In the words of Walter Benjamin, we can characterize this as one of the first cases of an "almost spectral melange" of two types of violence: the "violence that founded" the law, and the "violence that enforces" it.[10] The LGE established an authority empowered to decide and to command. The totalizing state interfered in the relationships of every actor with others and thus penetrated all areas of life. Likewise, the LGE institutionalized the transition toward the public control of private life. It established a mechanism of repression over the public behavior of the students, which moved in two directions: infringement of the privacy of the family and private social groups, and recourse to external control. The effect of the law was to establish the coercive collaboration of both parents and the state in the discipline of the children.[11]

The impact of the LGE on the behavior and the attitudes of the different actors must be interpreted in the light of what happened within the family. The family was compelled to become the instrument of the "violence that enforces" the new law. At the same time, the family's role as bearer of the threat has to be viewed in terms of what the state instructed the family to do and what it was really doing. Finally, we must also take into account the varying amount of freedom available to the actors. Only in this way is it possible to understand the meaning of the social results in both public and private realms.

Faced with the new political threat, the adults in charge of the family tended to withdraw into domesticity. They usually adopted the coercively required external behavior themselves and sought to force the members of their families to adopt it as well. By their capitulation, the parents internalized the mechanisms of control and thus contributed to the effectiveness of the controlling mechanisms of the state. This cooption of parents by the state inevitably produced a breakdown of communication between parents and children. Paradoxically, however, the external harassment by omnipresent authorities also contributed to the reinforcement of the family as an emotional base from which its members could draw strength and nourishment.

The new norms appeared to be constructed according to the axiom that everything that is not expressly permitted is automatically prohibited, with the proviso that it was impossible to gain access to any reliable information about what was expressly permitted. Although no concrete threat might be tied to specific actions, there was great uncertainty as to the limits of legality and to the correspondence between crime and punishment. Punishment could be certain only after the normative order and its hierarchy of in toto inviolable taboos were known.[12]

Parents, socialized according to the democratic principle that asserts that everything that is not expressly and publicly prohibited is automatically permitted, reacted to the transition with an active self-censorship that went beyond official prescriptions and proscriptions. For them, the threatening uncertainty colored all external behavior and attitudes that might be construed as violating the new laws.

The self-imposed restrictions first affected the parents' own personalities but then were extended to those who were considered more vulnerable: the youth. The tension produced by this situation was resolved by an intended inconsistency in the presentation of ego, between what Erving Goffman calls "front stage" and "back stage."[13]

In the same way, self-censorship was accompanied by a retreat into the family sphere, which was perceived as a refuge for the last remnants of sanity in a world characterized by the sudden loss of plausibility and verisimilitude. The family served as a reinforcing and compensatory mechanism. To retreat to this sphere involved not only an idealization but also a crystallization of the values and identities that had preceded the authoritarian regime. In this regard it is important to recall that Uruguay is a country in which one axis for the construction of the collective memory has traditionally been the postulate that "bygone times have always been better," and, therefore, it is only in the light of the past that the present is validated and legitimized. By means of this crystallization of previous values—a concealed form of delegitimization of the present—a countermessage emerged at the core of the family seized by fear, uncertainty, and distrust. Younger generations would be socialized, at least in a partial way, around this countermessage.

Meanwhile, at the other pole, the educational institutions were organized to counteract this counterideological tendency and later to destroy it. A multiplicity of ordinances, regulations, and circulars attempted to foresee and formalize—and ultimately to destroy—even the most minute and irrelevant details of everyday life in the educational community. Within the educational hierarchy a reification of positions and relations also occurred, to the detriment of whoever occupied them.[14]

Consequently, there was a sharp break in the criteria of socialization within the secondary schools. This step involved, first, the breaking of solidarity among teachers and students and, further, sharp divisions between young people and adults in general. The beginning of the period was marked by the mass dismissal of teachers and administrative workers, a fact that became a referent for the rest of the adult population. Nobody could be free of fear of inspections, not even those who held "positions of special trust."[15] Nobody could feel protected from the unexpected denunciation. The implicitly and explicitly repressive power of the imposed norms augmented self-censorship and the feeling of being always at fault that every adult experienced during that period. This fear should be kept in mind when analyzing the passivity, self-censorship, and atomization that characterized the teachers under the totalitarian regime.[16] Additionally, it is important to recognize that the wave of dismissals drained valuable people from the schools.

The regime's actions were aimed at eliminating any possibility of ideological "contamination" of the new generations. The regime blamed contact with "unreliable" adults, including many who had already been "cleared," for having generated the negative counterideology.[17] Hence, it exercised control over both the content of the curriculum and the teaching methods.

The regime also sought to break the links that persisted among the students in everyday school life and to prevent any new solidarity from arising.[18] This process gave rise to students' fantasies of spies and informers that were not sustained by reality.[19] However, the regime's greatest efforts were oriented toward constructing the secondary school as a sphere outside time and space, and divested of its formerly all-encompassing role.[20] The secondary school was transformed into a place of transition rather than a place where students matured socially as well as received formal education. The fact that the secondary school was intended merely as a market for the consumption and certification of official knowledge, however, impeded its ability to achieve control over its members. Consequently, the secondary schools had to induce uniform behavior and to impose acquiescence to coercive social norms, which students experienced as alien.[21] This coercion in turn facilitated the adoption of dissociated attitudes, which further reinforced the attitudes with which young people were socialized in their homes. Dissociation became the general way of life.

GENERATIONS

Each type of actor we will describe is at the same time (1) a product of the dominant mode of reaction to the new situation, (2) a (positive or negative) referent for the other reactive/creative types involved, and (3) a product of the manipulation of, subversion of, and acquiescence to the new norms—that is to say, a product of the effective possibilities of managing violence.

The actors lived in a state of dissociation that allowed them to cope with the "front stage" and "back stage" that each was compelled to adopt during the period. Such dissociation was a way to preserve identity. By putting on a mask, one could attempt to maintain intact the realm of what was real and to cope with the harassment of everyday life by constructing it as a dream. The result was doubly negative: on the one hand, there was a sclerosis of that which was experienced as real; on the other hand, it became difficult to communicate the frozen reality protected by the mask. Actors occupied two spaces at the same time: one in which they recognized themselves and another one in which they were recognized by others.

Those subjects who were already adults by 1971 and had strong family responsibilities may be regarded as true "social autists," to use Bettelheim's term, even though they would have characterized themselves as "prudent."[22] In the same way, once the coup had taken place, the adolescents of the early authoritarian period would be seen in the inquisitor's eye as *marranos*, while they would tend to consider themselves *amusim*.[23] As we will see, this distinction became increasingly blurred for the third group of subjects—namely, the adolescents who were entirely socialized during the dictatorship. In this group we can distinguish the external description of them as *iludente* (deviants)[24] from their self-reference as *Dionysian*.[25] These distinct reactions corresponded, in large part, to the generations' different ways of responding to the situation. At the same time, they corresponded to ways of manipulating, subverting, and acquiescing to the situation.

Obviously, these possibilities were contingent on the actors' ages, responsibilities, and orientations toward themselves and others. They were further influenced by their experience of time and, in particular, by perceptions about their own patterns of past behavior. Only in the light of such experiences and interpretations is it possible to construct one's identity and perhaps above all one's perception of the limits of the possible, the desirable, the feasible, and the tolerable—in other words, the frontiers of the real. It is in this sense that we can talk about generations and distinguish the dominant types of reaction of each.

Which, then, are these generations? What dominant types can we find in them? What significance does each type have in each configuration? What response to power does each of them involve?

In broad terms, we can distinguish three significant groups of actors. The criterion for this distinction is the position of each of the groups at a particular moment: the coup d'état of 1973. The relevant elements of these positions, in addition to the obvious characteristic of age, are the presence (or absence) of family responsibilities and the historical moment at which the subjects were socialized. The time of socialization was particularly significant in determining the kind of reaction actors might have to the new normative order because it conditioned both their perception of time as well as their perception of "normality" and, therefore, of reality.

The first generation comprised parents, who already had family responsibilities at the moment of the coup. Their socialization corresponded to a great extent to the period when Uruguay was confident of itself and of its institutions. For this group, the experience of the de facto regime can be compared only to shell shock.[26] The most visible effects of the trauma were withdrawal to more secure terrain, especially the family; reconstruction, preservation, and transmission of the myth of a democratic Uruguay; psychological regression and loss of confidence as well as of self-esteem; and a form of self-dissociation that was the most fearful but also the least carefully executed. We can classify their social behavior as "social autism."

The second group comprised those who were adolescents at the time of the authoritarian ascent. They were dependent on the first generation, although they had frequently rebelled against it. These were the children of socioeconomic crisis as well as of the institutional breakdown of the country. They were socialized in a context of chaos, characterized by a break with the old models and by naked violence. They consciously adopted the most meticulous dissociations, not so much as a result of their political commitments but rather because the de facto regime identified their age group as most closely associated with "revolutionarism." (In fact, although political militants did strongly influence this generation, in no way did they constitute the totality or even the majority of the militant group.) When youth is almost tantamount to evidence of crime, an individual is careful, sometimes excessively careful, not to give any grounds for confirming the suspicions.

At the social level, the behavior of this generation can be classified as *marrano*—perfect external obedience to imposed norms combined with the practice of forbidden rituals and with the maintenance of proscribed values. For the militant elite, those rituals involved clandestine work in the pockets of resistance. Being young was thus both a stigma and a catalyst of solidarity.

The third generation consisted of the young people who were products of both the new educational system and the dissociated family, which had been transformed into a sanctuary of counterideological mystification of the past. Their identity was constructed from contradictory referents and silencing practices. They were the ones who would take an active role in underground resistance movements, in an attempt to break with the self-imposed dissociation of the two previous generations. Because they attempted to remove the usual barriers and limits, they characterized their behavior, using the Nietzschean term, as Dionysian.[27]

Despite the fact that there was nothing left but nostalgia for the secondary school prior to 1973 and that the secondary school created by the regime was experienced as alien, the militant sectors of the last two generations sought, with different degrees of success, to organize resistance within the educational institution. The *marranos* had counterideological—political—objectives; the Dionysians, countercultural designs.

THE POCKETS OF RESISTANCE IN SECONDARY EDUCATION

Given the conditions described, the opposition to the regime was concentrated, until halfway through the "infamous decade," around two main axes: the countermessage of the autists and the construction of pockets of resistance by the *marranos*. Although these axes had discontinuous points of contact, they shared the same mystique. Both would eventually converge in the socialization of the Dionysians.

Hardly any of what went on during this period was visible on the surface, because of dissociation, which was at the heart of the culture of fear. The greater the degree of commitment and involvement in antiregime actions, the more complex and profound was the dissociation, especially among those at the core of the clandestine organizations created during those years.

In this period, the activities of these organizations were often devoted solely to the functions of surviving. The organizations were divided into compartments for security reasons and had a strict hierarchy of decision making. Between 1974 and 1980, the only apparent organized entities among secondary students were small clusters and study groups, which often lacked any continuity. Apart from the moral significance of the existence of such groups in the midst of generalized terror, these organizations had little influence on later events because their activities were not directed at the mass of students. They served more to preserve countermessages made possible by the tiny gaps left by the regime. In reality they appeared as a culture of catacombs, representative of autists, rather than as the creators of new and different spaces.

Not until the constitutional plebiscite of November 1980 did these groups begin to act politically. The plebiscite was the first attempt by the regime to legitimize its actions in a traditional political mode. The result was the first breakdown of regime control, brought about by the regime itself. The opposition was able to establish its first spaces for public discourse, as it seized the advantage and opened a gap in the culture of fear. In this tiny gap also appeared the first visible symptoms of the regime's failure to reformulate the secondary school system.

However, the first true organizational form that appeared in secondary schools under the dictatorship was constructed later in 1981. At that time there emerged a network of groups that functioned around the petition against the (university) entrance examination.[28] The network was organized with representation from each school in an area, with centralized coordination for the global campaign. The only goal of this first organization was to eliminate the entrance examination, an excellent tactic to unite the secondary students. This cause was also able to generate support among the parents, given the symbolic significance that education in general, and university education in particular, always held in the collective representations of the Uruguayan people. This first campaign was an important qualitative step in the conquest of fear because the opposition became visible and, more important, its actions entailed the individualization (self-incrimination) of those who signed the petition.[29]

Begun in the university, the campaign was then taken up by secondary students and used by the few politically committed students to mobilize and recruit other students. The petition became a major tool in the reorganization of the student union and the restructuring of the political party groups in secondary schools. The open activity around the petition was accompanied by the emergence of a stronger and more powerful—although often bitter and unstructured—political movement that sustained itself in the socially shared and legitimized space. Although the logic of the *marranos* prevailed in this period, its predominance implied an adaptation of old reflex actions to the new circumstances.

To some extent, the same shift occurred in society at large. The events that took place around this time took on greater significance because of the concealed meaning they acquired for the actors. Two events in particular that involved the participation of many levels of society played a major role in the cross-socialization of the generation of the Dionysians: the Canto Popular (popular song) and the publication of the first opposition weekly. One leader of the clandestine Federation of Secondary Students (FSS) reported:

> The Canto Popular was a kind of "sanctuary" for militants. . . . We suffered from a problem of communication, and, in a way, although it couldn't solve that problem entirely, at least it helped us socially. . . . It meant to go beyond listening to the record clandestinely at home. Although they did not have straightforward [political] lyrics, at least they hinted at something, and all this means a lot in Canto Popular. . . . And, besides, the fervor of that atmosphere created by all those people bound together by a certain common spirit, you could find it there and nowhere else. Even though you could gather with the rest of the militants of your secondary school, they were not more than five or six. Now . . . I don't know . . . a big room full of people, and a guy that sings you something more or less [meaningful], the people who clap hands and sing with one voice. . . . I mean, it turns you on.

Canto Popular became so important that attendance at the festivals was used to identify potential militants for the underground organization.

The second visible event of considerable relevance was the publication of *Opinar*, the first weekly that took a clearly opposition stance. It belonged to those elements within the Colorado Party who had supported the "NO" in the 1980 plebiscite. During 1981–82, this publication constituted, for this generation of adolescents, the first written and systematic public antiregime discourse. In fact, *Opinar* embodied what had been so far only part of the myth transmitted by the autists—a journal that opposed the government. It became so important that its audience came to be a second source of possible adherents, in addition to its use in study and discussions by the already organized groups.

As a result of these first gaps in the mystique of fear and the consequent visible manifestations of public dissent, there was an evolution—which later became a break—in the logic of the *marranos* and even a modification of the autists' reflex actions. In fact, the opening of spaces for opposition in the external world, in a way that was politically familiar to the autists, allowed them to return—at least formally—to the political arena and to a style of politics with which they felt confident. It allowed them to take an increasingly active role, which, in turn, had several repercussions in the patterns and referents of the cross-socialization of the new generations.

We should not, however, transform into myth the weight and influence that the opposition movement had among young people in this period. With the exception of politically committed militants—who, in this period, despite their age, responded more to the logic of the *marranos* than to new forms of politics—the movement remained unarticulated, atomized, and, therefore, lacking both a voice of its own and alternative projects. It was often no more than a protest by the repressed against the most irritating and formal manifestations of control. It was a form of defiance expressed through the characteristic weapons of the weak: attendance at events that were not approved by the regime, passive resistance, and a certain humor that could turn into mockery. A secondary student of the period narrates:

> In the classes of Moral and Civic Education, whenever we arrived at the critical point and the question of "democracy and totalitarianism" was posed, there was always some "weirdo" who would come out and say: "And this [totalitarianism], isn't this what is going on here?" . . . There was a general outburst of laughter. . . . During the national holidays . . . I remember one day, the "Day of the Fallen in the War against Subversion," we would all have to stand up and observe a minute of silence in class. . . . And when the headmistress told us, everyone was already a bit "pissed off," and so they made us all stand up and we managed to last for twenty seconds, twenty-five seconds. . . . The headmistress came round. . . . It was a hot day and we were all fed up. . . . Someone smothered his laughter, and there was a general outburst of laughter. . . . And I remember that it started to spread along the corridor until it became a general outburst.

Within this framework of desanctification of the imposed reality a debate concerning the possibility of using legal spaces arose in the students' coordinating committee and in the clandestine organizations connected to party politics. There was a confrontation between two antagonistic positions, at both the doctrinal and the strategic levels. The first group, which mainly comprised radicalized elements, supported a retreat to clandestine action in order to prevent new controls from being imposed on the already conquered open spaces of militancy. The second group, which basically comprised members of the League of Communist Youth and their sympathizers, wanted to keep a legal space that would be controlled by the clandestine movement. The debate centered on control and the use of newly opened space. It arose from contrasting ways of perceiving the alleged omnipotence and omnipresence of power. The two groups gave different meanings to the power of the other and the self, and to the diverse interpretations and representations of reality.

The debate culminated, however, in a tactical choice that did not result from doctrinal/strategic decisions but, rather, from the actions of the enemy. The militants were forced to withdraw to clandestine activities when it was discovered that their coordinating committee had been infiltrated by the security services. The magnitude of the infiltration threatened the security of the political-party groups. Therefore, after this short break, the adolescents were compelled to integrate themselves fully in the political spaces consolidated and led by the *marranos,* where the logic of dissociation prevailed.

With the return to clandestine activity, real pockets of resistance were organized, with a base/leadership hierarchical structure, around the FSS. Although the underground pockets of opposition had a clear political-party character, sympathizers were attracted by the FSS proposal and were recruited into its ranks.

The FSS suffered from the same limitations as other clandestine organizations of the period. It was unable to create activists in the traditional sense and therefore had a low level of theoretical support in the membership. The restricted nature of its activities often reflected members' reaction to their opponents' moves rather than their own initiatives. Although a hegemonic line prevailed in the leadership, a pluralist image was sought. An effort was made to coordinate with members of other organizations at the national level, but these other militants, mostly *marranos,* made the decisions in the last instance because they dominated the broad political spectrum. The general guidelines were later transmitted to the members of the coordinating committee, so that they could consider them and communicate them to the bases. In this context, only a rigidly hierarchical structure with an authoritarian bias seemed possible. Later, once new modalities appeared, a strong reaction against this bias emerged.

With the transition back to clandestine action, a strong cleavage was opened in the student population between those who were militants of the organizations and the noncommitted mass. The militants tended to constitute themselves as a group bound together by strong ties of solidarity, myths, rituals, and common values that increasingly separated them from the mass of their fellow students. Their separation reached such a point that, later on, they would require intermediaries to serve as links with the majority of students.[30]

The constant danger and harassment from outside necessarily reinforced the solidarity within the group. But at the same time, and almost inevitably, the group tended to generate its own mode of analysis and interpretation of reality, which confined its members to a circular "logic" and increasingly isolated them from the rest of the student population.[31] This "logic" eventually prevented the group from perceiving the signs of change in the environment and thus from developing accordingly.[32]

The increasing distance between the militants and the realities of the secondary schools was reinforced by the vertical structure that the organization adopted. Among the militants there was also an increasing contempt for legal activities, which they viewed as tantamount to scabbing. Moreover, the characteristic mystique of clandestinity carried a set of social values and habits of secrecy that could only deepen their estrangement from the mass of students. In the words of one leader: "In a way, the idea was that when everything fell, the clandestine organization would come to light, but not before." This biased vision of reality not only promoted estrangement but also interfered with the possible exploitation of situations among the student population that were more related to their common problems. Another leader points out:

> All the mobilizing efforts in secondary schools were carried out somehow in the wrong way, according to the hegemonic line that we had. It was a bit like coming on from above, instead of just posing the problems that annoyed you. And so, when the moment came to reorganize the secondary-school student movement, when it was necessary to tackle the things that upset you the most and that developed, for example, around the mobilization against wearing a uniform, they would call you for the demonstration in front of the U.S.A. Embassy to protest against the invasion of Grenada. . . . Sixty people would go who would be beaten up and no one would hear about it. And you didn't mobilize a damned thing! And when the moment came for secondary schools to become relevant at the national level, by putting pressure and taking part in an already organized form, then they realized that they had to mobilize it in some way, and so the mobilizations against the uniform and all the rest started.

This estrangement was critical because, among the mass of students, there were entire groups who did not want to or could not assume the commitment of working in the clandestine organization but who were prepared to be mobilized. They were more oriented toward participating in legal activities. When recalling the events of the period, another leader of the FSS maintains:

> Although among the masses neutrality prevailed, there was a kind of generalized spirit of noncooperation, of contributing so that things would go wrong, . . . so that they would not be successful. Now the national holidays, now the parades, or whenever there was an inspection by the head office, or when they wanted to show a certain image of the school in some place and the head office was going nuts, . . . and we tried our best to give a bad image: . . . singing loudly "Tiranos Temblar!" ["Tyrants Tremble!"—part of the lyrics of the national anthem], or lining up in disorderly fashion, or neglecting some part of the uniform.

These students, who often felt alien to the FSS, had a clear opinion about certain situations within the educational precincts. Such was the case concerning obligatory use of the uniform, school equipment, and prices in the canteen. Because of the increasing estrangement of the militants of the FSS from their fellow students, and because there was no possibility of protesting legally, these issues could not be made manifest. Only belatedly were these opinions channeled into action.

In 1982 there was a spontaneous strike in the secondary schools that followed a similar strike in the university. The strike, which had not been called by the FSS, demonstrated that this group of secondary students was prepared to be mobilized within certain limits. One leader accurately noted when evaluating the period:

> We contributed to the fact that the youth was rebellious and that it revolted against the framework that was imposed on them. . . . I would like to say that we worked at the organizational level for whatever developed later on. Now, for me, the influence of our work seems insignificant. I rather think that all the radicalization of the youth was, rather, generated by the authoritarian framework itself, by its own excesses. I think that if those guys had been more intelligent with respect to how things are done, they could have succeeded in shaping more docile youth. The thing is that there was an atmosphere of harassment. . . . It infuriated us! It did not produce a vision. . . . I don't know. . . . The guy who went to school was not anti-imperialist and he didn't even see clearly at the national level, but he was pissed off with the janitor, and he was fed up with the headmistress on account of the uniform. . . . And there were things that he did see clearly, about the school equipment, the excessively high prices in the canteen, and the generally repressive environment.

In this context and in this climate, the Association of Students of Public Education (ASCEEP) emerged at the initiative of the young students who had various leftist political tendencies. They sought to create an alternative organization within secondary education, one that might permit them to operate within legal spaces or, at least, from visible ones. During an entire year, both ASCEEP and FSS coexisted, the former criticizing the latter, the latter denying the former.

At the macrosocial level, there was a climate of increased openness, with successive positive experiences of public mobilization. The prevalence of the *marrano* mentality during the first period yielded and developed in the light of changing external realities. Finally, the feud between the two groups was resolved, at least at the organizational level. Thanks to the influence that the ASCEEP had acquired at the university, the FSS not only had to recognize its existence, even at the secondary level, but was also compelled to accept a merger into a larger organization. The merged organization was called ASCEEP-FSS.

A VISIBLE ORTHODOXY, AN EMERGING HERESY

At the beginning, the issues posed by ASCEEP were more in line with specific student demands than with political-party tendencies. They reflected the expectations of certain sectors of students who were dissatisfied with the FSS's performance. The FSS, which was perceived as estranged from the mass of students and which was notable for its rigidly hierarchical structure, had no power to unite the students. It remained separate from their realities and enclosed in its own logic. However, from the moment of its creation, ASCEEP attempted to mobilize the student population through novel and specific claims to which they could respond. Moreover, the activities were carried out by certain leaders who intuitively recognized the kinds of sabotage of the status quo that would appeal to the mass of secondary students. And the students could recognize themselves in these leaders.

Two important events exemplify the novel character of the measures taken to carry on the struggle: the "Day of Jeans" and the "Students' Week." Their common feature was their creative invention of new forms of struggle. The most visible manifestation of repression in secondary schools was the uniform, which was scrutinized in the most minute detail. The uniform thus became the symbol of authoritarianism in the educational system. This arbitrariness and harassment, typical of the educational system under "civilian/military" rule, transformed the uniform into the motive for and target of one of the most interesting mobilizations of the period. A significant number of students in one of the larger secondary schools of the capital responded to a call from ASCEEP-FSS and attempted to enter school wearing the piece of clothing that was anathema to authorities: jeans.

In this protest several novel elements were manifest—novel both for the period and for the environment—that were also, to a certain extent, discordant with the preceding tradition. In the first place, the militants were not the sole participants. The idea was also taken up by noncommitted students who acted without having to be pressured and with full knowledge of the punishment their actions might bring. In the second place, there was an active and intentional pursuit of sanctions, which were thereby transformed into an integral part of the mobilization. Such a pursuit was particularly relevant because (1) it tended to desanctify sanctions, thereby disarticulating some of the mythical connotations of power and reducing authority to a human scale; (2) it fulfilled the important function of dragging the parents into action, mobilized in the defense of their children's interests;[33] (3) it marked the start of a peculiar form of violence, which was extremely difficult to control and repress: peaceful violence. The action represented, perhaps, the first heretical endeavor of the generation of Dionysians.

The second important mobilization was led by the Federation of University Students, but it also attracted the participation of secondary students. The "Students' Week" was innovative in combining a clear antiregime protest with festive elements and a certain sarcastic humor that eventually transformed the whole event into a forthright mockery of the authorities.

In both struggles—and especially in the repercussions they had for the mass of students—there was a certain heretical bias. This bias, which recurred frequently in later events, had the following components:

1. A strong politicalization of everyday life, which eventually transcended the privatization of political life imposed by the dictatorship.

2. The dismantling of legitimacy based on the authority of age, knowledge, doctrine, or clandestine organization through peaceful violence and passive resistance.

3. The resort to atypical forms of struggle, which were not often perceived as such by the organizations or by society itself.[34]

4. A distinct break from the adult generation, which led to independent actions on the part of young people but did not extend to the emotional level.[35]

5.   A pronounced disbelief in the political and ideological apparatus that had gradually been extended to all areas of social life and to
social institutions, leaders, and values, and that increasingly confined
people to marginal, almost underground, spaces.

6.   A poorly structured, contradictory, and frequently incoherent
discourse, which resembled a mythical representation of the world rather
than an ideology.

7.   A concomitant distrust for every discursive practice that might
have a marked ideological character or was thought to espouse beliefs
and socially accepted reconstructions of the collective memory.

8.   The rejection of both the mystique of fear and sentimental
references to the communion of fear.

9.   The rejection of the myths of both autists and *marranos* of a
better yesterday and a happy tomorrow.

10.   The vindication of the present as a space for life and struggle and
of "here" as trench and refuge for those who were excluded from a
society they gradually rejected.

Such were the paradoxical, heretical signs of a generation that, in fact,
should have been socialized to obey.

NOTES

1.   "Abjurations" involved the publication of a declaration in the press in
which the accused asserted his or her innocence. Also, if the denunciations
eventually led to a trial, there could be a face-to-face verbal encounter (*careo*)
between the accuser and the accused.

2.   See *Aquí*, 7 January 1986, p. 7: "Harsh critiques of military justice by
civilian judges." "Serious irregularities" were proved.

3.   George Orwell, *Animal Farm* (New York: Harcourt Brace & Co., 1946),
112.

4.   *Inxile*, or *insile*, was a term coined in Uruguay (first used by Diego Pérez
Pintos) to refer to the marginality suffered by those who were either direct or
potential victims during the authoritarian period.

5.   Guillermo O'Donnell, paper presented at the SSRC-CEDES seminar, The
Culture of Fear in the Southern Cone, Buenos Aires, May 1985.

6.   The first reports about life in the prisons and resistance activities came to
public attention in March or April 1985. Until then, denunciations about the situation in the prisons circulated thanks to organizations of relatives and human-
rights organizations. Our interviews with leaders and militants of the Federation
of Secondary Students during the clandestine period took place from March
1985 onward.

7. José Maraval, *Dictadura y disentimiento político. Obreros y estudiantes bajo el franquismo* (Madrid: Alfaguara, 1978).

8. The expression was created before the military coup in an editorial in *Marcha* (date unavailable) written by Carlos Quijano.

9. The LGE was put forward by the then Minister of Education and Culture Julio Ma Sanguinetti, with the advice of other distinguished politicians. Sanguinetti was elected president of the restored democratic regime in November 1984.

10. Walter Benjamin, *Para una crítica de la violencia* (Mexico City: Premia, 1982).

11. Articles 33 to 37 of the LGE established the responsibility of parents for their children's behavior inside the secondary schools. Among the sanctions it proposed was suspension of the family allowance. However, this proposal was never put into practice.

12. For example, despite the fact that a 1975 decree forbade the introduction, distribution, and sale of books and records that were regarded as Marxist, no precise statement, lists, or reports ever indicated what was specifically banned. Neither the radio nor the television stations received precise guidelines. Oral suggestions were sufficient.

13. Erving Goffman, *Internados. Ensayo sobre la situación de los enfermos mentales* (Buenos Aires: Amorrortu, 1971).

14. The Protocol of Secondary Education was an attempt to foresee all the possible relations among people with positions in the educational community through a closed normative structure that completely depersonalized possible interactions among those in different positions.

15. The positions of special trust were conferred according to the link between the candidates and the powerful person who appointed them. In secondary education, to occupy one of these positions required full identification with the regime. Positions in critical areas such as moral and civic education, history, philosophy, and literature, and higher positions such as those in head-office inspection were considered with special care.

16. Marisa Silvia Schultze, "El liceo hoy: Testimonio de una profesora," *Punto* (CIEP, Montevideo) 21, no. 27 (September 1984).

17. The teachers who continued working or were incorporated into the system often had to answer written questionnaires in order to prove their "ideological purity," which had to be at a higher level than that of other civil servants.

18. The Ordinances for Secondary Education required students to report to the educational authorities any student or teacher whom they knew to be carrying out political activities. In the university this obligation was included in a commitment form that all students were obliged to sign. In neither case did it have any effect.

19. The myth of the *tira* (police informer) was present at all levels of society, and, as a result, created great distrust of certain people, even though the actual number of *tiras* was not high. This is another example of the uses of terror, of the "logic" whereby it was constructed. The library, as well as the canteen, ceased to be a social place for the students. In addition, there were *celadores* (invigilators

who were retired members of the police and armed forces), who barred any kind of meeting.

20. Erving Goffman, *Frames of Reference* (London: Penguin, 1974); and Georg Simmel, *Sociología* (Buenos Aires: Espasa Calpe, [1908] 1939), 2 vols.

21. The ritual actualizes the myth, in this case the myth of the omnipotence of power. Obedience, following external rituals, creates the subjective conditions for the affirmation of the myth. Ernst Cassirer, *The Myth of the State* (Mexico City: F.C.E., 1945).

22. Bruno Bettelheim, *Surviving and Other Essays* (New York: Vintage Books, Random House, [1952] 1980).

23. *Marranos* was the name the Christians gave to the fifteenth-century Jews who were forced to convert, although they maintained their original religion and practiced it in secret; the other fifteenth-century term, *amusim*, characterized those Jews who lived in expectation of better times for their own faith.

24. *Iludente* is a legal term used by the Inquisition to identify the crime of having apparently celestial visions, dealing directly with saints, or proselytizing.

25. Dionysian was the term Nietzsche used to describe the peculiarities of an individual (or culture) who typically actualized the instincts through action, a counterpart to the so-called man of reaction.

26. Shell shock is a state of deep shock, often catatonic. It was common among soldiers who fought in the trenches during World War I and was frequently caused by the explosion of shells.

27. Friedrich Nietzsche, *El nacimiento de la tragedia* (Madrid: Alianza, [1872] 1973).

28. The military regime's establishment of entrance quotas for the university brought strong reactions, beginning with the signing of petitions against the entrance examination organized by those who were most seriously affected by it: final-year secondary students.

29. Signing the petition against the entrance examination involved a high risk of incrimination, given that, by means of the signature and the number of the identity card, the student could be easily identified.

30. One FSS militant observed:

As for recruitment and political work in class, in a way we had to count on other people, the ones who were not so politically committed. They were not so schematic, and so they could talk about many topics and could communicate much more easily. What would normally happen is we would say, "So-and-so is a 'bullock' because he does not attend the meetings and he is late for a street meeting," and this guy could [explain] this because he was more in touch with the mentality of the other kids. Therefore, it was the most important channel of communications that we could have.

31. One militant of the FSS affirmed:

I had a good level of communication with the majority of my companions until I became a militant; I could communicate with them effectively because I could deal with a lot of topics: football, dancing, a lot of things that you need in order to start a conversation. Now, when I became a militant and also became the most committed member of the group, because I was a member of the Committee, I was almost entirely absorbed by internal problems. I would go to school just to be in class. Whenever I tried to strike up a conversation with someone, I would use a code of communication that was very different from what I needed to use there. Therefore, what normally happened was that I was there to *bancar* [take charge of] all the internal structure, all the organizational matters.

32. One militant of the FSS told the research team:

The activities with other people could be very thorough, in the sense that they were personal and that personal work would guide you. . . . Sometimes, . . . in the end, we were fed up and we would incorporate some guy within a week if he just said three or four nice things. Otherwise, we tried organizing. . . . I don't know . . . at the end-of-the-year outings, at some football match. But, in general, the problem was that we couldn't find the adequate language to remove those experiences from the conventional level of mucking around for a while, so as to be able to give them an organizational and participative character.

33. The authorities' imposition of severe sanctions against the students caused the parents to constitute themselves as a group and later as an assembly. What they sought at first was a solution to each individual student's particular problem, so several individual strategies were taken up for that purpose. However, as the situation evolved, the group found itself forced more and more to discuss the educational problem as a whole. Although this group was unable to grow sufficiently to transcend the original problem and, in fact, broke apart once the conflict was resolved, its creation and functioning were important in at least two ways. First, this was one of the first open critiques of the regime and educational authorities by the generation of autists that did not have a political-party character. This remained the case until an attempt was made to formalize the group, which led it to its final dissolution. Second, this mobilization was generated by an event related to the militancy of the youth, with which many parents were usually in disagreement given the different points of reference of these two generations and the symbolic significance that the authorities' injunctions had for each of them.

34. The following examples from interviews offer atypical forms of struggle. "In a private secondary school of the capital, the boys exchanged uniforms with the girls. Well, they were still wearing a uniform." In an assembly of the ASCEEP-FSS a "serious" speaker made a parody out of the platform of the organization as a way of critiquing it. Some years later, when this generation entered the university and was pressured by the politically committed militants to appoint class delegates, in many of the classes the most inadequate student was presented as candidate for the position. These events recall those of Cacareco in Brazil.

35. In the context of a communion of fear and the constant infantilization of adults by the regime, the family was reinforced in its role as the emotional center of social life. Yet because adults could not overcome their fixation on power, they could no longer fulfill their roles as parents. It was common to find reports noting that young people no longer asked for advice and would only announce, generally a posteriori, the actions they were going to take. This behavior, which might have been brought about by the mystique of fear and the "logic" of the militants, is still manifest today.

TWELVE

Strategies of the Literary Imagination

Beatriz Sarlo

THE INTELLECTUAL FIELD
AND THE LITERARY PROBLEM

The processes of producing a literary discourse are inseparable from the social space in which that discourse is written and read. The 1980s in Argentina proved no exception; on the contrary, some of the keys to present-day Argentine narrative can be found in its double correlation with the political and social domains and in that particular space that Pierre Bourdieu calls the intellectual field.

As a socially differentiated area, the intellectual field is the territory of a particular type of social actor: in it participate intellectuals, writers, critics, and those who decide what is to be produced and how the discourse and symbolic goods are to be distributed. This field is endowed with its own particular logic, which does not necessarily either contradict or reproduce the social logic but may do either. What truly constitutes the intellectual field is that in it all the other social processes undergo a series of ideological, intellectual, and aesthetic transfigurations. It follows its own laws and adjusts the balances and tensions that exist in the other social spaces.

As the field of artistic and intellectual relations, this space has its own criteria for conferring legitimacy; its rules are at once aesthetic and ideological, depending on the prevailing internal and external climate. Sometimes the aesthetic and the ideological are blended; at other times they are carefully separated. In Argentina (and I believe in all of Latin America) in the early through mid-1970s, the actors in the intellectual field wove aesthetic and ideological themes into the design of a cultural utopia in which the aesthetic and political revolutions were more or less identified with one another. Although we now know that this was only a utopia, like all utopias, it had profound aesthetic and political consequences.

The past or current state of an intellectual field may be defined by a hegemonic problem that cuts across the field as a whole or at least across its dominant tendencies. This problem encompasses specific relations among themes and subjects, ways of thinking about society, subjectivity, reason, strength, conflict, the place of the intellectual, and his or her relation with other social actors. It is a problem that, at given moments, crystallizes into formulas such as: artists should relate primarily to "the people" and derive their inspiration from the process of social change. In contrast, at other times (and as partisans of other tendencies) artists may insist that only their peers be their public or their judges; that they do not take their bearings from the grand destinies being played out in the other social spaces.

According to Bourdieu, such a problem confers ideological unity on a given period and, although their positions may vary, all the actors in the particular field must position themselves in relation to the set of hegemonic concerns. In this sense, the problem is defined by the questions to which intellectuals feel it incumbent upon them to respond; how they choose to answer is not particularly relevant.

I mentioned a utopia, the Argentine utopia of the 1970s. Revolution was not only thought possible then, it was the order of the day, and, moreover, it was deemed beautiful, aestheticizable. Perhaps Julio Cortázar best expressed this intellectual ideology when, at the Casa de las Américas in Havana, he stated that there was room for all the literary genres within the revolution and that outside of it no genuine art would be possible. Cortázar was literally quoting one of the most repeated slogans of those adolescent, and perhaps even happy, years. The long history of misunderstandings between politics and literature seemed to have been buried once and for all in the "new deal" in which Latin American artists and revolutionaries were collaborating.

This problem, expressed in slogans and in practice, was not exclusively Argentinian: Jean-Luc Godard's films, for instance, saturated with the intellectual and political climate of the events of May 1968 in France, come to mind. And in Argentina a system of metaphors, such as "the armored rose" (for militant literature) or "to use the camera like a rifle" (for militant cinema), was in vogue. These were the discursive manifestations of a *Zeitgeist* that profoundly marked writers and artists alike.

The social spectrum as a whole had shifted to the left during these years. The intellectual field not only shifted along with the rest of society but was one of the main forces of change. From it came many of the boldest impulses toward the left including, of course, the new left born inside Peronism. The shift to the left produced no great narrative texts. *Libro de Manuel* (A manual for Manuel) may not be Cortázar's greatest novel, but it was a product of an era when a new generation of writers was learning the dynamics of the relation between literature and politics.[1] Many men and women were beginning their literary careers in this intellectual climate, publishing first books, acquiring the means of production, and anticipating the certain arrival of socialism. An atmosphere of imminent revolution shaped the "structure of feeling" in the early 1970s, to borrow one of Raymond Williams's expressions. The intellectual field was deeply affected by the concerns and tensions spilling over from other social spaces. Antonio Gramsci, Louis Althusser, and the Mao conferences in the Yan'an forum, among others, provided the focus for the aesthetic debates. The tone of the era's hegemonic problem was profoundly political.

The 1976 coup took place in this aesthetic/ideological ambiance, and my intention is to examine some of the narrative texts published from that time on to find out what strategies they employed to challenge and represent recent history. The traumas of exile, repression, and the crisis all left their mark on the literature of the era, just as they marked the Argentine social fabric as a whole. The writers who published in those years were the contemporaries of the students and workers of the Cordobazo, of the Peronist leadership, of the prisoners, the disappeared, and the dead.[2] They too—because they were part of Argentine society— lived through that epoch; their lives too were connected to a liminal point, confronted as they always were with the absolutes, life and death. For those who want to explore these absolutes, literature is one of the privileged discourses. The question is, then, what instruments writers chose to use during those years, and what strategies they employed to convert the events and collective experience into discourse.

AESTHETIC MODERNITY

The Argentine intellectual field is defined by its modernity. What theories matter, what books are read, and which "authorities" impose their hegemony are those at the forefront of the European debate. This modernity is responsible for the demise of the mythical "naive novelist," and no writers had less in common with this figure than Argentine writers of the 1980s. Bits and pieces of literary theories and obvious and obscure references alike indicate in what direction writing had moved, reflecting on itself and on its own resources.

Argentine writing changed at the beginning of the 1970s: from the literary system dominated by Cortázar and a content-oriented reading of Jorge Luis Borges, it moved to a system dominated by a Borges reinterpreted according to the critical theory of the intertext.[3] Almost without exception, the writers who worked during these years took their bearing from this reinterpretation of Borges.

This move implies radical mistrust of "classical" narration and poses the question of how to continue telling the tale. There are two processes at work here. First, the crisis of the "story" form, which is just another chapter in the long crisis of realism. It is as though the writer were to say: this form has reached its limit; from here on in, if more can be told, it will invariably appear in quotes, to show that the once fluid relation between texts and the world is no longer operative. Second, writers search for narrative forms that allow one to reflect on tragic experience, that provoke bewilderment and the sense that an explanation is due. They explore narrative models capable of organizing a social experience whose horror initially appears to defy discourse.

A study of the writing produced during those years, then, might allow us to extract some meaning from the painful and chaotic experience of the 1970s.[4] Because its violence dissolved what they had taken most for granted about the recent political past, writers, besieged by history, chose not to speak in its name. Strictly speaking, the set of fragments that constituted Argentina during those years of questioning and fear can hardly be called history. Is there really a history? Several novels reiterated this question, revealing the prevailing uncertainty about whether discourse could in fact order a reality whose underlying logic seemed to be secret and inaccessible. What are we to do when the narrative forms themselves mistrust reality? How are we to deal with this second layer of disbelief, derived from Argentina itself, at a time when social experience is most fragmented?

Fiction could not aspire to restore the lost totality, which was in fact a figment of the collective imagination. Nor could it finish explaining something it had no answers for and could not reasonably be expected to have. Instead, it worked on the fragments of available experience so that, in fact, the best literature of those years bears the traces of history.

Once again, Argentina was invoked as a problem, a theme that, ever since 1930, has haunted the national literature like an obsession. None-theless, since the early 1980s, the Argentine question has been derived from social experiences and perspectives that are completely different from those that dominated the intellectual field of the 1930s. Martínez Estrada and Scalabrini Ortiz saw the essence of the "Argentinian charac-ter" as both pessimistic—a function of the process of material and intellectual construction since the colonial period—and open to change, a political rather than necessarily optimistic aspect.[5] At the present time, however, the Argentine question is focused not only on how we were constituted but on why we broke apart; what underlies the unjust and brutal order imposed on us? History itself has dislodged all the certain-ties that so jubilantly illuminated the earlier years, and ways had to be found to represent a society that has suffered from a process of physical and moral disaggregation.

Suppressing debate and dissent and liquidating the public sphere are more devastating even than censorship, and when the military dictator-ship froze public political forms of reflection, literary discourse was able to propose itself as a space for reflection. We cannot say that it invariably was, however. Although literature showed a certain reluctance to delve too deeply into all the dimensions and implications of the crisis, present history, stripped of none of its seriousness, magnetized the discourse. Because repression, censorship, and fear had effectively eliminated the other discursive forms and options, the inspiration to elaborate the Argentine experience of the most recent past found its way into litera-ture.

Some of the crucial problems that usually beset fiction came up: how to produce new images of oneself and of the other (wherefrom to nar-rate?); what strategies to invent to represent the other social actors and the subjective illusions sustained by them; how to reconstruct or reform the literary system and the story's place in it. As Bakhtin says, there are problems of linguistic and ideological representation of individual and social perspectives, whether these be discourses, practices, or the con-densation of experiences.[6]

Moreover, these constructive and internal issues of literary discourse sustained the dimension imposed by context, where a series of questions about Argentina began to come together. The violent fragmentation of the objective world had repercussions in the symbolic world. Having to come to terms with repression, death, failure, and lost illusions, fiction introduced bewilderment by using two basic strategies. On the one hand, it rejected mimesis as a unique form of representation, and, on the other, it proposed a discursive fragmentation of both subjectivity and social reality. Clearly these strategies were not used in everything published during this period. The narrative thread that runs through Jorge Asís's Canguros series suggests a stable pact between mimesis and its public: from mutual recognition in a system of moral, political, and ideological discourses to the mimesis of the clichés of middle-class and popular urban usage.[7] The writer/text/public circuit flows smoothly and accounts for the success of Canguros. Nevertheless, this success leads us to reflect on literature's capacity for symbolic (shifted) elaboration in relation to the mimetic complicity with the expectations of its public.

THE CODES

I want to turn now to some of the stories whose formal imagination, literary language and conventions, and capacity for figuration propose complex solutions to the problem of how to represent history. All are novels published in or after 1980, so they were written in the late 1970s. What these texts—which differ in every other respect—have in common is their aesthetic and ideological resistance to realist/naturalist representation. I have tried to explain above the reasons for this resistance and would like only to add that the point of using coded messages was not to get around censorship. This aesthetic option is more than a simply tactical one in my opinion; whether the writer is able to speak clearly is important but only circumstantial. Basically, these authors are expressing an opinion on the limits of realism, one that seems to me to be relatively independent of the circumstances in which those stories were written, published, and read. They are coded stories, and although this aspect meant that they were able to circulate under the military dictatorship, I believe that they would have been encoded in any case, under other circumstances. They treat Argentine history from an oblique, diagonal perspective; they glance over their shoulder at it, as it were. Each is encoded differently, and the variation reveals the aesthetic potential of the Argentine literature produced during that time.

Nadie nada nunca (No one, nothing, never), by Juan José Saer, was published in Mexico in 1980. Although Saer lived in France from the mid-1970s on, his work is connected to the Argentine intellectual field and is bound to an Argentine reading. This novel, superficially, tells an apparently absurd story. It is a local detective story that, however, presages a larger story. From the title on, the novel engages in this double play of language, first one meaning and then the other: no one, nothing, never, a verbal phrase; no one, nothing, never, a nominal phrase. The two-tiered title is a metaphor for the story itself: on the one hand, it is a bewildering text that poses perception as a basic novelistic problem and, on the other, an ambiguous story in which pleasure and death intersect.

In a town on the coast of the Parana River, someone is mysteriously shooting horses at night. A man, El Gato (cat), lives alone (maybe in hiding) near the river. His neighbor asks him to take care of a horse, thinking that maybe, if it were hidden in his house, it would come to no harm. The man's lover also comes to the house; and his brother who lives in France sends him a book, *Philosophy in the Bedroom* by the Marquis de Sade. His lover brings him news of a city that seems to be suffering from a heat wave and the plague. During the course of a long weekend, the superficial tranquility of daily life—meals, wine, suffocating siestas—seems to be punctuated by signs of violence: news is brought that more horses have been killed; cars are heard parking on the coast road at night; the local policeman, whose name is Caballo (horse) and whose specialty is "to make them talk," is also killed; the brother who lives in France (on the side of exile, in other words) sends, in a dream, a letter expressing his concern about the death of the horses. This dream is a code and the letter itself is a code within a code.

The unruffled surface of daily life has been disturbed by absurd death; later, the horror takes over a story that seemed concerned only to relate what had happened or to underscore the exasperating sameness of day-to-day life. El Gato hides the horse (as one hides a persecuted militant); the theme of the plague, a classic in Western literature, appears in the dreams of the characters and in the smells of the city; the newspapers do not report it, they cover it up, make wild comparisons, and pursue the real, although they are really trying to escape from it.

As in Sade's philosophical novel, the reader who is disposed to work with the text can fit together all the pieces of the puzzle: the images of eroticism and death, the evil that culminates in *Philosophy in the Bedroom*, and the concrete images of death—the horse killings—on the coast of the river. Superrefined, Saer's novel could be read on any of these levels: as a realistic novel; as a description of the way water refracts a ray of light or sun hits a beach or bathers move; or as a riddle concerning the absurdity and insanity of death. Fear, which haunts El Gato and his neighbors from the time the killings begin, is never mentioned. No one discusses fear in this literature: it is simply a presence, like the bay horse El Gato guards at the back of his house. It galvanizes the story and, at the same time, is absent, self-contained, silent, savage, and chaste.

The unification through narrative of what has been destroyed or fragmented can be only a fantasy of the rhetorical imagination. It is difficult, at this time, for writers to believe that history has an accessible and representable meaning. History appears, rather, as a mosaic of meanings and, on occasions, as a mystery that must be referred to although probably not resolved. In *Hay cenizas en el viento* (There are ashes in the wind), by Carlos Dámaso Martínez, published in 1982, we read: "Sarmiento believed that [Argentina] was a riddle that could be solved. If he had lived through what I have lived through, he would have written another *Facundo*. Or he wouldn't have written anything." Ricardo Piglia, in *Respiración artificial* (Artificial respiration), asks the same question through one of his characters: "Who would write *Facundo* today?"

Actually, *Facundo* is referred to almost obsessively in the fiction written during those years.[8] In contrast to what Sarmiento thought of the book, however—to which he attributed the unique power of having resolved the Argentine enigma—the writers of these years are more committed to asking questions than proposing answers. And when they do propose answers, they invariably appear as coded messages: blind messages and texts that do not compete with the chaos of the real by trying to organize it but attempt to draw semantic images with some of the materials that assault literature from reality.

They suggest symbolic spaces, for example. *Hay cenizas en el viento* encompasses all the spaces of death but without presenting them necessarily as the real spaces of Argentine death in the 1970s. Rather, the book looks at an almost paradoxical realm: the courtyard of a funeral parlor, where cardboard boxes and candelabra are dumped. Barbecues are held there; people get drunk, speak about anything but death, make love. The site also suggests a longer sequence of Bergmanesque reminiscences: bodies are dropped off at the morgue and prepared for the vicissitudes of a burial; the mourners speak of the smells of decay and of the corpse of a dog in the gully that runs across the city, presumably Córdoba. Two key characters in the novel are undertakers: "I am in the business of death; I am an undertaker," one of them says. And this business is constructed through perhaps the most ironic popular expression: the *pompa* (funeral ceremony).

In this novel, Argentinian death is represented in one of its classic forms: decapitation. A historic symbol of death, decapitation is the extreme of cruelty and barbarism on the one hand and, on the other, a thinkable form because the history of the last 150 years has made it so.

At the same time, decapitation, which fills the agonized delirium of one of the characters in the novel, becomes in theory the national violence:

> Then the decapitations came one on top of the other. Marco Avellandeda's, done with a notched machete so that he would suffer more; the series of decapitations in the Refalosa area; placing the victim in a certain position, plunging the knife in under the ear and sliding it slowly forward, feeling the flesh open, the blood spilling on the hands and the knife handle; the desperate cry, the twitching of the body tied on the floor; the final jerk and the head is grasped by the hair and held up in one hand like a trophy, while the mutilated body rolls around in the middle of a great puddle of blood and gore. And just beyond, a pile of heads; and further away, between the grass and the hard bloody ground, a headless body sliding around.

This novel opposes another strategy to the realist depiction of torture and death: representation of historic death, in all its cruelty, as a key to the present death. Forms and spaces of death—decapitation, the morgue, the funeral parlor—are always referred to in code when the subject is death or actual suffering: characters who disappear, demonstrations that are fired on, are represented as fragments, through a blurred lens, distant perspectives, or bits and pieces that the reader must put together and then fit into the story.

And when fear is named, it comes up in a conversation among drunks in the patio of the funeral parlor, amidst the belches and yawns that follow a barbecue. This presentation seems to affirm that it is impossible to discuss fear, that the only way to name it is to trivialize it, to compare it clinically to other feelings and situations. The novel does not refer directly to fear in any serious way.

Likewise, the disappearances are alluded to but never stressed; instead, they appear as gaps—characters who should be present but are not, fundamental actors whose absence is not represented as such at all but is the result of an unexplained interval after which the text reorganizes itself. These allusions occur not in *Hay cenizas en el viento* but also in *Respiración artificial*. This novel is entirely taken up with an investigation of absences. Renzi goes in search of his uncle, whom he will not find; he turns up instead some files in which his uncle collected the results of a prior investigation, an investigation of Ossorio, a Unitarian who worked for the dictator Juan Manual de Rosas as a secret agent, was exiled, went to pan for gold in California, and eventually committed suicide. Tardewski, an image of the European intellectual in the Rio de la Plata, brings the files to Renzi. Tardewski is an exile who has discovered that a secret meeting took place in Prague, in 1910, between Hitler and Kafka. He also investigates a certain Arocena, who opens and reads letters; Arocena represents the censor who uses the methods of the formalist literary critic to discover an evanescent and elusive literary message.

No clues as to the absences of characters or meanings are provided. Piglia's novel asks questions and opens lines that lead nowhere. And when there are answers, they are always coded messages: barely decipherable letters, diaries more than one hundred years old that speak of insanity and loneliness and, like a vision, of the political disintegration to come. The dispersed fragments of Argentine history and culture actually come together through the search for Renzi, in conversations, delirium, and manuscripts. The novel chooses the ellipse as a narrative form of response to the question on the Argentine malady because "what is most important should not be named." In fact, to name is to fix meaning, to give history a unique meaning, to pulverize the fragment into an undifferentiated mass. This novel, like the others, resists establishing a monopoly of meaning; instead it presents discourses that proliferate, withdraw, and then approach. Barely touching one other, they again distance themselves from that core question: How did we come to this? According to Renzi, "Argentine history is the interminable hallucinatory monologue of Sargeant Cabral at the moment of his death, transcribed by Roberto Arlt."

Other narrative strategies are used to think about Argentina: Juan Carlos Martini in *La vida entera* (The entire life), published in Spain in 1981, tells of the years prior to the coup, the conflicts unleashed by the political succession, and the new profile of the social struggles through an allegory of a power struggle in the brothels and in the space of sexuality. Martini's baroque novel works with the materials of Argentine political mythology (from the names of its characters to the toponymy) and with some forms of popular culture, such as the Gardel myths.[9] The violence that characterizes the narrative undoes, through literary reminiscence, the violence of the struggle for political and sexual power, providing instead a cheapened and common version of the episodes that can be read through the metaphors of the brothel and the mafia. The whole novel works with the idea that Argentine history cannot be articulated in rational and "elevated" discourse; that what has happened to us over these years can be distilled only in the chaos of a literary adventure. We are more or less sure that we will not understand history until we accept that its order is perverse. Furthermore, literature is one way to represent the disorder; a last resort is to exorcise it through representation.

Excess can also be a way of representing disorder. In *Cuerpo a cuerpo* (Hand to hand), published in Mexico in 1980, David Viñas presents an unrestrained narrative and discursive text. If the Argentine reality has exaggerated all forms of violence, Viñas makes this exaggeration the principal constructive feature of his writing and, by exaggeration, repetition, and excess, shatters every illusion of naturalist/realist mimesis. The text does not restrain the violence, the eroticism, or the language. Meanings and words are strung dizzily together to touch off multiple associations that work with the paradigm as a whole, with families of names: military life, journalism, the anarchism of the beginning of the century. These are the great universes of the novel, which expand all the narrative situations, repeating them and returning to them to deform and magnify them. Viñas works two meanings at once: the concrete (bodies, cavities, secretions, smells) and the historic (soldiers, bosses and underlings, journalists, politicians), which are inseparable. Paradoxically, *Cuerpo a cuerpo* sustains itself through the security of a possible representation and through the flaws the text shows in its excesses.

In fact, the narratives generated during those years faced up to extreme situations. Andrés Rivera published *En esta dulce tierra* (In this sweet life) in Buenos Aires in 1984; it is a tale whose irony begins with the title. In the story a man, being or believing himself to be in danger, hides for decades in an underground cave. Although these are the years of Rosas's dictatorship and the fugitive could be a Unitarian opponent, the story, punctuated with historical facts, manages simultaneously to allude to a more persistent history: persecution as an internal given of national destiny, in the sense that the fugitive becomes the victim of whoever shelters him, a prisoner of his fear and of the perversity of the other—in this case, his lover. A tense and tortuous story from the point of view of its writing, *En esta dulce tierra* defines the limits of historical representation. By examining the obsessions, violences, fears, and perversities in a closed universe that appears unable to divest itself of the fragmented history of those years, the novel, although apparently set in nineteenth-century Argentina, has the effect of shifting the dialogue into the late twentieth century, the 1970s. No one could be so naive as to read this novel as a text on *rosismo,* nor could they read it only as a description of erotic perversity. Fear and seclusion have been converted into situations and feelings that the literature locates in the past but that, on the horizon of reading, have the effect of being immediately displaced toward the present. The movement of the narrative is that of a permanently swinging pendulum that impels the history of nineteenth-century Argentina into the present day.

Persecution, exile, separation, fear. To close, I turn to *La casa y el viento* (The house and the wind) by Hector Tizón, published in Buenos Aires in 1984, when the author returned from his exile in Spain. A man has to escape from his country but before doing so goes on a long, sad visit to his home province. He stops because in order to leave he must listen to the voices that are going to be his only way of remembering once he is in exile. Only once does the novel refer specifically to fear, and it is a fear felt for others, a feeling that the narrative treats cautiously. Although persecution and fear set the text in motion, its theme is future memory—in other words, the literary production of fragments of memory that will make life in exile possible: "I know that what I wrote at night in these notebooks is not the truth. Or at least it is not the whole truth, but fragments, pieces of apparent life, of my life, and the lives of others, which they will soon return to tell. But what if this is not history? What if it is only a fistful of lucid, illuminated moments, a few broken images?" The theme of this book is memory, perhaps one of the great Argentine themes of coming years.

I have tried here to think what literature could do with the feelings, the practices, the situations of Argentine lives; what literature could do so that what happened might be given a form that can be grasped and thought about collectively. I have tried to respond to the question of how narrative represents, refracts, metaphorizes, and points toward the real. No matter how allusive and indirect, discourse that attempted to think about history was produced even during the most difficult years. Literature has tried and surely will continue to try to explain obscure and difficult facts. When the limits of reason seem to have been reached, aesthetic reason continues to illuminate, even when it seems most silent and obscure. As Theodore Adorno said, literature knows how to deal with its object and how to speak of it even when it appears to be saying nothing at all.

NOTES

1. Julio Cortázar, *Libro de Manuel* (Buenos Aires: Sudamericana, 1973).
2. The Cordobazol took place in the industrial and administrative city of Córdoba the last week in May 1969. Protests by students and workers, mass

demonstrations, and urban violence against the military regime of General Juan Carlos Onganía reached a high point of visibility and organization during the week that ended May 29 and were afterward considered a symbol of resistance to the military regime, a starting point of the leftist, "classist" trade unionism that developed in Córdoba, and a proof of the feasibility of an alliance of revolutionary students and workers. See Beatriz Balvé, *Lucha de calles, lucha de clases* (Buenos Aires: La Rosa Blindada, 1973); Claudia Hilb and Daniel Lutzky, *La nueva izquierda argentina; 1960–1980* (Buenos Aires: CEAL, 1984).

3. Julia Kristeva and the French Tel Quel group strongly influenced literary theory and critical reading in Argentina from the beginning of the 1970s. Major works that were then read and discussed included two by Julia Kristeva: *Le texte du roman* (The Hague: Mouton, 1970), and *Semeiotiké; recherches pour une sémanalyse* (Paris: Seuil, 1969).

4. Different critical readings of the narratives of this period and their links with history can be found in D. Balderston, D. W. Foster, T. Halperin Donghi, F. Masiello, M. Morello-Frosch, and B. Sarlo, *Ficción y política; la narrativa argentina durante el proceso militar* (Buenos Aires: Alianza, 1987).

5. Ezequiel Martínez Estrada, *Radiografía de la pampa* (Buenos Aires: Losada, 1942), and Raúl Scalabrini Ortiz, *El hombre que está solo y espera* (Buenos Aires: Gleizer, 1931).

6. See Katerina Clark and Michael Holquist, *Mikhail Bakhtin* (Cambridge, Mass.: Harvard University Press, 1984).

7. Publication information for novels referred to in this chapter can be found in the list of novels at the end of the chapter.

8. Domingo Faustino Sarmiento, *Vida de Facundo Quiroga* (Santiago, 1851).

9. On Carlos Gardel and his remarkable success story, from which many popular cultural topics developed, see Simon Collier, *The Life, Music and Times of Carlos Gardel* (Pittsburgh, Pa.: University of Pittsburgh Press, 1986).

LIST OF NOVELS

The following is a short list of novels written and published during the military regime or immediately afterward that address the problem of the relation of narrative and history.

Aira, César. *Ema, la cautiva*. Buenos Aires: Editorial de Belgrano, 1981.
Asís, Jorge. *Flores robadas en los jardines de Quilmes*. Buenos Aires: Losada, 1980.
———. *Carne picada*. Buenos Aires: Legasa, 1981.
———. *La calle de los caballos muertos*. Buenos Aires: Legasa, 1982.
Casullo, Nicolás. *El frutero de los ojos radiantes*. Buenos Aires: Folios, 1984.
Catania, Carlos. *El pintadedos*. Buenos Aires: Legasa, 1984.
Cohen, Marcelo. *El país de la dama eléctrica*. Buenos Aires: Bruguera, 1984.
Constantini, Humberto. *La larga noche de Francisco Sanctis*. Buenos Aires: Bruguera, 1984.

Dal Masetto, Antonio. *Fuego a discreción*. Buenos Aires: Folios, 1984.

Feinmann, Juan Pablo. *Ni el tiro del final*. Buenos Aires: Pomaire, 1982.

Fogwill, Enrique. *Los pichiciegos*. Buenos Aires: Ediciones de la Flor, 1983.

Manzur, Jorge. *Tinta roja*. Buenos Aires: Legasa, 1981.

Martínez, Carlos Dámaso. *Hay cenizas en el viento*. Buenos Aires: Centro Editor de América Latina, 1982.

Martini, Juan Carlos. *La vida entera*. Barcelona: Bruguera, 1981.

———. *Composición de lugar*. Buenos Aires: Bruguera, 1984.

———. *Copyright*. Buenos Aires: Sudamericana, 1979.

Medina, Enrique. *Las muecas del miedo*. Buenos Aires: Galerna, 1981.

Moyano, Daniel. *El libro de navíos y borrascas*. Buenos Aires: Legasa, 1983.

———. *El vuelo del tigre*. Buenos Aires: Legasa, 1983.

Orgambide, Pedro. *Hacer la América*. Buenos Aires: Bruguera, 1984.

Piglia, Ricardo. *Respiración artificial*. Buenos Aires: Pomaire, 1980.

Puig, Manuel. *El beso de la mujer araña*. Barcelona: Seix Barral, 1976.

———. *Pubis angelical*. Barcelona: Seix Barral, 1979.

Rabanal, Rodolfo. *El pasajero*. Buenos Aires: Emecé, 1984.

Rivera, Andrés. *Nada que perder*. Buenos Aires: Centro Editor de América Latina, 1982.

———. *En esta dulce tierra*. Buenos Aires: Folios, 1984.

Saer, Juan José. *Nadie nada nunca*. Mexico City: Siglo XXI, 1980.

Soriano, Osvaldo. *No habrá más penas ni olvido*. Barcelona: Bruguera, 1980.

———. *Cuarteles de invierno*. Barcelona: Bruguera, 1982.

Szichman, Mario. *A las 20.25 la señora entró en la inmortalidad*. Hanover: Ediciones del Norte, 1981.

Tizón, Héctor. *La casa y el viento*. Buenos Aires: Legasa, 1984.

Viñas, David. *Cuerpo a cuerpo*. Mexico City: Siglo XXI, 1980.

THIRTEEN

Beyond Fear

Forms of Justice and Compensation

Emilio F. Mignone

The armed forces accept no criticism for what took place during the war against subversion.

> *General Jorge Rafael Videla, de facto president,*
> *January 2, 1980*

A victorious army is not asked to give an account of itself.

> *General Roberto Eduardo Viola, former army*
> *chief of staff, April 12, 1980*

In terms of the actions against terrorism, no one is permitted
now nor will be permitted in the future to conduct any investigation whatsoever.

> *General José Antonio Vaquero, deputy chief of*
> *staff of the army, October 18, 1980*

Not long ago the army—in its capacity as a branch of the
armed forces—had to go to war against subversion. This situation, the growing and increasingly uncontrollable phenomenon of terrorism, and the particular characteristics of the
war dictated that the only viable option to preserve the
nation—other methods and institutional channels having
failed—was to annihilate terrorism. . . . The armed forces
have paid a high price for their military victory over subversion: long years of struggle against an insidious, clever, and
cruel enemy. They [the armed forces] have suffered their own
deaths and have their own martyrs; they have borne the hostility and indifference of fellow citizens, the indictment of
their commanders, and, finally, the trial of many comrades.
This is why the Argentine army, convinced that the war
against subversion was essential, has asked that the political
means that would cast the consequences of this war in a positive light be instrumentalized.

> *General José Dante Caride, army chief of staff,*
> *May 29, 1987*

The March 24, 1976, military coup in Argentina was different in many respects from its post-1930 predecessors. Although it modestly called itself a "process of national reorganization" (the vocabulary of revolution having been exhausted), this coup had military aspirations that were more ambitious than ever. The armed forces rebelled as an institution in 1976, and exercised power like a corporation—more precisely, like a mafia. The ministries, provincial governorships, and all important public positions, with the exception of key economic and educational posts, were occupied by either active or retired military officers. Positions were distributed evenly among the three branches of the service, and each branch had equal voting power in the military junta, which exercised absolute power illegally and with no constitutional or ethical limitations whatsoever. Positions were filled through an internal mechanism that overlapped to some extent the system of promotions and retirements. The dictatorship was an institutional one, not a personal one. Technically speaking it was a military dictatorship or a dictatorship of the armed forces, although fear generalized the euphemistic expression *proceso* (process) that was used to name it.

The political project of the armed forces was to stay in power for as long as it took to construct a political movement that would guarantee the continuity of the *proceso*. The goal of *national reorganization* alluded to a projected second republic, to be compared to the national organization of 1853, although in this case the process was totalitarian and fascist. This second stage of the plan, which came to be called MON, or Movimiento de Opinión Nacional (National Opinion Movement), foresaw the installation of a regime with limited political participation that was to govern under the permanent control of the armed forces, whose role was to serve as a reserve and strategic power. General Jorge Rafael Videla reiterated similar millennialist nonsense in his various speeches in 1976: "The 'process' has goals but no time frame." "There will be no shortcuts this time, only solutions." "The *proceso* will last until its legacy is secure." When it became obvious that the dictatorship was deteriorating, General Leopoldo Galtieri, commander in chief of the army, declared on March 28, 1980: "The ballot boxes are guarded and will stay well guarded."

THE CULTURE OF FEAR

A true culture of fear was born during this long and painful period of Argentine history. What set it apart from similar situations in neighboring countries was the fact that the repression was clandestine and illegal. There were no soldiers in the street, nor were there any public spectacles. There was no prior press censorship, and the authorities constantly proclaimed their respect for human rights, exalting the values of "Western and Christian" civilization. As I wrote during that period:

> The key to the method conceived and utilized by the military government against suspects and dissidents was the detention of persons followed by their disappearance and the official refusal of the responsible organizations to acknowledge their whereabouts. This was practiced in thousands of cases over a long period of time. It was state terrorism on a large scale that included, among other things, the indiscriminate use of torture, the withholding of information, the creation of a climate of fear, the marginalization of judicial power, the uncertainty of the families, and the deliberate confusion of public opinion.[1]

There is no doubt that the thousands of disappeared were assassinated in cold blood in clandestine prisons, usually local ones. Their bodies were buried in unmarked graves or thrown in the Río de la Plata or the Atlantic Ocean from air force planes.

For the most part, people either denied that the daily disappearances took place at all or seemed to accept the hypocritical official explanations. But there was an undifferentiated terror, a visceral uncertainty, beneath this guise of apparent conformity. No one was safe. Anyone's home could be broken into in the middle of the night and the occupants made to disappear. Books and magazines, and sometimes whole libraries, were hidden or burned. Journalists knew that an imprudent sentence could result in their disappearance or maybe a fire at the newspaper office. Lawyers refused to intervene or to sign even the most innocent legal papers, such as a writ of habeas corpus. They knew that dozens of their colleagues had been detained. Doctors denied treatment to those they suspected of being linked to the dissident organizations. Bookstores would not carry publications that could be described as subversive. And everyone knew how broadly the military defined this term. Almost everyone was silenced; people looked over their shoulders and parroted absurd justifications.

I could relate hundreds of episodes, in which I was a participant or to which I was a witness, when this terror manifested itself, even in people who were fervent supporters of the military dictatorship. Dozens of friends and acquaintances avoided meeting with me or with my family for fear that this contact might get them into some kind of trouble, given

my public stance as an active opponent of the regime and my position as
the father of a disappeared child.

The Argentine military believed they had discovered the ideal system
of repression. In their ignorance and stupidity they imagined they could
trick society and the world. They proposed exporting their methods and,
as was revealed in the Irangate hearings, actually sent advisors to Central
America with U.S. government approval. One of the most sadistic torturers, who was quite convinced of the messianic nature of his activities,
was General Ramón J. Camps. He wrote for the newspaper *La prensa*
and continued, from prison, to be a regular columnist.

> The antisubversive struggle in Argentina was first influenced by the French,
> then by the North Americans . . . until we came of age and applied our *own*
> doctrine, which enabled us to be victorious against the armed subversive
> movement.[2]

The revolutionary proclamation of March 24, 1976, declared that
one of the reasons for the military rebellion was "the lack of a concerted
antisubversive strategy on the part of the political leadership."[3] Six
months before, at the XI Conference of Latin American Armies, General
Videla had said in Montevideo that "if that is what it takes to achieve the
security of the state, all [of the subversives] must die."[4] Videla's statement shows that the military had clearly decided on genocide before the
coup d'état. The objective was not to eliminate terrorism. It was much
broader: to achieve the level of internal security that would permit the
installation of a political and socioeconomic regime that could subjugate
the nation.

Various military officers told me during this period that they would
not commit Franco's or Pinochet's mistake of executing people in public
or putting them on trial because then even the pope would intervene on
behalf of the victims. General José Antonio Vaquero once told me that
when he was visiting Uruguay, he had warned of the danger of keeping
subversives in prison: "They harden, and even convert their guards."
Although he did not say it in so many words, the implication of this
statement was not difficult to deduce.

LOST IMMUNITY

The armed forces' plan to stay in power for a long time and to install a
political regime that would carry on their program guaranteed them

immunity from their crimes. But it is said that God blinds those he wants to lose. Around 1980 the military dictatorship began to deteriorate rapidly on all fronts: political, economic, social, international, cultural, and educational. On March 28 of that year, the liquidation of the Banco de Intercambio Regional signaled the demise of the financial system built up by the military. The problems surrounding General Roberto Eduardo Viola's appointment as Videla's successor and the ambitions of Admiral Emilio Eduardo Massera exposed the internal disunity of the armed forces. Soon after, Viola was ousted by Galtieri, the commander in chief of the armed forces, who aspired to recover lost ground and pose as constitutional president. But the illusions of permanence soon dissipated, and the general staffs began to analyze the alternative of holding elections with the participation of the traditional parties. Only when they began to worry about immunity did the idea of coming to some kind of agreement with the political movements gain ground. For this reason the quotes at the beginning of this chapter date from 1980. The military dictatorship was in retreat by the beginning of that year and more obviously so by 1981. Everything, with the exception of immunity for the crimes committed during the repression, was now negotiable.[5]

Galtieri tried to use his personal power to revitalize the fading *proceso* at the same time as he declared his decision to curry the favor of the United States by cooperating with its efforts in Central America. These attempts were all futile. On March 30, 1982, a large, unruly demonstration of workers was violently suppressed by the police. His back against the wall and misinterpreting U.S. policies, Galtieri occupied the Malvinas Islands on April 2 with the approval of the other members of the military junta. This occupation brought immediate popular support that turned into fury and a sense of having been deceived once defeat exposed the professional incompetence of the Argentine military.

With defeat staring them in the face, the armed forces offered the political parties unconditional elections. It was the right moment to form a provisory civil government and to break the back of the military power base once and for all. Although I proposed this publicly, the idea was not taken up; the political leaders preferred to accept the military's offer of elections. The military junta was reshuffled, and General Reynaldo Bignone was appointed acting president during the transition period. Elections were held, and the military was able to retire defeated but intact.

During the Bignone period, there were two attempts to guarantee the military immunity from the crimes committed during the dictatorship. The first was the publication, on April 28, 1983, of an official declaration called the *documento final* (final document). It attempted to close the book on all investigations of the "dirty-war" period. It declared that the disappeared were dead and gave no further explanations; it also stated, to satisfy the middle-ranking officers, that operations against the so-called subversives had been acts of service, carried out under superior orders and as part of a policy approved at the highest levels. Not only was the final document rejected by all representative sectors of society; it also lacked practicality. Thus, on September 23, 1983, the military junta declared a so-called amnesty (in reality a self-amnesty) under which it revoked all criminal charges against members of the armed forces, the security forces, and the police, and against prison personnel.

The first act of the new Congress was to declare the amnesty "absolutely null and void." The annulment (Act 23.040) was signed into law by President Raúl Alfonsín on December 27, 1983. Three days after taking office Alfonsín announced a series of measures covering human rights and the sanctions for past violations. Two of these deserve particular mention. The first was a bill (23.049) passed by Congress in February of the following year. Under the provisions of this law, military tribunals were to try crimes committed during the dictatorship by members of the armed forces, the security forces, and the police, and by prison personnel. To offset this provision, which was criticized by the human-rights organizations, sentences handed down by the Supreme Council of the Armed Forces could be appealed to the federal courts—in other words, the civil justice system—and the federal courts also had jurisdiction wherever there was evidence that the Supreme Council was dragging its feet. It was a political decision: Alfonsín was giving the armed forces the option of cleaning house themselves, while avoiding public trials. The proposal failed because of the strength of the military's esprit de corps and their conviction that their actions were legitimate. After almost three years and a backlog of more than 2,000 cases, the Supreme Council pronounced only one verdict: it held that Navy Captain Alfredo Astiz, whose crimes had received international attention, was not guilty.

The second measure announced by Alfonsín ordered the military tribunals to try the members of the three military juntas: Videla, Massera, Orlando Ramón Agosti, Viola, Armando Lambruschini, Omar Graffigna, Galtieri, Jorge Isaac Anaya, Basilio Arturo Lami Dozo. A little later Alfonsín included Generals Carlos Guillermo Suarez Masón and Luciano B. Menéndez, Admiral Rubén Chamorro, and General Camps to the list. When the Supreme Council refused to try the junta members, the Federal Criminal Appeals Court in Buenos Aires claimed jurisdiction. The public trial, the first of its kind in Latin America, took place between May and November 1985. Almost a thousand witnesses ap-

256 Emilio F. Mignone

peared to testify. Extensive media coverage revealed to the Argentine public and the world the magnitude and gravity of the crimes committed by the military regime. The court sentenced Videla and Massera to life imprisonment, gave lighter terms to Viola, Lambruschini, and Agosti, and acquitted the others. Not only was the court's verdict—in which it declared that the junta members planned and carried out a criminal project—historically significant, but it constituted one form of justice and compensation for the climate of fear created by the regime over which the accused presided.

Another compensatory mechanism was the actual exposure of the terrorist methods employed by the state. This was the work of human-rights organizations such as the Asamblea Permanente por los Derechos Humanos (Permanent Assembly for Human Rights), the Centro de Estudios Legales y Sociales (Center for Legal and Social Studies), and the Madres y Abuelas de la Plaza de Mayo (Mothers and Grandmothers of the Plaza de Mayo). The presidential Comisión Nacional Sobre la Desaparición de Personas (National Commission on the Disappeared) expanded on and completed the work begun by the human-rights groups. A diverse panel chaired by the writer Ernesto Sabato, it overcame a lack of investigative powers to gather a considerable amount of material, which was published under the title *Nunca más* (Never again). The book was a bestseller in Argentina and has been translated into several languages.[6]

The memory of the tragic years of the military dictatorship stimulated the production of literary works, plays, movies, and plastic art, as well as many studies and research projects. Human-rights commissions were set up throughout the country, in labor unions, educational centers, and social and cultural institutions, constituting a broad movement. And although fear is internalized in Argentine society and could reappear at any moment, as we will see at the end of this chapter, the democratic transition and the freedom of expression it brought with it attest to a people's effort, through memory and sanctions, to exorcise the demons of the past.

THE MILITARY POLICY

President Alfonsín's military policy, which was characterized by weakness and vacillation, conspired against the disappearance of fear. A good analysis of this attitude can be found in a book written by the retired colonels Horacio Ballester, José Luis García, Carlos Mariano Gazcón, and Augusto Benjamin Rattenbach, members of the Center of Military Men for Argentina (composed solely of retired officers). It says:

> Since the very first day, the radical government adopted a military policy based on the following premises:
>
> Respect for the military institutions in the hope that they would voluntarily incorporate themselves into the democratic process.
>
> Trial of the superior officers responsible for the excesses of the repression to ensure that the mass of junior officers—who always acted under the principle of "due obedience"—would not have to face trial.
>
> Allowing the military institutions to restructure themselves in harmonious and group form under the presumption that they would discard the doctrine of national security and understand and come to terms with the unavoidable budget cuts warranted by the present situation and the changes in foreign policy.
>
> Three years later the results are self-evident. In sum: The respect that the government accorded the military sectors was highly controversial and was interpreted as a symptom of the weakness of the democratic regime. With the exception of a few isolated voices the vast majority of the military, both active and retired, repudiated the present government, casting aspersions on it both privately and in public. The general staffs are filled with officers who for the most part were active participants in and "descendants" of those who conducted the process.
>
> Military justice works against the commander in chief of the armed forces [the president of the nation], and public discussion of the legal reasoning of their superior, who inexplicably tolerates such excesses, is permitted.
>
> The military has not restructured itself. The doctrine of "internal security" persists, and, as a result, the former organization and deployment remain in place because if "the enemy [the people and its government] is internal," the forces of order must have control over all the national territory if they are to operate on the day that our Christian, Western way of life is threatened by the traitorous enemy.
>
> On the other hand, the combination of military budget cuts with little reduction in overall manpower has meant that combat units are skeletal and lack resources. Spare parts are insufficient even to maintain war materiel, and officers and junior officers receive only limited theoretical instruction. The doctrine of "the process" is still included in the curriculum, and the "destruction" of the armed forces is explained as a maneuver of the traitorous enemy that has lodged in sectors of the constitutional government and is now taking advantage of the fledgling democracy.
>
> Although these days it seems totally unrealistic to speak of a coup, we cannot ignore the fact that every coup is a process that is conceived, planned, and finally executed in a way that touches on all aspects of national life. We perceive that considerable parts of the military sector still nurture hopes for a coup, hopes that must be prevented from materializing at all costs because the people of the republic do not deserve any more grief. There are no easy answers, but the attempt is worth making and success is still possible.[7]

I am quoting at length and without omission. The failure of Alfonsín's military policy facilitated the consolidation and growth of the armed forces as an autonomous power. Moreover, the armed forces considered themselves to be the aggrieved and humiliated party, and held the government responsible for this situation.

In fact, the armed forces have been largely discredited and are marginalized from civil society. Although the military consider that they acted legitimately during the repression and see themselves as saviors of the republic, the vast majority of the civil population thinks that the methods used during this period were immoral and aberrant. The armed forces have proved incapable of cleaning their own house or of engaging in self-criticism, and they hold unswervingly to the doctrine of national security. The Alfonsín government was a constitutional government, not a revolutionary one. It did not propose that the armed forces be dissolved. It knew that it must share power with them and come to terms, in one way or another, with their ideology. As I said above, however, no effective reform has taken place.

THE FULL-STOP LAW

In 1986, the Federal Criminal Appeals Courts began to try the backlog of criminal cases from the Supreme Council. Military unrest was growing. As a result of the erroneous policies described above, the armed forces were gaining ground and were beginning to publicly declare their opposition to trials for crimes committed during the dictatorship. Devoid of any capacity for self-criticism, the military saw themselves as besieged, slandered by society, the media, and the government. Their conspiratorial and Manichean mentality led them to conclude that these attacks came from the so-called subversives, who, having been beaten militarily, were now winning a political victory.

Afraid that one of the officers might refuse to appear before the judges, thereby breaking a key piece of the legal chain and challenging the rule of law—an action that would have unforeseeable consequences—Alfonsín was prepared to bring the trials to an end. Although he acted under the pressure of events, this was not a new position for Alfonsín, who always maintained the policy of condemning those at the top and exempting the rest, the majority of active officers. Because the armed forces could not be changed, he believed that only thus could they be incorporated into his democratic political project.

During the election campaign, Alfonsín constantly said, "We have to distinguish between those who gave the orders, those who carried them out, and those who committed the excesses." Although he did not go into detail, the message was clear. The first and the third groups had to be punished and the second group, the majority, pardoned. As I told the president during an interview, the slogan was realistic for two basic reasons. In the first place, those who had committed the crimes were aware of their criminality. And second, it is difficult to determine what "excesses" were. Were torture and assassination of prisoners excesses? Obviously not, because these deeds, from the point of view of the military, were performed in the line of duty and were committed against thousands of people.

Reality and social pressure overruled the presidential will, and, given the stalling of the military tribunals, the federal courts prepared—a large volume of evidence having been gathered—to try dozens of officers, many of them in active service. To obstruct these trials, Alfonsín allowed the Minister of Defense to instruct the public prosecutor of the armed forces to absolve those officers who had acted under the principle of due obedience. These instructions had no effect whatsoever. On the contrary, the Federal Criminal Appeals Court in the capital indicted General Camps, the former chief of police in the province of Buenos Aires (General Riccheri), and three police officers, one of them a medical doctor, who were guilty of serious crimes.

Afraid of military insubordination, and under pressure from an increasingly unified and vociferous military, Alfonsín threw all the weight of his authority behind a bill that was popularly named the *punto final* (full stop), passed just before Christmas, on December 23, 1986. Alfonsín denied that he was declaring an amnesty, as the military with the support of the rightist parties and political leaders and conservative sectors of society maintained. Instead, he proposed a semi-amnesty without using the word. The law (23.492) had two main provisions. The first called a halt to criminal actions against members of the armed forces and against security, police, and prison personnel for crimes committed between March 24, 1976, and December 10, 1986. Deserters (like General Suarez Masón) or officers who received summonses during the seventy days prior to enactment of the law—in other words, before February 22, 1987—were exempt from this provision. Thus, the act provided a deadline for the filing of criminal charges. The second provision established that the members of the armed forces who were to be jailed before their trials could be arrested only at the barracks or establishments where they were in service.

This legal order also failed to achieve the president's objectives. During the seventy days at their disposal, the federal courts convened to take depositions from almost 400 officers and police, many of whom were in active service. Although many were then exonerated, the large number of indictments and, above all, the fact that the defendants were active officers proved to be too much for the military, who had become increasingly sensitive to the government's vulnerability. The judges, for their part, clearly did not want to have the historic responsibility of providing torturers and assassins with immunity. Over a two-month period they indicted more officers than in the three previous years.

FEAR AGAIN

The dreaded incident finally took place. On April 15, 1987, the Federal Criminal Appeals Court in Córdoba summoned Major Rubén Barreiro, who was accused, among other crimes, of torturing prisoners he was interrogating in the clandestine prison La Perla. Barreiro took refuge in the 14th Airborne Infantry Regiment and announced that he would not appear. The regiment's commander refused to arrest him. The brigade commander ordered other guard units to arrest him, and although no one replied that the order would be disobeyed, no one carried it out. In the words of Horacio Verbitsky:

> So began the Holy Week rebellion. The Buenos Aires infantry school was occupied by Lieutenant Colonel Aldo Rico, a commando who arrived there after deserting his infantry regiment at the Brazilian border. A decorated veteran, commander of the 602nd Commandos, who fought in the Malvinas, he had been disciplined on several occasions for insubordination, disrespectful behavior toward superior officers, and problems with his fellow soldiers. Rico demanded the ouster of Carlos Ríos Erenu (army chief of staff) and what he called a political solution for the officers of the "dirty war." Two weeks before, Rico had discussed the details of the revolt with Barreiro in a Buenos Aires pizzeria.[8]

The Córdoba episode was resolved through a secret agreement mediated by the archbishop of that city, Cardinal Raúl F. Primatesta, and Federal Judge Jorge Becerra Ferrer. Barreiro was allowed to escape, and because he was a deserter, his superiors did not appear to be disobeying the judicial order. He was later detained and arrested in his regiment under the provisions of Law 23.492.

Meanwhile there was an outpouring of popular support for the constitutional regime. It was clear that Argentines did not want the military to return to power. The political leaders convened at the Casa Rosada and declared their loyalty to the president. On Holy Thursday, April 16, he convened the two houses of the legislature, made a strong speech, and was applauded both by the legislators and by the crowd that had gathered in front of the Congress building. "There is nothing to negotiate," said Alfonsín. "Argentine democracy does not negotiate. The era of the coups has gone forever, along with the era of pressure, declarations, and deals." Insisting on his old idea, however, he announced: "We will reaffirm in concrete actions the criteria of responsibility that will permit national reconciliation."

The following day, Good Friday, Alfonsín had to face what he lacked the power to repress. He gave orders that the generals repeated, but nobody moved. The armed forces, without actually rebelling against the constitutional order, formed a united front behind the proposals of the revolt. They then opened tentative secret negotiations. At the same time, the president and the political parties gathered the people. On a sunny autumn Easter Sunday, a million people gathered in the Plaza de Mayo in Buenos Aires in front of the Casa de Gobierno, in the main squares of all the cities of the republic, and around the Campo de Mayo, peacefully surrounding the barracks of the rebel soldiers and insulting them. The previous Saturday, political leaders and leaders of social, business, and union organizations among others, had signed the Defense of Democracy Law at the Casa de Gobierno, which gave the green light to a new set of criminal liabilities.

At three o'clock in the afternoon, when the negotiations were stalled, Alfonsín announced from the balcony of the Casa Rosada to the crowd that had gathered beneath that he was going to the Campo de Mayo. He returned a few hours later to wish everyone a Happy Easter and explain that the rebels had surrendered. Although the country calmed down, the speculation soon began. Obviously the president had negotiated. Army Chief of Staff Ríos Ereñu had to retire, as the junior officers had demanded. On Wednesday April 21, two guard units, in Salta and Tucuman, announced their refusal to recognize the appointment of the new army chief of staff, General José Dante Caride. The episode, although troubling, was resolved, but it exposed the rupture in the chain of command.

After that the armed forces stepped up their verbal offensive. Two speeches, one by the navy chief of staff and one by his army counterpart, which I quoted at the beginning of this chapter, exemplified this defiant attitude. The president sent a bill to the Congress that exempted from

prosecution officers in the lower and middle ranks—officers up to the
rank of lieutenant colonel and their counterparts in the other branches of
the service—who acted under orders. The bill was approved in the
Chamber of Deputies but broadened in the Senate—with Alfonsín's
agreement—to include almost all officers with the exception of the
commanders, the unit chiefs, and the police. It was called the Law of Due
Obedience because it used this legal principle to justify the grant of
immunity. The most troubling aspect was that it included those who
committed such crimes as torture and secret assassination of prisoners.
To all intents and purposes, it was a total amnesty. Alfonsín must have
exercised the full weight of his personal authority to make the legislators
of his party, who held a majority in the Chamber of Deputies, accept the
modification. The bill became law on June 4, 1987.

Such are the facts. The population asked itself whether the military,
aware of their power, would be satisfied or whether they would demand
further concessions, maybe amnesty or pardon for those who had been
sentenced. Argentina's history of making concessions to the military is
instructive. One has to go back only as far as the Frondizi (1958–62)
and Illia (1964–66) administrations. The armed forces, moreover, demanded moral and social vindication for the actions during the so-called
antisubversive struggle. And some thought that they even demanded
political power. But the military knew that they could not exercise
power. Besides, that would have meant civil war, or the Lebanonization
of the country.

A coup d'état is impossible under the present internal and external
conditions but perhaps not if the socioeconomic and political situation
were to deteriorate. Although I continue to be optimistic that Argentine democracy will be consolidated, there is no doubt that something
changed in the country after the events of April and May 1987. The
relation of forces changed. Confidence diminished. The euphoria over
the military's subordination to civilian power was lost.

Most serious, fear has returned, although not in the same way as
during 1976–83. People do not think that they could be dragged out of
their houses at dawn. The legal system works, and there is freedom of
expression. But the memories of that time have resurfaced. There is fear
of a surprise move and a new witch-hunt, maybe bloodier than the
previous one. The former prisoners, the exiles, the families of the disappeared—those who were tortured and abused—are having nightmares.
Knowing the truth of what happened between 1976 and 1983, the social
sanction of the military, and the condemnation of the commanders have

made some of the fear go away. But it will take more time for the wounds to heal completely. The culture of fear has deep roots in Argentina, and episodes like the Easter Rebellion could easily happen again. Only time will tell if we Argentines will be able to live, once and for all, beyond fear.

NOTES

1. Augusto Conte, Noemi Labrune, and Emilio F. Mignone, *El secuestro como método de detención* (Buenos Aires: Centro de Estudios Legales y Sociales, 1982). See also the preface to Emilio F. Mignone, "Les déclarations abusives de disparations, instrument d'une politique," in *Le refus de l'oubli: La politique de disparitions forcées de personnes* (Paris: Berger Levraut, 1982), 6, 151–83.

2. *La prensa* (Buenos Aires), 4 January 1981.

3. *La nación* (Buenos Aires), 24 March 1976.

4. "*Clarín*" (Buenos Aires), 24 October 1975.

5. Andrés Fontana, *Fuerzas armadas, partidos políticos y transición a la democracia en Argentina (1981–1982)* (Notre Dame, Ind.: Helen Kellogg Institute for International Studies, University of Notre Dame, 1987).

6. *Nunca más: Informe de la Comisión Nacional Sobre la Desaparición de Personas* (Buenos Aires: Editorial Universitaria, 1984). English version: *Nunca Más: The Report of the Argentine National Commission on the Disappeared* (New York: Farrar, Straus & Giroux, 1986).

7. José Luis García, Horacio Ballester, Augusto Benjamin Rattenbach, Carlos Mariano Gazcón, *Fuerzas armadas argentinas, el cambio necesario, bases políticas y técnicas para una reforma militar* (Buenos Aires: Editorial Galerna, 1987), 136–38.

8. Horacio Verbitsky, *Civiles y militares: Memoria secreta de la transición* (Buenos Aires: Editorial Contrapunto, 1987), 360.

PART FOUR

A Look Ahead

FOURTEEN

Toward Societies without Fear

Juan E. Corradi

Le XVIIᵉ siècle a été le siècle des mathématiques, le XVIIIᵉ celui des sciences physiques, et le XIXᵉ celui de la biologie. Notre XXᵉ siècle est le siècle de la peur.

Albert Camus, Combat

There are several powerful reasons why a society in which fear is unknown has not existed and is unlikely ever to exist, and there are other—equally powerful—reasons why such an outcome, even if remotely possible, would be undesirable. It is possible to avoid, under specific conditions, however, the institutionalized (especially political) exploitation of irrational fears. History offers many instances in which fear-mongering upstaged other public concerns and alternative orientations of public policies.[1] On a more general plane, however, as far as I am aware, the record of social arrangements in the most disparate places and times—from simple, nonliterate societies to modern, complex ones—does not register the absence of the emotion, at least in some of its many forms, nor the absence of at least some of the known mechanisms to exorcize or cope with fear. What do vary are the occasion for fear and its object, its intensity, and the manner of managing it.

GENERAL CONSIDERATIONS

THE SOCIAL ORGANIZATION OF EMOTIONS

The emotional repertoire of human beings is limited and standard. But every culture holds some of these reactions to be unacceptable and attempts to warp the emotional makeup of its participants in some peculiar way. This cultural shaping of human emotions is eased by compartmentalization: there are special times and situations where the disparaged responses are permitted or classes of people who can provide vicarious satisfaction of emotional needs. Yet every society and every individual has difficulty with a few of these responses. They must be suppressed continually, although they are usually visible to the outsider. Thus, although authoritarian cultures place great stress on order, precision, and obedience to authority, they periodically explode into chaos or are driven by romantic fantasies. Rather than saying that members of those systems are obedient, we can more correctly say that they are preoccupied with issues of authority. The opposing forces are more equally balanced than the society's participants like to recognize.

Life would be much less frantic and cruel if people were all able to recognize the diversity of responses and feelings and could abandon the somewhat futile efforts to present a monolithic self-portrait to the world. In this sense pluralistic democratic institutions offer safeguards against fear that authoritarian systems—conservative and revolutionary—lack. Our attention should therefore be directed to the various distributions and regimes of fear, insofar as they are socially structured. In other words, what is interesting and worthy of study, from a sociological perspective, is not the existence of fear as such but the social and psychological operations to which it is subjected and which it stimulates—substitutions, displacements, condensations, exchanges—within specified cultural matrices. The proper object of study is the avatars and metamorphoses of fear in different social situations.

From this perspective, it is quite possible to envisage social arrangements in which fear has less destructive and pernicious effects on both the individual and the group than it does in other social arrangements. In this chapter, I present a nonexhaustive repertoire of historically salient fears and analyze their interaction with an equally nonexhaustive set of social institutions and processes, in particular those that have to do with acquiring and preserving power.

From the standpoint of the individual, fear can be seen as the basic response to an assault on one's integrity—primarily physical in the case of all organisms but also psychological, moral, and symbolic in the case of humans.[2] This is especially the case when the assault takes place in sudden and arbitrary (unpredictable) fashion or when it is expected to occur suddenly and arbitrarily. Some of the responses that we associate with fear are preprogrammed—that is, they are activated regardless of actual experience, as a sort of innate repertoire. Others are acquired through personal and social experience. Of course, the assault may be intraspecific or it may come from other forms of life or inanimate phenomena. For most animals, the intensity and variety of threats vary on account of several factors, the last but not least of which is the encroachment of human cultures. For humans, there has been a rather rapid tilt of the balance in favor of self-made dangers.

All human groups "organize" fear. They provide protection to their members against external enemies. They facilitate coping with the environment and its dangers. They regulate conflicts that otherwise would have catastrophic results for the integrity of the antagonists. They provide, in short, a modicum of law and order, cooperation, and solidarity. However, fear is a frequent and perhaps unavoidable resource for attaining those very objectives. It is used to deter potential deviants, to punish those who break the rules, to impose public or communal obligations on recalcitrant or simply lazy members of society, to bring up children, to maintain social cohesion itself. Social life, whether stateless or sporting political institutions, does not abolish fear: it puts it to work. In this respect too the circularity of the civilizing process is quite evident: that against which human beings seek to protect themselves must be used to keep them together. In many cases, the circle is not a vicious one: danger is transcended or sublimated.[3]

In some instances however—as Freud and others have surmised—the civilizing process may become self-defeating.[4] Though one of the functions of society is to make its inhabitants feel safe, they often do not feel safe, despite or because of the investment of resources in security. This observation is of particular relevance in the specialized realm of politics, where it seems to me that the conventional reading of Hobbes must be modified. Fear is not just the terminus a quo of sovereign power; it is just as often its terminus ad quem. About Hobbes's ceaseless struggle for power—the "war of all against all"—two important points have been made: "that Hobbes's vision of the dangers of anarchy captured an important dimension of the human condition, and that to call that condition 'the state of nature' is a remarkable misnomer."[5] In fact, Hobbes was pointing to a dynamic typical of a species that has stepped across the threshold of civilization and has stumbled into a chaos that did not exist before: the uncontrolled system of relations among societies. Security devices—from guns in the closet to nuclear missiles overhead—produce as much fear as they contain.[6]

FEAR AND CIVILIZATION

Human perceptions of threats change historically along with the capacity to cope with calamities, a capacity that reflects specific cultural, social, and technical resources. As humans gained control of the physical aspects of the body and of the environment, secular explanations eventually permeated the understanding of social and political affairs even if they did not yield in them the same degree of control as in the physical aspects. At any given point in time the perception of threat and its remedies provide the basis for defining friend and foe, self and other. Such perceptions are the emotional bases of politics. In a religious age, the enemy is sacrilege and those engaged in impious acts. Sentiments about purity and pollution remain under modern secular perceptions of danger.

The plague haunted Europe for four centuries (roughly from 1348 to 1720).[7] The term is a generic one covering a wide variety of epidemic diseases. The plague ravaged Europe from one end to the other. It flowed and ebbed, with longer intervening lapses, until it disappeared after 1721. It claimed the lives of 20 to 40 percent of the population in the affected regions. It was strong in town and country. It killed rich and poor, dignitaries and commoners. The plague was perceived as one of the great calamities to befall humanity—a cruel event that triggered, in turn, the cruelty of people. Because of its terrific impact, it was, for many decades, the very paradigm of collective fear.

Until the nineteenth century, ignorance and impotence in the face of the plague gave rise to a rich iconography and a varied repertoire of exorcisms. The plague was attributed to pollution, to the stars, to a miasma from the soil. It was exorcized through rituals of purification, through atonement, persecution, avoidance, and isolation. The imagery that accompanied the health crises of those centuries was drawn from other natural catastrophes (fire, famine, war). Texts and pictures portrayed it as a rain of arrows thrown at sinful humans by an enraged god. It was a sudden, indiscriminate attack. And people were easily led to believe that it was not, perhaps, undeserved. Attempts to cope with a disease of such proportions were many, desperate, and ineffective. The calamity was so great, and the practical means to fight it so inadequate, that people turned to the examination of themselves in a way that confused cause with responsibility and event with retribution.

Not until the nineteenth century did a new explanation of physical suffering establish itself. It came largely from the successful application of science to the etiology and treatment of disease. The advance of the scientific and technical outlook blunted the moral poignancy of some age-old fears. Modernization redeployed fear. A legion of ancient scares faded away with the relentless disenchantment of the world. Not only the dimming of certain images—ghosts, demons, and the dead—but the progressive discredit of both their ritual and spontaneous exorcism mark our modernity.

Moderns do not seek to keep the unknown at bay. Rather, it becomes a challenge. Modern research is "value neutral" rather than persecutory—a change that must be seen, in retrospect, as rather benign. Modern ignorance is neither wondrous nor prone to teasing guilt; it is either stoic (perseverance in the face of baffling failures, especially in medicine) or blasé (the ignorance of the specialist about specialities other than one's own). A technical culture does not honor fear: it reduces it to objectified and manipulable dimensions. It is a neutral and neutralizing enterprise.

In such a light, remaining phobias may be seen as unsuccessful attempts to reenchant a depoeticized world. They are failures of metaphor. The successful attempts are to be found in certain genres of fiction. In short, many ancient fears become either the object of treatment or the occasion for nostalgia. That fear may be the object of nostalgia is not so surprising if we interpret it as resistance against the blights of a matter-of-fact civilization. Nineteenth-century romantics and twentieth-century surrealists sought to keep the endangered sense of mystery alive. The tension between enlightenment and enchantment quivers through detective novels, tales of horror, thrillers, fantastic stories, and science fiction. Those genres function like the archive of the uncanny creatures that once stalked society in the open.

It seems clear that a secular scientific ethos had been important in redefining notions of friend and foe and in transforming the landscapes of fear. But the cultural impact of modern science has not entirely dissipated ancient fears or prevented the periodic relapse of entire populations into a politics of anxiety.[8] In some instances, scientific techniques have been put at the service of political demonologies, with devastating results in both the scope and the intensity of human suffering. But these serious shortcomings should not make us lose sight of larger cultural trends in secularization. The most frightening cases of persecution in the modern world involve a perverse overdetermination (or intersection) of secular and religious approaches—a fateful mixture of notions of scientific objectivity (objectifying other human beings), ritual pollution, and sacrilege. The religious and magical definitions place categories of people "beyond the pale," whereupon they are subjected to "technical" modes of disposal. The paradox of modernity can be put thus: the harnessing of technical means to totalizing political projects results in an unprecedented revival of fear. The attempt to overcome this fateful paradox defines the project of a responsible (not just fashionable) post-modernity.

PRIVATE AND PUBLIC FEARS

Leaving aside, for the moment, the fear of strangers and the fear of known enemies, fear of fellow members of society is affected by the degree of differentiation between the public and the private spheres—a distinction that first developed and that has been carried farthest in the West. Much ink has been spent critically describing the cycles of public and private investment of peoples' interests and efforts in modern history. From my own perspective, suffice it to say at this point that the unique Western contribution has been to make such shifting involvements possible. In modern, civilized democracies today, most people use one sphere as an escape from and compensation for intrusions into the other. When such intrusions amount to an assault on physical or moral integrity (or both), the very differentiation of society into a private and a public sphere offers the possibility of protection—that is, of surcease at least from some if not from all fears. There are however, situations in which the distinction offers no protection, either because it has not been allowed to emerge or because an older version of it has collapsed.[9]

Especially when the public/private distinction has collapsed, a system may develop that combines the worst features of both assaults on personal integrity. As we shall see, terrorism, state terror, and various intermediate or combined forms of both may succeed in establishing true "cultures of fear." In such instances, the blurring of boundaries between a private and a public sphere takes on the form of a perverse dialectic. On the one hand, the private sphere becomes vulnerable to sudden, brutal, and arbitrary intrusions on the part of the authorities. On the other hand, the authorities cease to operate in a true public fashion. Punishment becomes secretive, unavowed, in what amounts to the privatization of state coercion. Under terroristic regimes there is a dual structure: a public facade of business as usual beneath which a network of lawless areas grows unimpeded. This perverse dialectic allows, in turn, the proliferation of inadequate adaptations—a mixture of secondary responses and defense mechanisms. Thus, the ostensive concern with safety covers a mounting sense of insecurity; manifest loquacity envelops a desolate silence; sheepishness coexists with bravado. Moreover, this perverse dialectic is both synchronic and diachronic. It operates both in depth and across time. Some societies accumulate fears over time, and these fears are about one another. In the remarks that follow, I shall seek to sketch a model of the social and political circulation of fear.

THE CIRCLE OF FEAR IN POLITICS

SOCIAL INERTIA

When Montesquieu recast the ancient classification of governments in modern terms, he pointed to the operating principles underlying each basic type of political arrangement. Thus, a republic for Montesquieu was based on civic virtue, a monarchy on honor, and despotism on fear. Because Montesquieu viewed institutions as interrelated in functional wholes, he surmised that each of the visible types of government was imbued with a different spirit and that each spirit expressed a determinate social structure.

Although civic virtue, honor, and fear are not mutually exclusive, they do not mix well as social principles. The first two can be combined but each and both of them seem to repel the third. Since ancient times it has been assumed that, for both the proud aristocrat and the virtuous citizen, courage is intrinsic to status.

I shall seek to explain here why civic virtue—the republican spirit par excellence—is normally in short supply and especially difficult to generate and sustain in a rational and voluntary manner in large, complex societies. I shall also show how, despite this difficulty, some civic virtue (or its functional equivalent) is nonetheless produced by specific social arrangements. In short, in the modern world Montesquieu's republicanism lapses into Tocquevillian democracy. The slippage generates a deficit of legitimacy, but there is no acceptable return.

Both theoretical logic and empirical observation show that, contrary to common sense or social mythologies, individuals behaving in a rational and voluntary manner—that is, in terms of the standard assumptions of economic theory—do not undertake action in the pursuit of a demonstrable common interest or a public good. In other words, diffidence in the pursuit of the public interest is the rule and not the exception.[10] If we were to translate this argument into the idiom of Marxian analysis, we would have to say that the drift of collective action is toward classes-in-themselves and away from classes-for-themselves, and that such analysis is logically condemned to the frustration of its expectations.

The reason for this paradox is not hard to fathom. The very fact that an interest or objective is common means that the gain from any sacrifice an individual makes to serve this common purpose is shared with everyone else in the group. Hence, the individual in any large group with a common interest will reap only a small share of the gains from the sacrifices made to achieve this common objective. Because any gain goes to everyone in the group, those who contributed nothing to the effort will get just as much as those who made the sacrifice. Therefore, it pays to let the next fellow do it, but the next fellow has little incentive to do anything in the group interest either, so in the absence of factors that are alien to rational-choice assumptions, there will be little, if any, collective action. I shall call this argument the argument of *social inertia*. It follows that any organization, group, or individual seeking to produce public goods that inevitably go to everyone in some category is subject to this social inertia: those they serve have little incentive voluntarily to contribute to their support. Something other than the collective goods that these organizations, groups, or individuals provide accounts for their existence.

OVERCOMING INERTIA

Groups and organizations have managed to overcome social inertia and gain support for common-interest activities through a series of interesting inventions. Compulsion is one such arrangement. Since time immemorial, governments have resorted to the military draft and compulsory taxation to support their activities. Such forceful impositions are often legitimized by the intuitive understanding on the part of the underlying population that public goods cannot be sold in the marketplace or provided by voluntary contributions. Other incentives can be applied selectively depending on whether individuals contribute to the public good. Shame and social ostracism have always been powerful negative selective incentives. Violence has been another.[11] Perks and privileges for those who contribute to an organization are examples of positive incentives. In short, any organization (governmental, nongovernmental, or antigovernmental) that seeks support for the production of a public good or common outcome (even when there is full consensus about the desirability of such a good among its constituents) cannot count on getting it from the rational and voluntary behavior of individuals, but must find the appropriate selective incentives—that is, an effective mix of rewards and coercion.

Small, interactive groups have an advantage over large ones in that they can more easily provide both positive and negative inducements for their members to get involved in the pursuit of some public good. In other words, a small, cooperative, and homogeneous group can more easily be organized for the pursuit of its common interest—and even larger public goals—than a large, heterogeneous, and complex group. In the absence of selective inducements, the incentive for group action diminishes as group size increases, so that large groups are less able to act in their common interest than small ones. In addition, collective action can take place without selective incentives if and when the groups that would benefit from collective action are only a few. Under such oligopolistic circumstances, collective action can take place even if the groups in question are large.

What, however, leads an individual to commit time, energy, and resources to a common cause, given the rational propensity not to get involved? One answer lies in a special kind of participatory, or "Kantian," altruism, as when a material sacrifice for the common good brings a significant return in moral satisfaction, regardless of the ultimate impact on the level of the public good that results. Max Weber's notion of a "politics of ultimate ends" is a case in point. In a more general sense, and always following Weber, we could say that means/end rationality is subject to the paradox of social inertia, while value rationality is not. This sort of "high altruism" seems rare. Its existence, however, even in short supply, does make a difference.

The propensity to social inertia explained so far applies not only to social action but to social knowledge as well. Just as individuals are reluctant to invest time or resources in the production of public goods, given the disproportion between effort and final share, and given the expectation that they can freeload on somebody else's efforts, so will they be reluctant to take the trouble to inform themselves about the public good. Information about a public good is itself a public good and hence subject to the same paradox. The propensity to social inertia therefore will be paralleled by a propensity to remain rationally ignorant about the public interest. Here too selective incentives, in the form of compulsions and rewards, are necessary to jolt individuals away from a peculiar cognitive sloth.

In addition to selective incentives, which apply to all members of a group, there are differential incentives that motivate some members to devote themselves fully to action and knowledge. Whereas the typical citizen will find that his or her income, life chances, and status will not be improved by zealous study of public affairs, professionals will be so rewarded. In this context I have in mind vocations like politician, lobbyist, social scientist, labor organizer, human-rights activist, professional revolutionary. Tensions will of course develop between the larger public good that a profession seeks and its narrower interest qua profession. Professions have been criticized for sacrificing the larger goals to their own corporate interests, yet fantasies about the thorough deprofessionalization of society deliver us back to the paradoxes of social inertia and rational ignorance. The fact remains that some professionalization is always necessary to transcend the propensity for social inertia and cognitive sloth. I shall call this focused pursuit of public goods as a profession *political and social entrepreneurship.*

When social entrepreneurship combines with high altruism, the intensity that results is enough to propel a small group into action. A small number of zealots eager for a particular collective good are more likely to act collectively to obtain that good than a larger number with the same aggregate willingness (but one that is less intense for each member). This consideration explains the great historical significance of small groups of saints or fanatics (depending on who views them). Weber's observation that social inertia is sometimes effectively overcome by charismatic phenomena (which become routinized in turn) no doubt owes something to this consideration.

THE PASSAGE TO ANOMIC FEAR

So far I have pictured, in the manner of a snapshot, only the limited production of public goods (virtue) in nonrepressive regimes. I shall now seek to present some processes that facilitate a further passage—not one, this time, from republican virtue to democratic "normality" but from that normality to anomic fear. To put the question once again in Montesquieu's terms, what allows the perversion of government into despotism? In drawing this second model, or theoretical fiction, I keep Argentina and Uruguay in mind as the closest approximations to anomic, or failed, modernity.[12]

We have seen that, in an open society, although virtue is not spontaneous, it is nonetheless supplied by special institutional arrangements: legitimate government, political parties, associations, unions, and professions, as well as a dose of Kantian altruism and nonmarket conventions here and there. Each of these arrangements provides selective and differential incentives for people to contribute to the attainment of public goods. In the absence of such arrangements, social inertia would prevail. If no one voluntarily pursues the public interest, the only hope for the realization of it lies with the "invisible hand." That, however, is not enough. In Bernard de Mandeville's expression, one would hope that out of private vices unintended public virtues would flow. I do not think it necessary to show here that no such automatic guarantee exists. One can easily list examples in which the exact opposite occurs. Think only of the deterioration in the social environment that is produced by the increased competition of individuals. The ironies of thousands of drivers each trying to beat traffic at the same time or of the flight to the suburbs or of the tourists who, in search for something different, inevitably destroy that difference by their very enjoyment of it, are well known. The invisible hand produces as much social ill as public wealth.[13]

By encouraging self-regarding individual objectives, a market economy makes social objectives difficult to reach. Individualistic calculation leaves the community with less social orientation than individuals themselves would choose if they felt the full consequences of their actions. Special institutional arrangements and extramarket conventions of responsibility and obligation are necessary to counter such tendencies. The preservation of such arrangements seems to me indispensable for producing, sustaining, and even imagining a public interest. The political and social systems of socialism, by replacing the market with bureaucratic planning, solve the problem in a Pyrrhic manner. Because the state both generalizes and preempts the pursuit of public goods, it acts like a doctor who kills the patient together with the disease. I shall not dwell on the differences between systems. Such considerations fall outside the purview of this chapter. I shall focus instead on the deterioration of the public interest and the rise of a culture of fear.

A prolonged social crisis may weaken and destroy many of the institutional arrangements that supply public goods in an open society. Governments lose their legitimacy, parties their representativeness, professions and unions their regular ability to motivate their members. In each case, the capacity to provide the customary mix of selective incentives is impaired. Furthermore, a protracted economic crisis may also disrupt calculations and distort choices. The net result is an accumulation of social power outside institutions (corporate deals, short-circuiting of legitimate procedures, *sottogoverno*,[14] ad hoc improvisation of rewards and coercion, corruption, violence). Entire social networks function like wild markets. The tacit convention is *sauve qui peut*.

Because in such situations most social actors are anomic and working at cross-purposes, because black markets and "black" institutional arrangements replace the damaged ones, the likelihood increases that some groups will offer no-nonsense approaches to the pursuit of the elusive public interest through a mixture of high moralism and coercion. Moreover, because the crisis disrupts the natural propensity of the population to be left alone (social inertia), these groups of zealots gain saliency. They compete with each other for "the hearts and minds," the monies and the bodies of the population, who watch them as they would watch a contest of gladiators. In short, the crisis disrupts both the general inertia of the population and the institutional arrangements that supply public goods.

One or several groups of zealots may press for totalizing and exclusive notions of the public interest. A fight among those groups for a monopoly on such notions and on selective incentives will then take place. The fight will, for a while, further disrupt residual legitimate institutions and upset social inertia, as each of the competing groups of zealots tries to show that the other is the worse bully.

Finally, the quest to restore inertia will result in an inchoate demand for the minimal public good—order. The stage will then be set for the seizure of power by a group with access to large means of violence and to administrative and economic resources. In modern complex societies, the odds favor those groups close to or on the fringes of the establishment. Certainly in the Southern Cone that has been the rule. Their intervention installs a conservative authoritarian regime that seeks the forceful reintegration of society. In the rarer cases when a general collapse of most groups gives radical insurgents the chance to seize power, the consequence is a thorough overhauling of the institutional fabric. This is a revolution. Both reactionary and revolutionary regimes exploit fear and produce it as an instrument of policy. To use the language of thermodynamics, the system goes then into a new steady state—into a phase where it can reproduce itself in a repressive mode.

THE INERTIA OF FEAR

A byproduct of institutional crisis is a special culture of fear—what we may call anomic, or Hobbesian, fear. This fear, in turn, generates a strong demand for forceful reintegration. Forceful reintegration returns the system to a new—albeit simpler and more repressive—steady state. A second culture of fear then appears, and the circle is closed.

Let us now try to apply the initial considerations of social inertia to the social conditions that prevail under a highly repressive or a terroristic regime. In the terms dear to Montesquieu, the question is no longer "What makes civic virtue so scarce in a republic?" but "What makes it so difficult to break the spell of fear in a despotic regime?"

The conditions that prevail under despotism can be treated as the negative of the social conditions discussed in the previous section. I use the term *negative* both in a direct and in a metaphorical sense. In a direct sense, the conditions are negative in that negative commands or prohibitions predominate over the positive reception of initiatives from below. The characteristic behavior of authorities is the refusal of consent to existing or proposed measures, backed by severe sanctions or countermeasures. Despotic governments appear as formidable barriers to social demands and as a source of arbitrary impositions, including harsh and arbitrary punishment. Individuals and groups are faced with a systematic official denial of requests, of protection, of orienting information. In a metaphorical sense, the conditions are similar to those obtaining in a photographic negative, in which natural lights and shadows are reversed.

The sacrifice an individual has to make to serve the common purpose of the group is much higher in a despotic than in an open regime. Moreover, the individual in such straits cannot be sure to reap gains at all from sacrifices made to achieve a common objective. In fact, the individual may reasonably suspect that sacrifice could make matters distinctly worse for everyone in the group. The citizen's reasoning is likely to go as follows: "What can you do? If you stick your neck out, they'll get you. And nothing is going to change, except maybe for the worse. It's better to sit still and keep your mouth shut." In a terroristic regime, the very capacity to calculate rationally the consequences of an action (that is, the relation between action and sanction) is damaged. Because there is a distinct possibility that violent countermeasures on the part of the authorities will affect everyone in the group, those who do not make a sacrifice for the common good will be afraid of those who take initiatives and will seek to dissociate themselves from such acts and persons.

The logic of collective inaction, only half-acknowledged in everyday life, applies to both atomized individuals and fragmented groups as they face repressive regimes. In one case, there is no solidarity at all among isolated, frightened individuals. In the other, fragmented groups have a retreatist orientation—a sort of amoral familism—away from the public sphere. The absence of solidarity and the wrong kind of solidarity have similar effects. Under these circumstances, most of the explanations offered by people for inaction are rationalizations. Nevertheless, the rationalizations exemplify the logic. For the sake of convenience I shall present only some of the justifications that seem most prevalent.

The most common justification for inaction takes this form: "I'll just stick to my business. I'll do nothing, just as long as nobody interferes with my work. In that way, I'll make my contribution to society." In this familiar account, the opposition between one's concern for public problems and one's activity in a narrow field is clear. Such a justification, the retrenchment into one's niche within the division of labor, is merely the expression of social inertia reinforced by fear. A conviction that nothing can be done usually accompanies the justification. A sense of inevitability, whether pessimistic or cynical, provides a powerful shield for the logic of collective inaction. It is no use to point out to such people that change does, after all, take place constantly in the world and in our lives because the change stems from factors outside the purview of standard rational and voluntary behavior. The justifiers are not being unusually selfish or craven, just "regular guys." In fact, they are likely to resent moral admonitions and to see them as calls to perform extraordinary duties. This attitude may well coexist with a clear awareness of social and political ills, even with full knowledge of atrocities.

If somebody else sticks his or her neck out and succeeds in stopping an abuse, justifiers will either shrug or bestow on such action a belated approval. More often however, under severely repressive conditions, the sacrifice incurred by others will elicit a gloating response: "See? We told you!" And the justifiers rejoice that no one managed to "provoke" them into an "imprudent" act. There is also another variety of this inertia, which is the attitude of wait and see—the belief that improvement will happen by itself. Actually this is a disguised form of freeloading on others, the hope that a faceless somebody will pull one out of a bad situation.

Inaction is maintained through the reciprocal deferral of responsibility, which we can view as a social exchange of excuses. People in high positions say that conscientious behaviors are all right for "ordinary people" who have nothing to lose. "Ordinary people" say such things are all right for those in high places because nobody will give them any trouble. One person says he is just finishing his degree. Another does not want to make things hard on her family or boss. Yet another is afraid his passport will not be renewed. The young say they are too young; the old say they are too old. And there is worse yet. People behaving, as we all do, on the basis of standard rational and voluntary premises will sometimes feel a real hatred toward anyone who sets an example of coura-geous behavior and confronts them with a serious moral choice. Some-times we not only lie and feel afraid: we do not want to stop lying and feeling afraid. This is a particular case of the logic of collective action that I have called social inertia.

In authoritarian and totalitarian regimes, the natural propensity to inaction in the voluntary pursuit of public goods is reinforced by the higher probability of severe negative rewards. In general, authoritarian regimes mute the very notion of a public good (except for order). Total-itarian regimes, however, preempt and expropriate the notion of public duty through the planned imposition of collective activities.

Here it pays not to rock the boat and to watch the next fellow. Obedience to fear-inspiring authority is guaranteed by mutual surveil-lance. In his historical survey of the social bases of obedience and resistance, Barrington Moore, Jr., states:

> To this sociologist the most striking set of facts to turn up in these examples is the way solidarity among an oppressed group forms readily *against* an individual protester or protector. This social mechanism appears not only in the concentration camps but also in ordinary prisons. In the less overtly threatening form of the Hindu caste system it occurs in the fully institutionalized form of lower-caste councils who punish their own members for the infraction of caste rules. The reasons for this solidarity are clear enough: any single act of defiance runs the risk of retaliation that threatens the whole group. Thus the group's spontaneous efforts at defense can easily and almost unavoidably serve to perpetuate and even intensify its submis-sion.[15]

Under special circumstances, and especially if fear is prolonged, an intense form of self-surveillance may develop. Notions of guilt, sin, and discipline owe much to these processes.[16]

A different, perverse sort of inertia is therefore produced in authori-tarian and totalitarian regimes. Borrowing an expression from Valentin Turchin, I shall call this perverse condition the *inertia of fear*.[17] It is a paradoxical form of action that explains why people participate in the maintenance of oppressive conditions.[18] Under these special circum-stances too, in the absence of factors that are alien to the assumptions of rational-choice theory, there will be little, if any, collective resistance, except the inertial resistance of fear itself. In this model, *homo econo-micus* or his socialist counterpart, *homo committicus,* may be expected to toe the line or, at best, to drag his feet.

All these social, cultural, and discursive processes work jointly or separately to produce a culture of fear and even tinge oppression with a perverse aura of legitimacy. The key to this quasi-legitimacy of fear is the sense that oppressive arrangements are somehow natural and unavoidable. Therefore, the conquest of inevitability in any number of areas (action, perception, emotion, thought) seems to be the clue to understanding how, despite inertia, fear is overcome.

BREAKING THE CIRCLE

CRISIS

Argentina offers a good example of protracted crisis. The rapid, discontinuous modernization of that country crowded into the life span of just two generations the simultaneous ferment of economic, social, political, and cultural movements that elsewhere grew more gradually: the extension of citizenship to the middle and the working classes, an industrial revolution, the breakdown of old values. The result was a plethora of crises: of distribution, of legitimacy, of participation, of institutions. The overload of demands from successively mobilized groups could be neither processed politically nor satisfied economically. This failure allowed a considerable amount of power to accumulate outside institutions, whence it broke out in various forms of violence: military coups, popular insurrections, armed insurgency, state terror, and external war, in that sequence. The multiple crises and the crescendo of violence that accompanied them posed, on the institutional surface, an acute problem of governability, and threatened, on a deeper structural level, the stability of class domination. The crises were detrimental not only to democratic values and the rule of law but to the functioning of the state as well.

In such a context, dominant groups tended to place as a first item on their agenda the reestablishment of a monopoly on coercion. Few countries in the modern world have seen in so few years so many attempts to "re-found" themselves. However, utter fragmentation and anomie generated among subordinate groups—in particular the middle sectors—an inchoate demand for order and a generalized readiness to subscribe to a Hobbesian covenant or "pact of fear." These general and particular pressures granted temporary autonomy to authoritarian regimes. They opened, as it were, a credit line of power that those regimes in turn sought to consolidate by mixing a variety of incentives (coercion against target groups, internal and external alliances, economic programs, ideological indoctrination). Against this background terror made its appearance in Argentina.

In short, over the course of several decades Argentina has been subjected to three types of authoritarian regimes: arbitrationist dictatorships of a temporary sort (which rule by arbitration between interest groups), a dictatorship sine die with developmental goals, and a dictatorship sine die with negative reconstructionist objectives. They have differed from one another in several respects: the intended length of tenure, the degree of autonomy from social and political forces, the pattern of economic development, the depth of penetration into and control over civil society. All emerged from complex distributions of fear, all engaged in some sort of fear-mongering, and the last type resorted to terror as an instrument of policy.

In cases like this, the same processes that facilitate repressive policies also impose checks on the power holders. Developments are best described by fitting them in a sequence of partially overlapping crises. These crises begin with the decay of institutions, which fail to fulfill and unify the expectations placed on them by organized groups. The consequence of institutional failure is an added flow of power to military authorities and an attempt by the military to overhaul the system extensively. The rulers impose draconian models of order and seek frantically to prevent other groups from developing alternatives. A terror phase is usually part of this process. Eventually, the projects of the power holders are subject to contradictions and self-checks. Inconsistencies develop among regime objectives, and tensions develop among support groups. Moreover, the extreme and autonomous nature of its policies deprives the regime of stable and reliable connections with civil society. Civil society becomes opaque to the rulers; no substitute structures of participation develop to replace the destroyed ones; and opposition becomes unpredictable. The lack of societal feedback makes mistakes difficult to correct. Policy becomes erratic and irrational. In short, the subsidiary dysfunctions of power management constitute a final crisis that paralyzes or brings down the repressive regime. In the end, weakened regimes rule over weakened societies. To describe such a process as a transition to democracy would be misleading. The crisis merely provides an opportunity for a transition to start but does not by itself break the circle of fear.

CONSTRUCTING BOUNDARIES

As we have seen, the distinction between a private and a public sphere makes individual protection against arbitrary assaults on integrity possible. But, for it to be effective, this distinction must be sanctioned by legally defined boundaries and by a culturally based notion of individual rights vis-à-vis the state. The emergence and maintenance of such legal boundaries depend, in turn, on social experiences that have solidified into values. Without these experiences, legal safeguards easily turn into fig leaves for arbitrary practices.

Moreover, these legal safeguards must be reinforced by larger conceptions of politics and by widely shared structures of political discourse. In Latin America, the dominant political formations have not supported individual rights.[19] On the one hand, populism, as an overinclusive political and rhetorical formula, has operated under the tacit motto: "Whoever is not against us is with us." On the other hand, authoritarianism—traditional or bureaucratic—has conveyed the opposite message: "Whoever is not with us is against us." The alternation of inclusionary and exclusionary politics has taken place at the expense of the notion of a legitimate opposition. Both power holders and opponents have tended to assume that the winner takes all. This tendency has had sometimes curious consequences. For instance, in periods of redemocratization or "rediscovery" of democracy, democracy is embraced as a panacea for all ills, is worshiped as a deity, or is reified as an entelechy, but continues to be sidestepped as a practice. The sometimes enthusiastic endorsement of democracy thus betrays the persistence of authoritarian habits. These political cultures seem to lack a proper respect for boundaries—legal, cultural, symbolic.

It is not difficult to detect fear as the origin of both overinclusionary or exclusionary ideologies. Because the emotion is being continuously translated into thoughts, certain manifestations are rationalized and justified in certain periods, while others are criticized and rejected. What is justified or rejected varies, but what remains constant is a comprehensive doctrine of political good and political evil in which the main emphasis is on the intimidating and hate-inspiring enemy (who can be "subversives" when the ruling group is military, "destabilizing forces" when the regime is constitutional, or "counterrevolutionaries" when the regime is revolutionary).

The legacy of fear shows also in the emotional investment in crucial political concepts. Order is one such concept. When spoken of by the right, it points to values that spring from old but fragile sources—values that can endure only as long as the world's primeval brutality does not turn against them. They are always threatened; they offer a homily of fear. Rightist emotion sees all order within the state threatened by the assault of barbarians. Sponsors of order feel themselves hemmed in, crushed, by alien and hostile forces, some of which are invisible and some inside themselves.

But these metaphysics are not absent from discourses on democracy. In them the political system is deified—"goddess democracy," fragile, tender, threatened. The term *democracy* is the functional equivalent of *motherland* in the nationalistic right-wing discourse. As a goddess, democracy becomes an absolute, simultaneously satisfying the old need for worship and the modern desire for security. The tendency for political systems, abstract entities, or concrete leaders to become objects of cults persists behind the transitions from authoritarian to democratic regimes. The residue of fear turns politics into a degraded religion.

SUCCESSOR JUSTICE

The deconstruction of cultures of fear is a long, fragile, and incomplete process. For those who embark on such a journey there are no magic formulas nor a clearly charted course. The appropriate mixture of political skill, constraining and enabling conditions, and sheer luck can be ascertained only after the success or failure of the enterprise. Ultimately, only the historian can tell. But those involved do not enjoy the benefits of hindsight and calm—in other words, the privileges of scholarship. They must act, pass judgment, find or improvise yardsticks with which to measure past behaviors, ideally in such a way that the values they promulgate transcend the lifetime of political regimes and the vagaries of the moment.

This need and this difficulty constitute the special significance of what I would like to call *transitional justice,* which is a particular and intensive type of political justice: the trial by fiat of a previous regime.[20] Such trials are especially intense because they pose before the entire community an ultimate problem: the fact that the exercise of justice is at the same time indispensable and impossible. Only the archangel descending on judgment day would be exempt from the reproach that blame and praise have not been distributed according to everyone's due. In contrast to ordinary justice, transitional justice implies arguments addressed to the public at large and to future historians.

Transitional justice is both more and less than ordinary justice. It is more because it aims beyond the simple ordering of human relations: it seeks to achieve moral and political regeneration. It is less than ordinary justice because it is subject to serious irregularities, it is a political formula for the formal elimination of a scapegoat,[21] it is imbued with problematic judgments by the power holders of the moment on the qualities and policies of their predecessors, and it is a constitutive act of a new regime.

There is little that justice per se can do to end a reign of fear. Political justice meted out by successor regimes at best sanctions a new legitimacy and prefigures a course of events before it actually takes place. It prefigures the uncertain verdict of history. Transitional justice is in this sense half constitutive and half symbolic, partly performative and partly a morality play. It faces two contradictory sets of pressures that reproduce on the plane of the law the two cultures of fear discussed above: the steady state and the anomic.

First, the supporters of the new regime and those who might have suffered most from the oppression of the old regime cry not only for revenge but for the construction of a permanent, clear wall between the new beginnings and the old despotism. They demand a break with the steady-state culture of fear of the predecessor regime. The rallying cry is the title of the book produced by the Argentine National Commission on the Disappearance of Persons: *Never Again.*[22] Second, there is pressure, somewhat more subtle but nonetheless strong and persistent, toward minimizing the insecurity from widespread prosecution and the indiscriminate rejection of the record of the previous regime. An important component of this second type of pressure is the concern with avoiding the recurrence of anomic fear that precedes the establishment of repressive regimes.

Transitional justice must balance these contradictory pressures. That balance depends, in turn, on the nature of the transition to the new regime. The length and bloodiness of the battle or, conversely, the relative ease with which the transition took place conditions the attitude of the new authorities. Historical and comparative evidence supports, in my view, this contention. I will merely illustrate the point, for reasons of elegance, by using the French example in this century. It is the fable of "the two de Gaulles." At one end of the spectrum, there is the French provisional government in 1944, liquidating the heritage of Pétain and collaboration, which accentuated repression after the bloody battles of the liberation. At the other end there is the shift from the Fourth to the Fifth Republic in 1958, which occurred within the framework of constitutional change and which was designed so as to obliterate the categories of winners and losers, accusers and accused. In the first instance, de

Gaulle appeared as a punitive victor. In the second, he projected the image of a father lovingly embracing all his children.

In the South American cases that concern us here, the two aspects are intertwined with various accents and proportions: punishment and reconciliation, revenge and catharsis. In the relative ease and length of the transition to a new democratic order, Argentina could be placed at one end of the spectrum and Brazil at the other, with Uruguay and Chile somewhat in between.

Often the balance not only reflects the dynamics of the transition but is also embodied in the political structure of the successor regime. The same fundamental tasks may be accomplished in various countries by different organs, and similar or comparable institutions may fulfill, in various countries, different tasks. By way of simplification, one could say that the president of Argentina, in his role as supreme magistrate, fulfills three functions, like his counterpart in France: a symbolic one, which makes him the representative of the nation; an executive one, which makes him the chief officer; and a partisan one, which makes him the leader of the dominant party or coalition. In Italy, these three functions are distributed among three persons; in Spain and in Greece, between two.

And these functional differences dovetail in turn with the various modes of determining jurisdiction in politically tinged trials. In general, we may say that there are three main forms of jurisdiction in the administration of this type of justice: a political assembly that doubles in selected cases (like impeachment) as a political court; the constitutional court, which functions as an arbiter for the highest organs of the state; and, most common, the highest civil court or lower civil courts, which can shift cases to military jurisdiction.

I will not explore these arrangements further here. I will mention instead the substantive issues raised by political justice in regimes that succeed despotic or terroristic governments. The quest for a yardstick with which to judge the actions of predecessors in power is fraught with legal difficulties. It is difficult to determine values that transcend the lifetime of a political regime against which acts can be judged. Furthermore, it is difficult to relate the attitude of individuals to the sum total of the record of the regime served. And, finally, it is difficult to determine a precise point at which action in the service of a past political goal turns into criminal conduct.

As a result of these difficulties, and especially in cases in which the transition to the new state of affairs is not drastic or revolutionary, the original political intent is likely to be deflected by supervening pressures. As in Italy after the war, modification in the structure of the new regime, reinforced by obstruction from the administrative and judicial corps, may redirect and soften repressive policies. In anticipation of this predictable erosion because of the relative weakness of the successor regime, the new authorities may decide to give assurances of limited prosecution, exempting only a selected few from this show of benevolence.

Yet even limited prosecution may well be the occasion for the entire community to focus on fundamental notions that all groups and nations must examine.[23] A national debate on the notion of a criminal state could help the community find a new sense of purpose. In an ideal world, I would venture the formula of "limited repression, maximum debate" as the one that could help the most in abhorring and transcending a culture of fear. That the importance of a debate should be stressed over the mechanisms of justice stems from the fact that whereas the structure and function of a criminal state are unfortunately clear, the legal formulas that could cover and repress such a state's actions remain problematic. To ignore their problematic nature is to frame a political trial as a spectacle with prearranged results. Ordinary justice is bound to fail to ever answer adequately the silent questions of the victims of the charnel houses. But this very failure, when revealed in a dignified manner, can provide the occasion for the community to glimpse the boundaries between the humane and the inhumane. In other words, the value of the exercise is independent of its concrete results—perhaps even inversely related to the extent of repressive outcomes.

DEMOCRACY WITH A DIFFERENCE

What lies beyond the circle—the *corsi e ricorsi*—of fear and beyond the crossing of symbolic boundaries through acts of successor justice? To begin to answer this question we must turn to the construction and consolidation of democratic alternatives—that is, to reformist possibilities in state, culture, and society. This is a vast project, and others are technically better qualified to undertake it than I. I will limit myself to general and preliminary remarks and leave the reader with a query.

There seldom is a completely peaceful and uneventful change. Historically, the process has been difficult, involving a measure of violence, unexpected turns, paradoxes, and crises, including, as we have seen, the unintended but very real dysfunctions and self-checks of fear-mongering regimes. By removing a variety of obstacles, these nonpeaceful processes have played their part in creating institutions that have made subsequent peaceful change possible. In the past, peaceable and democratic change did take root, even though it started from a relatively repressive and fearful base.[24] And several contemporary cases provide a good comparative database. Is there anything that can be learned from these experiences and applied to Latin America? Tentatively one can argue that there is, if we determine the causes for the present situation and ascertain whether functional substitutes may be discovered or encouraged given the different conditions of each country.

The kind of changes that this perspective implies can be summed up as establishing a democracy-with-a-difference—that is, a democracy that lives up to its rhetoric instead of using it as a cover for the perpetuation of the status quo. To make such a democracy a reality in the Southern Cone means to take a step back from the established conditions of Western industrial democracies, where the issue is one of preserving and extending considerable historical achievements. In the Southern Cone, civil liberties, protection against arbitrary authority, and a considerable degree of participation in the political process have to be rediscovered and reassumed, even though these achievements fail to produce enthusiasm in the advanced West as it crosses the threshold to new forms of participation and legitimacy.

In response to this modernity/postmodernity debate, the task for Latin Americans seems to be to take one step backward and two forward. The task is extraordinarily difficult because it means experimenting with democratic forms in the face of a legacy of failed, or pseudomorphic, modernity. The task requires resocialization and experimentation—in other words, renovating the old structures of bourgeois liberalism and redirecting social efforts away from militarism and toward humane ends, sponsoring passionate debate about positive goals, and finding an appropriate mixture of public and private institutions that can generate growth and promote talent.

Just what segments of our societies, if any, might be expected to exert pressures in this general direction? I resolutely reject global structural models as inadequate. I doubt very much that there are uniquely altruistic groups—in fact, that they have ever existed outside the imagination of a few theorists and ideologues. Relatively small sectors within the various strata are the ones that could be expected to become active, often in loose, cross-class coalitions formed for limited and specific purposes. Nor does the outcome need to exist in many of these actors' heads, except in the case of a few strategic thinkers and statesmen.

The task, hence, is to ascertain what aspects of a democratic program do or can appeal to what elements among the population. The potential clientele may be heterogeneous and have crisscrossing interests and traditions. These characteristics are not decisive. What seems crucial is the association of one or some of these segments with a new and growing social function comparable to capitalist industry in the nineteenth century. At this delicate point the economic and political problems dovetail. The social function needs to be one that is likely to gain recognition from the social order as a whole. The incentive would be only partly material. A great deal of the reward may come from the effective performance of a highly regarded social task.

If the general drift of this chapter is correct, the sociological guiding thread for leaving the circle of fear—that is, the sociological substance of hope—can only be a network of social activities that has three interrelated functions: they generate in individuals strong moral convictions concerning their social importance, produce larger economic pickings, and provide room for innovators. Conversely, the less articulated these functions are, the more likely anomic fear becomes.

In order for a democratic transition to succeed, a non-zero-sum counterpoint must develop between a substantial section of the elite and other elements in the society—a game of pressure and concession with enough room to maneuver. In addition, as we have seen, elites must invent new ways of satisfying the perceived needs of society, shift to the new tasks, and perform them adequately. However, demands for the elimination of entire social functions *tout court* make a relapse into anomic or steady-state fear a distinct possibility. Room for material concessions and a change in the social function of strategic elites in a nonrepressive direction seem the bottom line for democratization beyond initial and prefiguring gestures. Such a bottom line is and will continue to be in grave jeopardy in Latin America. Conditions, however, can never be determined with precision. Social processes do not take place, after all, inside rigid containers. There is no automatic translation of hardship or prosperity into chaotic conflict or social bliss.

At any rate, the simple point I want to make is that democratization is not a distillate of direct, frontal interaction but a transversal and mediated process. For such a process to sustain itself, there has to be an overlap of values in the various arenas of contestation, with a strong reluctance on all sides to use force. If all these conditions exist, occasional crises that test the boundaries of the process may in the end reinforce it, provided they are not frequent, convergent, or left unresolved. The forceful handling of insurrection—from above or from below—is both possible and beneficial when a process has been previously engaged whereby a significant portion of popular demands and of elite status are reciprocally legitimate.

Beyond the sometimes confusing ebb and flow of opinion, fear will be controlled only if democracy is consolidated. Yet, without some concrete success, the democratic process cannot sustain itself. How can success be gauged? Provisionally, it behooves us to discover the range of socially useful activities that can generate commitment and that can be rewarded only in a democracy.

NOTES

1. See the now-classical study by Jean Delumeau, *La peur en Occident* (Paris: Grasset, 1972), as well as his more recent *Le péché et la peur* (Paris: Fayard, 1983), English translation: *Sin and Fear* (New York: St. Martin's Press, 1990).

2. Cf. Pierre Mannoni, *La peur* (Paris: PUF, 1982).

3. This is the argument put forth by Norbert Elias, "Civilization and Violence," *Telos,* no. 54 (winter 1982–83).

4. The most eloquent formulation of this pessimistic view remains Sigmund Freud, *Civilization and Its Discontents* (New York: Norton, [1930] 1961).

5. Andrew Bard Schmookler, *The Parable of the Tribes* (Berkeley: University of California Press, 1984), 19.

6. A more recent use of fear as a point of departure for political theory may be found in the writings of Guglielmo Ferrero, *Potere, i geni invisibili della città* (Milan: SugarCo, 1981). See also Luciano Pellicani, "Saggio introduttivo," in Ferrero, *Potere,* and Antonio Cavicchia Scalamonti, "La paura e il potere," *Mondoperaio* 38, no. 1–2 (January–February 1985).

7. See the excellent work of Giulia Calvi, *Storie di un anno di peste* (Milan: Bompiani, 1984).

8. See Franz Neumann, *The Democratic and the Authoritarian State* (New York: Free Press, 1964).

9. Cf. Ferrero, *Potere.*

10. A formulation of this rational-choice principle appears in Mancur Olson, *The Logic of Collective Action* (Cambridge, Mass.: Harvard University Press, 1965, 1971). See also Mancur Olson, *The Rise and Decline of Nations* (New Haven, Conn., and London: Yale University Press, 1982).

11. Zealous violence in the pursuit of virtue produces generalized fear. See Laurent Dispot, *La machine à terreur* (Paris: Grasset, 1978).

12. For Argentina, see Juan E. Corradi, *The Fitful Republic* (Boulder, Colo., and London: Westview Press, 1985). For Uruguay, see Charles Gillespie,

Louis W. Goodman, Juan Rial, and Peter Wynn, eds., *Uruguay y la democracía* (Montevideo: Ediciones de la Banda Oriental, 1985).

13. Cf. Thomas Schelling, *Micromotives and Microbehavior* (New York: Basic Books, 1978). For an expanded model including many participants, see Garrett Harding, "The Tragedy of the Commons," *Science* 162, no. 3869 (13 December 1968). An interesting application to Britain can be found in Samuel Beer, *Britain against Herself* (New York: Norton, 1982). For Uruguay, see Juan Rial, *Partidos políticos, democracia y autoritarismo* (Montevideo: CIESU, 1984).

14. See Norberto Bobbio, "Italy's Permanent Crisis," *Telos*, no. 54 (winter 1982–83).

15. Barrington Moore, Jr., *Injustice: The Social Bases of Obedience and Revolt* (London: Macmillan, 1978), 79.

16. On the connection between cultures of fear and the development of a sense of guilt, see the massive study by Delumeau, *Le péché et la peur.*

17. Valentin Turchin, *The Inertia of Fear and the Scientific Worldview* (New York: Columbia University Press, 1981).

18. To my knowledge, the first thinker to address the paradox in a systematic way was Etienne de la Boétie, *Discours sur la servitude volontaire* (Paris: PUF, 1979).

19. See Juan E. Corradi, "The Avatars of Socio-Political Discourse in Latin America," *Social Science Information* 18, no. 1 (1979).

20. See Otto Kirchheimer, *Political Justice: The Use of Legal Procedure for Political Ends* (Princeton, N.J.: Princeton University Press, 1961).

21. See René Girard, *Le bouc emissaire* (Paris: Grasset, 1982).

22. *Nunca más: Informe de la Comisión Nacional Sobre la Desaparición de Personas* (Buenos Aires: Editorial Universitaria, 1984).

23. See Paul Boyer and Stephan Nissenbaum, *Salem Possessed* (Cambridge: Harvard University Press, 1974).

24. See the discussion of English reformism in Barrington Moore, Jr., *Social Origins of Dictatorship and Democracy* (Boston: Beacon Press, 1966).

Index

Compositor:	Keystone Typesetting, Inc.
Text:	10/13 Sabon
Display:	Sabon
Printer and Binder:	BookCrafters, Inc.